Holy Fable

Volume III
The Epistles and the Apocalypse
Undistorted by Faith

❖

Robert M. Price

Mindvendor

This volume completes the Holy Fable Trilogy

- ❖ **Holy Fable Volume I:** The Old Testament Undistorted by Faith
- ❖ **Holy Fable Volume II:** The Gospels and Acts Undistorted by Faith
- ❖ **Holy Fable Volume III:** The Epistles and the Apocalypse Undistorted by Faith

Other Titles by Robert M. Price

Beyond Born Again: Toward Evangelical Maturity
Inerrant the Wind: The Evangelical Crisis of Biblical Authority
Deconstructing Jesus: How Reliable is the Gospel Tradition?
The Widow Traditions in Luke-Acts: A Feminist-Critical Scrutiny
The Da Vinci Fraud: Why the Truth Is Stranger than Fiction
The Paperback Apocalypse: How the Christian Church Was Left Behind
The Pre-Nicene New Testament: 54 Formative Texts
Jesus Is Dead
Atheism and Faitheism
Evolving out of Eden: Christian Responses to Evolution (with Edwin Suominen)
The Reason-Driven Life: What Am I Here on Earth for?
Moses and Minimalism: Form Criticism versus Fiction in the Pentateuch
The Christ Myth Theory and Its Problems
The Case Against "The Case for Christ": A New Testament Scholar Refutes the Reverend Lee Strobel
The Tommentary: Interpreting the Gospel of Thomas
The Needletoe Letters: A Parody of "The Screwtape Letters"
Top Secret: The Truth Behind Today's Pop Mysticisms
The Politically Correct Bible
Jesus Christ Superstar: The Making of a Modern Gospel
Biblical Buddhism: Tales and Sermons of Saint Iodasaph
Bart Ehrman Interpreted: How One Radical New Testament Scholar Understands Another
Latter-day Scripture: Studies in the Book of Mormon
The Sage of Aquarius: A Centennial Study of "The Aquarian Gospel of Jesus the Christ"
The Amazing Colossal Apostle: The Search for the Historical Paul
Night of the Living Savior
Blaming Jesus for Jehovah: Rethinking the Righteousness of Christianity
The Human Bible New Testament
Secret Scrolls: Revelations from the Lost Gospel Novels
Killing History: Jesus in the No-Spin Zone
The Historical Bejeezus: What a Long, Strange Quest it's Been
Preaching Deconstruction

For B. Keith Brewer,
colleague in the Higher Criticism

CONTENTS OF HOLY FABLE
VOL. III

INTRODUCTION

Texts, like all sets of data, can look altogether different when read through different interpretive paradigms. It reminds me of the Kabbalistic belief that, when the Kingdom of God dawns, the text of the Torah, while eternal and unchanging, will nonetheless read very differently because a hitherto invisible letter will become visible, changing everything. (That is because there will then be no sin and therefore no need for the many "Thou shalt nots.") Or think of the difference it makes when one casts off the worn-out garment of biblical inerrantism with its obscuring web of harmonizations and theologically controlled interpretations. The text becomes, in Karl Barth's words, "the strange new world of the Bible." In that moment of *Satori* it makes sense, though not the sense you had previously been told it makes. I recall how, one evening while attending Campus Crusade for Christ's mega-rally Explo '72 in Dallas, it occurred to me to ask our youth director, a Bible Institute student, if there might be another way to construe the Bible and biblical thought other than the way we fundamentalists put it together. His answer, not surprisingly, was "No." If you were going to read the Bible, ours was the only way to read it. Of course, now, some forty-five years later, I know that is not so.

Different "interpretive communities," as Stanley Fish calls them, utilize different paradigms, so very different, in fact, that meaningful dialogue between them is often impossible. Tertullian warned his readers never to engage in debates with heretics over scripture because one can only understand the text rightly by reading it in accord with official "apostolic tradition." But what factors determine which interpretive community one belongs to? Maybe just the luck of the draw: the church you were raised in, your parents' instruction, the beliefs of the sect you joined because you found its members were friendly and promised you an exciting life of faith. Who knows?

But it is not merely a matter of competing religiosities. The same diversity of paradigms and perspectives prevails among learned scholars in all fields including biblical studies. At any Society of Biblical Literature convention you will find a whole zoo full of exotic creatures. There are adepts in Structuralism, Narratology, Deconstruction, Social Science criticism, Women's Studies, Jungian analysis, Postcolonialism, etc. But it is not the Babel-din you might imagine. The common understanding is that of collegiality, of being workers in different corners of one vast vineyard, or of each being one of the blind men trying to get an idea of the shape of an unseen elephant by grasping the tail, an ear, a tusk, the trunk, a leg, or the side. Maybe by comparing notes all of you can get a better idea of the whole.

In my books I have operated within the paradigm of the Dutch Radical Critics, taking much inspiration from W.C. van Manen, but making my own individual judgments. My approach has been to explain the New Testament writings from the standpoint that there was no historical Jesus, a view I once thought bizarre and wholly implausible but eventually came to find quite compelling (though of course unprovable). You have seen some of that in the previous volume of *Holy Fable*, though I have not hesitated to note when some other perspective makes good sense of the text. Another cardinal conclusion (not, please note, a *presupposition*) of the Dutch Radical position is that *none* of the thirteen epistles traditionally assigned to Paul are genuine. Though unthinkable to most, the idea should not seem unreasonable in view of the facts that, first, all critical scholars already consider about *half* of the Pauline Corpus to be spurious anyway and, second, that most also dismiss both ostensibly Petrine letters as pseudepigraphic, consigned to the same bin with the Gospel of Peter, the Letter of Peter to Philip, the Letter of Peter to James, the Apocalypse of Peter, the Nag Hammadi Revelation of Peter, and the

Preachings of Peter. If all of Peter turns out to be spurious, why not Paul, as long as there are good arguments?

Nonetheless, in this volume of *Holy Fable* I am adopting the perspective of mainstream New Testament scholars and treating Romans, 1 and 2 Corinthians, Galatians, Philippians, 1 Thessalonians, and Philemon as, in the main, authentically Pauline. If you have read my books *The Pre-Nicene New Testament* and *The Amazing Colossal Apostle*, you are already familiar with my preferred approach to these epistles, the approach I think makes the most sense. But I by no means dismiss the work of the majority of critical Pauline scholars as bunk and nonsense. So here I want to work their side of the street (Mark 9:38), to show what sense I should make of the Pauline letters on the assumption that Paul *did* write the "lucky seven" just listed. (In occasional footnotes I will, however, remind you of difficulties posed by the text for Pauline authorship.) Remember, scholarship isn't a race of hobbyhorses. We need to remain honest and open to "competing" views even while doing our colleagues the service of developing alternative paradigms for them to consider. Let a hundred flowers bloom!

Robert M. Price
August 16, 2017

14
The Epistle to the Romans
Protestant Papyrus

The Sitz-im-Leben[1]

Paul wrote Romans for one very practical reason: he was in Corinth planning an evangelistic mission to Spain. For this he needed a unified and supportive base of operations and a stepping stone. Rome might provide both. He writes to secure their hospitality and financial support. But there is, as always, a problem. A division between Torah-keeping and Torah-free Christianity runs through the landscape of the Roman churches, which must have been "organized" as a string of congregations meeting weekly in the homes of wealthier members who had enough space. Some of these congregations leaned one way on the issues, some the other. Paul had never visited Rome, but his reputation had preceded him there, and some apparently did not like what they'd heard (cf., Acts 21:18-22). Legalist Christians viewed law-free Christians as dangerous libertines and Paul as aiding and abetting such moral anarchism by preaching that "works" were irrelevant to salvation. Apparently, some of the law-free Christians had drawn the same inference and scandalized their more conservative brethren! Thus Paul writes to clarify his teaching, trying to make it amenable to both factions in order to reconcile them—behind *him*. The ultimate aim was to prepare the ground for his planned stopover in Rome on the way to Spain.

We may suppose that the core of the Torah-observant faction was composed of Jewish Christians (though they would not have used that word, nor did anyone else at the time), and that the law-free faction were Gentiles, probably both converts from paganism and "God-fearers," Gentiles who admired Jewish ethical monotheism and had already been attending synagogues.[2] This latter sub-group would

---

[1] This is a technical term translated as the "setting in life" of any particular writing (or saying). With ancient documents, we have to try to infer from the text itself why and in what circumstances the work was composed, since we are, so to speak, hearing only one half of a conversation.

[2] My approach to Romans, presupposing this profile of the Roman church(es), owes a great debt to Paul S. Minear, *The Obedience of Faith: The Purposes of Paul in the Epistle to the Romans*. Studies in Biblical Theology, Second Series 19 (Naperville, IL: Alec R. Allenson, 1971) and J.C. O'Neill, *Paul's Letter to the Romans* (Baltimore: Penguin

have had familiarity with Jewish scripture, hearing it read (from the Greek Septuagint translation) in the synagogues. However, they had not become full-fledged proselytes, card-carrying converts to Judaism, because the many ceremonial and dietary requirements were utterly alien to them, and they balked at the prospect. The Roman centurion Cornelius in Acts chapters 10-11 is usually understood as one of these "pious Gentiles."

It was a bit messier than "Jews versus Gentiles," though. No doubt there were Christians who had already been Hellenistic Diaspora Jews who did not feel obliged to keep the Jewish laws, having assimilated to the surrounding Gentile milieu. Likewise, there were probably Gentile Christians who, at the urging of Jewish Torah-Christians, had decided to embrace the whole Law and to get circumcised, as in Galatians 5:2-12.

It looks as if Paul has based this epistle on his earlier epistle to the Galatians.[3] The two have significant differences and yet much in common. They were both probably written while Paul had returned to Corinth to pick up the funds he had raised for the Jerusalem church. This would have been just after he composed 2 Corinthians 1-9 (originally a separate letter unto itself, as we will see later). Once he had written (actually dictated) Romans, Paul may have seen the value of a general statement of his gospel message and directed his assistants to make more copies of Romans to be used as an encyclical to any and all congregations. This might explain why some manuscripts of the epistle lack any specific address ("to the church at Rome"). Or perhaps the Romans themselves saw the general value of the great epistle and sent such copies around to other congregations.[4] Just a guess, of course.

Opening Salvo of Salvation

The opening salutation (1:1-7) mentions Paul's divine ordination to preach the gospel to all nations, something relevant to his agenda of

---

Books, 1975).

[3] Hans Hübner, *Law in Paul's Thought*. Trans. James Greig. Studies of the New Testament and its World. (Edinburgh: T&T Clark, 1984), pp. 51-55.

[4] One major qualm about this theory is that, in the second century, major churches were jockeying for clout by boasting that they had received privileged teaching from Paul, Peter, or other big-name apostles, so it seems unlikely for the Roman church, of all people, to humbly erase their collective name from the epistle.

requesting Roman assistance in carrying out this mission. Most scholars detect in verses 3-4 a fragment of a creed. Partly this is because of the poetic structure and meter of the lines, and partly because it does not reflect what we usually think of as Paul's doctrine of Christ. He wouldn't have put it this way *de novo*. Paul commonly speaks of the heavenly pre-existence of Christ, but verses 3-4 seem to stipulate *adoptionism*, the very widespread doctrine[5] that Jesus was a mortal man subsequently awarded divine (or messianic) honors in heaven.[6]

Paul announces, right up front, that he plans to visit Rome (verses 8-15). At once (verses 16-17) he states the theme of his exposition: God himself provides saving righteousness to both Jews and Gentiles, to be accepted by faith, which means that both Jews and Gentiles have equal access to it, i.e., without ceremonial Torah observance. And both *need* that saving righteousness. In verses 18-32 Paul aims his rhetorical guns at the Gentile world, detailing the tragic fall of humanity into sin and depravity, largely the result of their having turned from the genuine God to serve mere idols. His readers from the ranks of the Gentile God-fearers had probably heard such ideas in synagogue sermons; it was their own disgust at the pitiful morality ascribed to their traditional deities (like the rapists Zeus and Apollo) that made Judaism so attractive to them. This whole section is so close to Wisdom of Solomon 14:8-16:1 that it may actually have served as the model for this passage of Romans.

As of chapter 2, Paul turns to the Jews, warning that they, too, sin and are really in no superior position to the unwashed Gentiles. Sure, Jews are guardians of the precious Torah, but what good does it do them if they neglect to obey it? Conversely, the *lack* of the Torah is no real disadvantage for the Gentiles (theoretically even in their pre-Christian state) since they *can* be righteous by the moral law which

---

[5] Also on display in the early Christian book, authored in Rome, The Shepherd of Hermas, Similitude 5.2.1-11.

[6] However, it seems a bit early in the institutional evolution of Christianity to imagine the existence of official creeds and formulae. This does not mean verses 3-4 are not a piece of a creed, but it might suggest that, if Paul wrote the rest of the letter, a later scribe inserted a creed familiar in his own day. Or it might imply that the whole epistle is a much later, post-Pauline pseudepigraph (Willem Christiaan van Manen, "Epistle to the Romans." In Van Manen, *A Wave of Hypercriticism: The English Writings of W.C. van Manen* (Valley, WA: Tellectual Press, 2014), pp. 175-212. In my books *The Pre-Nicene New Testament* and *The Amazing Colossal Apostle* I follow the approach of Van Manen, but here I am adopting the approach of mainstream criticism, to see what sense the epistles make when read that way.

God has placed within every human heart. Again, this idea is part and parcel of Hellenistic Jewish missionary preaching and well describes the condition of the Gentile God-fearers (if not even the "noble pagans" whom Justin Martyr regarded as "Christians before Christ"). Jews and Gentiles would both seem to be on the same footing before God, both being liable to punishment for sin and reward for righteousness. As John C. O'Neill[7] pointed out, the whole of Romans 1:18-32; 2:1-29, seems out of sync with Pauline thought as we meet it elsewhere even in this same epistle; thus it looks like a large interpolation. Does Paul really believe that, apparently under their own steam, Jews and Gentiles may succeed in keeping the commandments of God? As we will soon see, Paul (Rom. 3:10) believes in the universal depravity of the whole human race, and that the proud self-assurance of religious Jews is, if anything, even worse than the overt and unapologetic wickedness of the benighted heathen (cf., Matt.23:14; Luke 18:9-14).[8] No one has any means of escaping divine judgment except through the atoning death of Christ. But in the present section, the closest we come to this is 2:16, "on that day when, according to my gospel, God judges the secrets of men by Christ Jesus," which then must be an interpolation intended to tack the rest of the passage into the letter. So the bulk of these two chapters must have originated as the text of a Hellenistic missionary tract or sermon. Considered in isolation, it has nothing to do with any doctrine of salvation by faith.

In chapter 3 Paul delivers his verdict: all have sinned and stand equally condemned in the sight of God, a fact which serves to glorify God by way of contrast. But Paul is quick to point out that this doesn't mean we *should* sin because the worse we look, the more brightly God shines! Paul is taking the opportunity to repudiate the libertinism[9] some of his critics infer from his doctrine of salvation

---

[7] O'Neill, pp. 52-54; William O. Walker, Jr., *Interpolations in the Pauline Letters*. Journal for the Study of the New Testament Supplement Series 213 (Sheffield Academic Press, 2001), Chapter 8, "Romans 1.18-2.29," pp. 166-189, defends and buttresses O'Neill's argument. Alfred Loisy already suggested the same in *The Birth of the Christian Religion*. Trans. L.P. Jacks (London: George Allen & Unwin, 1948), p. 26. E.P. Sanders, *Paul, the Law, and the Jewish People* (Minneapolis: Fortress Press, 1983), "Appendix: Romans 2," pp. 123-132, agrees with O'Neill, too, but he thinks it was Paul himself who integrated someone else's sermon text into his epistle.

[8] Rudolf Bultmann, *Theology of the New Testament*. Volume I. Trans. Kendrick Grobel. Scribner Studies in Contemporary Theology (New York: Scribners, 1951), pp. 240, 264.

[9] Though Gnostics have commonly been vilified as immoral rioters and orgiasts (e.g., Jude 8-13), their own writings, discovered in 1945 in Egypt, show no trace of this.

through grace. And of course if any Roman Christians are actually misbehaving on this basis,[10] Paul wants to yank that particular rug out from under them, too.

Just a Vacation by Faith

Lucky for us, God has himself provided the righteousness which we so sorely lacked. He has done this by the expiatory death of Jesus, bestowed upon the human race as a gift (2:21ff.). Therefore, no one has any right to boast: salvation comes only from God. All, whether Jew or Gentile, can be saved in this way, but it is equally true that *no one can be saved by any other means.* And most especially not by Torah observance.[11] But then, why on earth did God give Moses the Law in the first place? You can bet the Roman Torah-Christians would be asking this question at this very point. Is Paul, then, anti-Torah, as they have heard?

Many scholars[12] have challenged the traditional Protestant (Lutheran) interpretation of Romans and Galatians, suggesting that

---

Instead, they appear as dour ascetics. But there certainly have been Jewish and Christian libertines. The eighteenth-century sect of Jacob Frank engaged in lights-out liturgical orgies because they believed their messiah had ushered in the Kingdom of God, in which nothing any longer counted as sin (Gershom Scholem, "Redemption Through Sin." Trans. Hillel Halkin. In Scholem, *The Messianic Idea in Judaism and Other Essays on Jewish Spirituality* (New York: Schocken Books, 1971), pp. 78-141. Countess Elisabeth Bathory, who used to bathe in the blood of virgins, seeking to renew her youth, was a member of the Reformed Church of Hungary. She thought the grace of God made all things lawful for her. In the twentieth century, Elvis Presley and James Dean were both libertine Pentecostals.

[10] As my seminary pal Michael Di Gregorio used to put it (not endorsing the idea, mind you!), "Saved by grace, O blessed thought! Sin as I will and never get caught!"

[11] We might have a parallel to this in Luke 17:20 if we translate it as "The kingdom of God is not coming by (Torah) observance," supplying "Torah" in place of "signs," which is not in the text either. The reference would be to the Jewish belief that if all Israel would only keep a single Sabbath perfectly in every detail, the messianic era would immediately dawn. *Shemot Rabba* 25:12; *Yerushalmi, Ta'anit* 1:10: "Though I have set a limit to 'the end,' that it will happen in its time regardless of whether they will do *teshuvah* or not... the scion of David (Mashiach) will come if they keep just one Shabbat, because the Shabbat is equivalent to all the *mitzvoth* [commandments]."

[12] Krister Stendahl, "The Apostle Paul and the Introspective Conscience of the West," in Stendahl, *Paul Among Jews and Gentiles and other Essays* (Philadelphia: Fortress Press, 1976), pp. 78-96; Francis Watson, *Paul, Judaism and the Gentiles: A Sociological Approach.* Society for New Testament Studies Monograph Series 56 (New York: Cambridge University Press, 1986), Chapter 1, "Paul, the Reformation and Modern Scholarship," pp. 10-22.

Protestants have made a milder version of the mistake committed by Paul's ancient opponents, in the background here and on display in James 2:14-26. Protestants have always read Paul's epistles as implying a division between moral, ceremonial, and civil laws in the Old Testament. Old Testament civil, tort, and criminal laws were obviously moot in Paul's day while there was no autonomous Jewish authority to enforce them, so that kind of law was off the table (no pun intended). Ceremonial law had nothing in the first instance to do with morality. It dealt instead with ritual defilement, kosher versus non-kosher food, the calendar of holy days, etc.

No one ever thought it was *immoral* to eat pork barbeque, or for spouses to have intercourse within the woman's menstrual period. No, these deeds violated *ceremonial* taboos. They were "wrong" for a different reason and in a different way. They were purely ritual transgressions, as, say, spitting out the Communion host would be. Accordingly, Protestant interpreters have long taught that when Paul declared the Torah over and done with, he was referring *strictly to the ceremonial law, not the moral law*. They were right. But they did not take the next logical step, to recognize that it was equally the ceremonial law, *not the moral*, that Paul said was not required for salvation. Salvation did not require "works of the Law," things like circumcision, kosher laws, and fast days (Rom. 14:17; Col. 2:16). This meant that Gentile God-fearer Christians, who made no pretense of observing the ritual regulations, had the same status before God as Jewish believers in Christ. As for moral behavior, "good works" in that sense, they are not even under discussion here.

In one sense, this was nothing new. Judaism had long admitted that Gentiles who kept the minimal regulations of the Covenant of Noah (Gen. 9:4-6) could and would be saved. So what were Paul and his opponents worried about? The issue had emerged as an unforeseen consequence of gospel preaching. It seems that Jewish Christians kept the Torah, never having had it occur to them that Jesus had come to retire the Law (Matt. 5:17). After all, why would anyone imagine that the Jewish Messiah would make it his business to get rid of the Jewish scripture? And at first they seem to have thought it unnecessary to preach the gospel of Jesus to non-Jews. What would Gentiles care if Jesus or Alfred E. Neuman was the rightful king of some tiny Middle-Eastern postage-stamp country they would never even have occasion to visit? Imagine the surprise of Jewish Torah-Christians at learning that Gentiles here and there had embraced the gospel (Acts 10:45-48; 11:18)! Now the unanticipated question popped up: "Uh, if we Christians (up to now, only Jews) keep our ancestral Law, easy since we're Jews, does it mean Gentile converts to the gospel have to keep it, too?" Paul's answer, basically, was "No! What's natural for *you*, raised in Judaism, is culture shock for *them*.[13] Why make Christian conversion more of a hurdle than it has to be? Jew or Gentile, isn't belief in Jesus enough?" When the New Testament authors characterize the Torah as an unbearable burden (Matt. 23:4; Luke 11:46; Acts 15:10; Gal. 5:1), they are presupposing the daunting prospect of a Gentile becoming a full proselyte to the Torah. Jews considered the Torah a gift, not a ball and chain.

Scofflaw Salvation?

Though he's never quite explicit, Paul seems to have thought that Jews were free to continue Torah-observance, no problem. But to require it of those used to a different set of cultural mores is to elevate Torah-observance to a shibboleth of salvation, at least in effect if not intent. Likewise, Gentile Christians who are persuaded by Jewish Christians that they must embrace full Torah-observance to be legitimate Christians are in effect doing the same thing. It would be like the United Pentecostal sect today denying salvation to any who do not speak in tongues. They don't *mean* to make glossolalia a saving work, but that's the logical consequence. Either way, Saint Peter turns you away from the Pearly Gates, right?

Was the code of 613 commandments all a mass of neurotic superstition? By no means! These laws set up a high wall of ethnic identity, rendering it difficult for Jews to blend in (e.g., to intermarry) with pagan Gentiles. (Remember, this is why the Gentile God-fearers would not go the whole way and fully convert to Judaism.) And the reason had nothing to do with racism. Since Jews (like Gentile God-fearers) saw a causal link between pagan religion (polytheism, idol-worship, and sexual fertility magic) on the one hand and immorality of character on the other, they regarded assimilation, the dilution of Jewish identity, as the infiltration of pagan religion with the consequent moral degeneracy. The high walls erected by the ceremonial commandments was a "hedge about the Torah," a barrier to keep Jews as far as possible from temptation. So, albeit a bit indirectly, the ceremonial law *did* serve an ethical purpose. So why does Paul want to ditch it? As we will see, it was because he thought

---

[13] Sanders, *Paul, the Law, and the Jewish People*, p. 29.

the Torah an ineffective safeguard against sin.

Chapter 4 deals with the Patriarch Abraham in an attempt to do an end-run around the Torah in order to undermine the centrality of the Torah for salvation. If the basis for salvation had been settled hundreds of years before Moses, then, whatever role might be assigned to the Torah, it can't have been the criterion for salvation either then or now.[14] Before the Torah ever existed, salvation was promised to Abraham and his progeny on the basis of faith. He believed God's wildly improbable promise that he and his centenarian wife would have a baby son and heir. And this trust earned him merit in God's eyes. (This reasoning, however, appears extremely dubious when one remembers that salvation in Paul's sense, deliverance from eternal death, was not even in view in Genesis or most of the Old Testament. Did Abraham believe God for a blessed life after death? Did God promise him such a thing?)

The Torah was not even on the horizon, and neither God nor Abraham had to wait for Moses to show up. If Abraham received the promise of salvation under these circumstances, one can hardly make Torah-observance a requirement for salvation. (In our day theologians have raised the same problem with regard to faith in Jesus Christ: if it wasn't required of Adam or Nehemiah, why should God require it of us? Wouldn't that make Christian belief a "false stumbling-block"[15] like circumcision?)

Paul infers that the Mosaic Law cannot enter into salvation even once it exists because that would confine the promise's eligibility to the one nation who possessed the Torah, namely the Jews. That can't be so; how then could all who have a faith like Abraham's (i.e., without regard to the Torah) obtain the promised salvation? And that is the kind of faith shared equally by Jews and Gentiles who believe in the resurrection of Jesus. Just as Abraham believed that Isaac would emerge alive from a long-barren womb, so Jesus emerged alive from an empty tomb.

---

[14] It might have been simpler had Paul written something like this: "the works of the law of Moses do not avail unto salvation; neither were they intended to do so. Anyone who reads the law can see for himself that Moses is not even concerned to tell us how we may be saved from anything greater than exile from the people or from the worldly punishment of the evil-doer, whether a murderer or a thief. Of the soul's salvation Moses says nothing at all. Above all, the law was taken up with rites of purity which served to shield the people of God from the pollutions of the Gentiles" (Cilicians 2:6-10 [Robert M. Price, *Paul: The Lost Epistles*]).

[15] Rudolf Bultmann, *Jesus Christ and Mythology* (New York: Scribners, 1958), p. 36.

THE EPISTLE TO THE ROMANS

Adam and Evil

Romans chapter 5 sets forth a parallel between Adam and Jesus Christ: Christ died for us as an act of grace, dying for his enemies, reconciling us to the God from whom we had been estranged, and this was an act of obedience to his Father's will proportionate in impact to Adam's race-wide act of disobedience in the Garden of Eden. Whereas Adam's sin implicated all mankind in death, Jesus' self-sacrifice provided life for all. His death atones for all the sin of the whole human race throughout history. (Paul does not think to address the question whether the cross atoned for the sin of generations yet to come, apparently because he assumed his own generation would be the last. See 1 Corinthians 7:26 and 1 Thessalonians 4:15.)

This chapter (verses 12-14) plants the seed from which sprouted the notorious doctrine of Original Sin. Some take this text to imply that Adam's sin and guilt, plus a tendency to sin, were passed genetically to all subsequent human beings (though that would make Paul a Lamarckian, a believer in the discredited theory of the inheritance of acquired characteristics). Where, if anywhere, does the text say this? It depends on how one separates the Greek words which all ran together in ancient manuscripts. Should we read verse 12 as saying, as Augustine of Hippo thought, "*In him* all sinned," or "*because* all sinned"? I can only say that, especially in view of verse 14, "even over those *whose sins were not like the transgression of Adam*," the point seems more likely (to me) that Adam's sin was like the first domino knocking down the second, which knocks down the third until all have fallen over: a chain reaction.[16]

This opens the door to the Pelagian understanding, revived by liberal Protestant theologian Albrecht Ritschl, that Adam's sin was inevitably reflected in the society set up by him and his descendants, which evolved along the lines of a "wisdom" that "is not that which comes down from above, but is earthly, unspiritual, diabolical" (James 3:15), a well-oiled system with its own sinister rationale, aptly embodied in, e.g., Machiavelli and Saul Alinsky. This "environmentalist" view of sin recognizes the virtual impossibility of

---

[16] Buddhism faces the same problem in explaining what it is that gets reborn from one incarnation to the next, since there is no immortal soul to re-clothe itself in body after body. Their analogy is like the one I have just suggested. It is like lighting a second candle from a first, a third from the second, and so on. Same flame, or just a chain reaction?

anyone raised in such a social system ever being able to transcend it. "When in Rome..." One can safely predict that no one will wind up sinless, though theoretically they have the freedom not to sin. Practically speaking, though, what are the chances? This is the sad realization of 1 Corinthians 5:9-10 and Matthew 13:24-30.

Baptism of Blood

Does all this talk of negating God's Law imply libertinism? In chapter 6 Paul explains it does not. He raises the question at this point because he knows that what he has just said will sound dangerous to Torah-keeping Roman Christians, and he will now seek to allay their fears. He hastens to assure them that freedom from the Torah is *not* freedom from morality. Just the reverse: it is freedom from *immorality*. You see, what gives us freedom from the Law is our *dying* to the Law through baptism, our inclusion in Jesus' death.[17] Baptism also includes the Christian in Christ's resurrection, which imparts freedom from sin and sinning, just as surely as we should expect to have put sin behind us once and for all when we emerge from our graves on Resurrection Morning. The great devotional writer Watchman Nee (Nee To-sheng) recounted his *Satori*-like realization of this Pauline teaching.

> I remember one morning I was upstairs at my desk reading the Word and praying, and I said, "Lord, open my eyes!" And then in a flash I saw it. I saw my oneness with Christ. I saw that I was in him, and that when he died I died. I saw that the question of my death was a matter of the past and not of the future, and that I was just as truly dead as he was because I was in him when he died. The whole thing had dawned upon me. I was carried away with such joy at this discovery that I

---

[17] Albert Schweitzer ingeniously attempts (*The Mysticism of Paul the Apostle*. Trans. William Montgomery [New York: Seabury Press/ A Crossroad Book, 1968], Chapter II, "Hellenistic or Judaic?" pp. 26-40) to explain this mechanism of ritual incorporation into the savior's sacrificial death, within the context of Jewish apocalyptic eschatology. But the notion is plainly cut from the cloth of the Hellenistic Mystery Religions (Richard Reitzenstein, *The Hellenistic Mystery-Religions: Their Basic Ideas and Significance*. Trans. John E. Steely. Pittsburgh Theological Monograph Series 15 (Pittsburgh: Pickwick Press, 1978); Harold R. Willoughby, *Pagan Regeneration: A Study of Mystery Initiations in the Graeco-Roman World* (Chicago: University of Chicago Press, 1929).

jumped from my chair and cried, "Praise the Lord, I am dead!" I ran downstairs and met one of the brothers helping in the kitchen and laid hold of him. "Brother," I said, "do you know that I have died?" I must admit he looked puzzled. "What do you mean?" he said, so I went on: "Do you not know that Christ has died? Do you not know that I died with him? Do you not know that my death is no less truly a fact than his?" Oh, it was so real to me! I longed to go through the streets of Shanghai shouting the news of my discovery.[18]

Chapter 7 pursues this question. The "statute of limitations" on Torah-observance is like the death of one spouse making a second marriage legal, not adulterous. The analogy seems a bit off-kilter. Wouldn't it have been more to the point if Paul had said it was the *Torah* that had died, leaving us free to seek another husband, Christ? I can't help wondering if he'd rather have said this but feared affronting Law-observant Roman Christians. He couldn't very well give the impression that the Torah had been simply abrogated, nullified.

Verses 5-7 tell us that sin and the Torah are linked in such a way that to die to one is automatically to die to the other. *What?* Is the Law tantamount to sin? Again, Paul knows that what he just said will suggest this. But it is not so. The real purpose of the Law, he says, was never to provide salvation. If it were, it must be the grossest failure since no one has ever been able to keep it perfectly. Instead, the Law was introduced in order to pique our awareness of underlying sin, to bring it to the surface, actually to *provoke* sin! As Nee put it, "The law was given to make us law-breakers!"[19] Jolted from our complacency, we are spurred by the commandments to seek a salvation we blithely assumed we had. The commandments show us what God's standards really are. This makes us eager to keep them but rapidly makes it clear that we cannot.

Where did Paul get this notion that everyone is a sinner, that no one can keep the Law and that no one ever has? E.P. Sanders argues[20] forcefully that this dogmatic claim does not issue from some existential analysis of the human condition, or from any inductive study of scripture, but rather that it is reverse-engineered from Paul's

---

[18] Watchman Nee, *The Normal Christian Life* (Bombay: Gospel Literature Service, 1957; rpt. Wheaton: Tyndale House / Fort Washington: Christian Literature Crusade, 1983), pp. 64-65.

[19] Nee, p. 159.

[20] Sanders, *Paul, the Law, and the Jewish People*, pp. 25-27, 68, 80-81.

enthusiasm for the notion that Christ came into the world in order to save the human race. If this is true, why, then, the human race must have needed it! Otherwise, what's the point? Similarly, what's so wrong with the Torah? The big problem with the Torah is that it's not the gospel. Paul is reasoning backward from a conviction arrived at on other grounds, namely a religious epiphany.

The Confessions of Saint Paul?

Once again, one wonders if the whole discussion does not presuppose a distinctly Gentile viewpoint, that of a God-fearer attracted to Judaism but daunted by the prospect of full conversion, as this would entail not only circumcision (ouch!) but the wholesale teaching of new tricks to old dogs. Interestingly, Ebionite[21] (Jewish Christian) critics of Paulinism claimed that Paul himself was a Gentile who tried to convert to Judaism but just could not handle it, gave up in frustration, and invented a new sour-grapes theology of the abrogation of the Torah. Maybe they were right. Would a Jew born and bred really regard Torah-observance as such an albatross? Only about 100 out of the total 613 commandments had any bearing on the individual, and a combination of peer-pressure and habit would make it second nature to keep most of these. How tempted could you have been to fry up some bacon, much less to boil a baby goat in its mother's milk?

It is significant that Paul takes as his illustrative example of temptation the commandment against coveting, one of the very few that treat of interior motivation. It would be downright ludicrous to picture his Hamlet-like introspection as a wrestling over whether or not to allow his ox to gore his neighbor. And how difficult is it to avoid committing murder, theft, perjury, or adultery? The stance taken here is that of introspective conscience-policing. We seem here to be far from the issue of whether the specifically Jewish laws are still binding.

Paul doesn't seem to be speaking autobiographically in the

---

[21] "They say that he was a pagan, with a pagan mother and father, that he went up to Jerusalem and stayed there a while, that he desired to marry the priest's daughter and therefore became a proselyte and was circumcised, but then did not obtain the girl, who was of such high station, and in his anger wrote against circumcision, the Sabbath, and the law" (Epiphanius, *Panarion* 30.16.9). Philip R. Amidon, ed. and trans., *The* Panarion *of St. Epiphanius, Bishop of Salamis: Selected Passages* (New York: Oxford University Press, 1990), pp. 103-104.

soliloquy in verses 7-25. I think it makes more sense if "I" is used to mean "one," describing the general situation of people in general. But then wouldn't the whole thing still apply to him as well? Well, yes, but the subject is the general predicament of sin and transgression, not an Augustine-style confession by a rueful individual. After all, Philippians 3:4-7, which *is* explicitly autobiographical, portrays Paul as a man proud of his perfect Torah-piety. He does not come across like someone tormented by a bad conscience, like an alcoholic who repeatedly falls off the wagon like Joe Clay (Jack Lemmon) in *Days of Wine and Roses*. "Romans 7:7f does not contain Paul's confessions, or a description of the spiritual state of unredeemed man, but the presentation of the objective nature of unredeemed man from the viewpoint of the one who is redeemed."[22] The discourse certainly seems to be contrasting the ineffectiveness of the Torah in reining in sin with the moral rejuvenation that comes to those baptized in Christ. It is he who liberates one from the state of being dead in sin (cf., Eph. 2:1-2).[23]

One reads along to the triumphant conclusion in Romans 7:25a: "Thanks be to God through Jesus Christ our Lord!" But hold on! The second half of the verse seems to pop that balloon: "So then, I of myself serve the law of God with my mind, but with my flesh I serve the law of sin" (Rom. 7:25b). Huh? *This* is the summation? We are *still* mired in moral paralysis? I have to wonder if some scribe, as pessimistic as Augustine[24] concerning any post-baptismal "victorious Christian life," added this "corrective" note. He perhaps thought the discourse smacked too much of "enthusiasm,"[25] and tried to rein it in. I'd bet on it.

Sin Is Over if You Want It

Chapter 8 continues the discussion of the victorious Christian life, a fact implying all the more that 7:25b is an interpolation. Christ's death makes it possible for us actually to fulfill the standards of God

---

[22] Rudolf Bultmann, "The Problem of Ethics in the Writings of Paul," in Bultmann, *The Old and the New Man in the Letters of Paul*. Trans Keith R. Crim (Richmond: John Knox Press, 1967), p. 16.

[23] Reitzenstein, *Hellenistic Mystery Religions*, shows the Mandaean-Manichean character of the phrase Paul uses here, "the body of death" (p. 449).

[24] Elaine Pagels, *Adam, Eve and the Serpent* (New York: Random House, 1988).

[25] Ronald A. Knox, *Enthusiasm: A Chapter in the History of Religion* (New York: Oxford University Press, 1950).

once revealed in the Torah. How? Christ gives us the Spirit, a new source of power. This does not mean that we will henceforward *automatically* live righteously. That is still in our hands, and we run the risk of still being condemned if we voluntarily submit again to slavery to sin, which, of course, we need no longer do. The fact that we *can* overcome sin makes our failure to do so even more egregious than it was before. We shouldn't be slaves to sin, since we *needn't* be anymore (and if we are, we are like the inmates in *One Flew over the Cuckoo's Nest*, holding the key to our own manacles), but rather the liberated sons (and daughters) of God, much as in John 8:34-36.

We cannot help noticing a couple of important differences between the argument here and the largely parallel discussion of the same theme in Galatians. Here Paul drops the role of the angels as administrators (or even originators) of the Torah on Sinai (see Gal. 3:19-20) and thus as our guardians/schoolmasters during our minority (Gal. 3:23-26). Accordingly, when Paul speaks in Romans of submitting again to slavery, he is referring to Gentile Christians returning to their once-accustomed pagan immorality (cf., 1 Pet. 4:3-4), whereas in Galatians he had in mind Gentile Christians embracing the Torah (Gal. 4:8-11). Quite a difference! Why the change? Perhaps because he has in view Roman Gentile Christians who have been persuaded to embrace full Torah-observance. We know such people were in mind when he wrote Galatians, but they were his own converts, and in Galatians he was chastising them for apostatizing from the *Pauline* Torah-free gospel. But Paul had not yet visited Rome, so none of these church members could be considered his (lapsed) disciples. They had, so to speak, come by their legalism honestly, and Paul knew he had no right to rebuke them. So who is he talking to in Romans 8? It must be Roman Torah-free Christians, whom he is warning not to succumb to libertinism.

In verse 11 Paul comes very close to saying that baptism means not only that believers have died with Christ, but also that they have risen with him as well. He does not cross that line, though, seemingly deferring the spiritual resurrection of believers to coincide with the End-Time resurrection of the body. Colossians 3:1 and Ephesians 2:5-6, however, do say that believers have already been raised with Christ. The hot potato here is the "enthusiasm" of Gnostic Paulinists (2 Tim. 2:18) who taught that the resurrection of believers is altogether spiritual, non-corporeal, and fully accomplished in baptism (cf., 1 Cor. 15:12, which seems to attack a belief that there is to be no *future* resurrection). The hair-splitting difference between Romans and Colossians/Ephesians at this point is one of the reasons many scholars deny that Colossians and Ephesians are really the work of Paul, stemming instead from those Gnostic Paulinists.

Verses 18-39 develop the theme further, suggesting that the inner renewal experienced now will one day eventuate in an outer, bodily resurrection, when Christ returns. Verse 23 equates the eschatological resurrection with the adoption of believers as God's sons (and, of course, daughters). This reflects the formula in Romans 1:3-4, where Jesus' own resurrection denoted his designation as God's Son.

It must be noted that this language would seem to make the most sense on a Marcionite reading. Marcion taught that human beings were the creations, the children, of the Creator God Jehovah, who was *not* the Father of Jesus. When Jesus revealed the latter's existence (Matt. 11:27), he offered the Creator's children the opportunity to *become* the children of his own Father, hence adoption. (The ransom and redemption language describing the death of Jesus would also seem to make the best sense in Marcionite terms, according to which Jesus' death was the price paid to Jehovah for the freedom of his creations.)

Romans 8:29 offers another potent piece of soteriology, that of our being "conformed to the image of his Son." In modern Christian devotionalism, this phrase is taken to describe the gradual process of sanctification whereby we take up the slack between how God sees us *de jure* in Christ (or "through the blood of Jesus") and *de facto* Christ-like character. That is certainly a fine application of the language, but I think it does not represent Paul's intent. For him, the phrase really must denote the putting on of the resurrection body on the Last Day. Philippians 3:20-21 makes the same point: "our commonwealth is in heaven, and from it we await a Savior, the Lord Jesus Christ, who will change our lowly body to be like his glorious body." Besides, unlike the gospels, the Pauline epistles have little if anything to say about either the personality or the character of Jesus, of whom Paul speaks only as an abstract savior figure, so there's no reason to think he has this in mind here.

Metaphysical Mystery Tour

The New English Bible translates verses 26-27 as follows:

> In the same way, the Spirit helps us in our weakness, for we

do not know how we should pray, but the Spirit himself intercedes for us with inexpressible groanings. And he who searches our hearts knows the mind of the Spirit, because the Spirit intercedes on behalf of the saints according to God's will.

This very likely refers to glossolalic prayer (praying in tongues) as in 1 Corinthians 14:14.[26] As for the idea of the divine Searcher of the human heart discerning the mind of the divine Spirit as expressed in these prayers, does it not imply that God is at both ends of the same conversation? This is a prime example of those places where scripture, as Tillich says, raises ontological (philosophical) questions but leaves it to us to answer them.[27]

Do verses 29-30 teach the doctrine of predestination? I should say that they do, as "foreknow" seems to mean "choose," just as in Jeremiah 1:5 ("Before I formed you in the womb I knew you, and before you were born I consecrated you; I appointed you a prophet to the nations."), which the New English Translation[28] renders as follows: "Before I formed you in your mother's womb I chose you. Before you were born I set you apart. I appointed you to be a prophet to the nations." The implication would seem to be that only those who are chosen beforehand are then summoned to salvation.

Roger T. Forster and V. Paul Marston[29] argue that the divine foreknowledge of believers is tantamount to the psalmist's lyric, "he knows our frame; he remembers that we are dust" (Ps. 103:14), and that in context with the business about our cluelessness vis-à-vis prayer, the point is that, even in view of human incompetence, God has still chosen to appoint us to the task of world evangelization. But the idea that God demonstrates his grace by entrusting the evangelistic task to buffoons incapable of carrying it out seems far-fetched to me,

---

[26] Ernst Käsemann, *Perspectives on Paul*. Trans. Margaret Kohl (Philadelphia: Fortress Press, 1971), Chapter VI, "The Cry for Liberty in the Worship of the Church," pp. 130-131; John L. Sherrill, *They Speak with Other Tongues* (Old Tappan, NJ: Spire Books/Fleming H. Revell, 1965), p. 75.

[27] Paul Tillich, *Biblical Religion and the Search for Ultimate Reality*. James W. Richards Lectures for 1951-52 at the University of Virginia (Chicago: University of Chicago Press, 1955), p. 81. Also p. vii, "each of the biblical symbols drives inescapably to an ontological question." And p. 83: "If one starts to think about the meaning of biblical symbols, one is already in the midst of ontological problems."

[28] To be distinguished from the older and unrelated New English Bible.

[29] Roger T. Forster and V. Paul Marston, *God's Strategy in Human History* (Wheaton: Tyndale House, 1974), pp. 202-203.

an *ad hoc* hypothesis to wriggle out of predestinarianism. And the typical Arminian[30] dismissal of the passage is almost a tautology: God knew ahead of time who would accept salvation, and so he decided they would. Tautology? Maybe it's an oxymoron.

Forster and Marston are certainly correct to point out that "he predestined" need by no means imply that God wrote a script which, as mere puppets, we have no choice but to follow.[31] It can simply mean appointment to a task, whether or not one successfully carries it out. In this case, it looks to me as if Paul means that those whom God chose, he slotted for eschatological resurrection/transfiguration (though whether they *make* it that far is another matter).

From Mediator to Messiah

Verse 34 depicts the ascended Christ as going to bat for his elect, putting in a good word on our behalf, presumably pleading for mercy when we screw up.[32] This notion appears also in Hebrews 7:25 and 1 John 2:1. It may have originated in (or at least reflects) 2 Maccabees 15:12-15. There Judas Maccabeus relates a vision of the heavenly court.

> What he saw was this: Onias, who had been high priest, a noble and good man, of modest bearing and gentle manner, one who spoke fittingly and had been trained from childhood in all that belongs to excellence, was praying with outstretched hands for the whole body of the Jews. Then likewise a man appeared, distinguished by his gray hair and dignity, and of marvelous majesty and authority. And Onias spoke, saying, "This is a man who loves the brethren and prays much for the people and the holy city, Jeremiah, the prophet of God." Jeremiah stretched out his right hand and gave to Judas a golden sword, and as he gave it he addressed him thus: "Take this holy sword, a gift from God, with which you will strike down your adversaries."

---

[30] Of course, "Arminian" refers to Jacob Arminius and his "Remonstrant" opponents of predestinarian Calvinism. It has nothing to do with ethnic Armenians or the Armenian Orthodox Church. You can't take anything for granted anymore.

[31] O'Neill, p. 151.

[32] Theologian Norman Greenbaum got it exactly right: "I've got a friend named Jesus; he's gonna set me up with the Spirit in the sky."

Judas beholds two holy figures, the martyred high priest Onias III (the "anointed one" of Daniel 9:25) and the prophet Jeremiah. Both serve as mediators with God on behalf of his people Israel. Benjamin W. Bacon[33] suggested that, before devotees of the crucified Jesus came to believe he had been enthroned at God's right hand, they held a more modest belief in Jesus as a martyr interceding in heaven for his earthly followers, just as he appears in Acts 7:55-56, standing before God as an advocate in court, as Onias and Jeremiah do in 2 Maccabees, not sitting enthroned. Think of the scene in John 18:15-16 in which one disciple, who has inside connections with the high priest, pulls some strings to get Peter admitted: "He's with me." In the same way, Romans tells us, we have gained access to God's favor thanks to Jesus and his privileged "connections" with God.

Verse 38 features a list of demonic entities (not mere abstractions) which threaten to separate souls from God, but which Paul says are rendered impotent by the saving work of Jesus Christ.[34] Understandably, most readers have just looked at the bottom line and taken from the passage the simple notion that "nothing shall separate us from the love of God." One imagines that readers picture something like the situation of Job, whose steadfast devotion to God could not be shaken by even the worst vicissitudes. And that indeed might be a good demythologization of the text, but Paul is referring to the widespread ancient belief that the souls of the righteous did not ascend directly to heaven but must needs fight (or slip past) a gauntlet of planetary spirits, devils, fallen angels, or Gnostic Archons, posted like guards along the Berlin Wall. The enlightened initiates possessed the knowledge, the "passwords," to evade the angels' butterfly nets. This is no doubt why the members of the Dead Sea Scrolls sect had to memorize long lists of the names of the angels, to be ready to meet them and to get past them. When Paul declares that Christ has opened the way to heaven for us, the fiendish efforts of Principalities, Powers, and Archons, etc.,[35] notwithstanding, this is what he means. Christ has "disarmed the Principalities and Powers, triumphing over

---

[33] Benjamin W. Bacon, *The Story of Jesus and the Beginnings of the Church: A Valuation of the Synoptic Record for History and for Religion* (London: George Allen & Unwin, 1928), pp. 283-284.

[34] Elaine H. Pagels, *The Gnostic Paul: Gnostic Exegesis of the Pauline Epistles* (Philadelphia: Fortress Press, 1975), p. 37.

[35] G.B. Caird, *Principalities and Powers: A Study in Pauline Theology*. Chancellor's Lectures for 1954 at Queen's University, Kingston Ontario (Oxford at the Clarendon Press, 1956).

them" (Col. 2:15a).

The First Shall Be Last
and the Last Shall Be First
and the First Shall Be First Again

We move next to consider chapters 9-11, where Paul sets forth his missionary strategy, in the course of which he explains God's plans for the Jewish and Gentile communities. One preliminary note: the Marcionite edition of Romans, earlier than any of our extant manuscripts, lacked most or all of these three chapters.[36] And as Van Manen[37] pointed out, in them we meet, almost exclusively, the term "Israel" rather than "the Jews," which predominates in the rest of Romans. These and other oddities suggest that chapters 9-11 may be a later addition (or series of additions) to the epistle. But here I plan to make the best sense I can of the text on the usual assumption that Romans is a single, coherent document.[38]

Paul's explanation here is intended to justify his mission and to seek the Romans' support for it. To do this he must again mediate problems between the Roman church's factions. It has become evident that most Jews have rejected Christianity,[39] and this development has raised new difficulties. Jewish Christians in Rome may hold their Law-free "brethren" responsible for this, as their disregard for the Torah has scandalized traditionalist Jews who dismiss Christianity as half-pagan antinomianism (cf., Acts 15:21).[40]

(Here we see an anticipation of the withering away of Jewish Christianity as a whole a few centuries down the line. It attracted few Gentiles given its strenuous legal demands, and, especially in view of Christian belief in Jesus as a divine being, Jews disdained Christianity as a species of syncretistic polytheism and Jewish Christians as

---

[36] Jason D. BeDuhn, *The First New Testament: Marcion's Scriptural Canon* (Salem, OR: Polebridge Press, 2013), p. 222.

[37] Van Manen, p. 190.

[38] I interpret Romans with a more critical model in my book *The Amazing Colossal Apostle: The Search for the Historical Paul* (Salt Lake City: Signature Books, 2012), Chapter 9, "The Epistle to the Romans," pp. 253-298.

[39] Wait a minute! Can this really have happened already during the lifetime of Paul? It seems to presuppose a considerably later historical perspective.

[40] Hugh J. Schonfield, *The History of Jewish Christianity from the First to the Twentieth Century* (London: Duckworth, 1936; new ed. Lexington: Biblical Life College & Seminary/Messianic Bible Institute, Yeshiva, 2009), Chapter III, pp. 30-34.

heretics.)

Gentile Christians in Paul's Roman audience seem to regard the Jewish rejection of Christianity as the vindication of their belief that Christianity is at heart a non-Jewish religion (the essence of the later Marcionite doctrine). This Paul regards as sheer arrogance (see 11:17 ff.), though Paul himself seems to share the same opinion in 1 Thessalonians 2:14-16.

Paul explains that it is all a matter of God's choice as to who believes and who doesn't. As (he says) Isaiah predicted, only a small remnant would believe in Jesus. The rest fail to believe because they mistakenly persist in seeking salvation/righteousness through the Law of Moses. Only faith will save, though of course this assumes people have the opportunity to hear the gospel preached. (Obviously, Paul is here leading up to his planned evangelistic mission for which he seeks to recruit the aid of the Roman Christians.)

Yet the Jews *have* heard, as Paul implausibly "proves" by quoting scripture! And besides, a remnant of Jews, like Paul himself, *did* believe, though admittedly most did not. The reason they didn't was that God in his mysterious wisdom has temporarily blinded them in order to force Paul and others to turn to the Gentiles, a new and surprisingly receptive field. If Jews *en masse had* accepted the gospel, Paul and his colleagues would have been so busy with them that they would never have been able to get around to the Gentile Mission. The poor benighted heathen would never have had the chance to hear the glad tidings. But as things are, they have. And in due time, the spectacular growth of Christianity among the nations[41] will prompt the astonished Jews to jealousy: "Wow! Maybe it's not too late to jump on the bandwagon!" I have to guess Paul is thinking that Jews, otherwise unpersuaded of Jesus' messianic qualifications, will be impressed that *anything* got the pagans to embrace the God of Israel. Could they have been a bit hasty about that Jesus fellow? Then they, too, will convert. (*Right.*)[42]

Uh, so what? Well, Gentile Christians in Rome should stop boasting of having replaced Israel, since God has not in fact abandoned his ancient people. (Apparently, Catholics and Calvinists

---

[41] Again, doesn't this sound just a little bit anachronistic? Retrospective?

[42] In fact, many modern Jewish thinkers *are* impressed with Christianity as a quasi-Jewish instrument for getting Gentiles to drop Zeus and Odin for Jehovah, but the theological result is the Double Covenant doctrine: that Christians have their own, quite different, relation to God, much as Vatican II described Protestants vis-a-vis Catholicism.

were playing hooky when this part of Romans was taught in Sunday School.) Jewish Christians in Rome should not oppose (or remain aloof from) Paul's mission to Gentiles for thinking it is gradually (?) undermining Jewish Christianity,[43] since, as Paul has just explained, his Gentile Mission is actually a kind of back-door way to convert Jews.

As to the predestination texts in Chapter 9, some have suggested Paul is discussing collective groups (Jews and Gentiles), not individuals, as of course he does in Chapter 11. Yet in Chapters 1-3 he certainly refers to the universal guilt both of whole groups (Jews and Gentiles) *and* of all individuals in them. So we must not introduce a false "either/or" into Chapter 11. Besides, since he distinguishes a believing minority from a larger unbelieving majority of one of these groups, he must have in mind God's predestination of individuals within the two groups.

Is Jesus Feeding Paul his Lines?

Chapter 12 provides a welcome respite from these theological profundities. It is something of a book of proverbs tucked away in Romans. Much of the material is strikingly reminiscent of the Sermon on the Mount, and many conservative scholars, seemingly trying to meet the objections of critics who point out the utter neglect of any historical Jesus in the Pauline epistles, suggest that Paul is here quoting Jesus without attribution. This way they can pretend, er, contend, that Paul did have knowledge of Jesus and his teachings. What is the issue here? Radical critics[44] hold that the lack of both biographical details for Jesus and teaching materials by him implies that Christians did not yet believe in a historical Jesus but were content to worship him as a celestial Savior who may have granted visions and epiphanies on occasion (like Asclepius, for instance) but who had never actually walked the earth.

Paul and his epistles, they aver, come from the earlier period

---

[43] What a coincidence! That's exactly what happened! More historical hindsight?

[44] E.g., G.A. Wells, *The Jesus of the Early Christians: A Study in Christian Origins* (London: Pemberton Books, 1971), Chapter 6, "Evidence of Early Christian Writers," pp. 131-150; Earl Doherty, *The Jesus Puzzle: Did Christianity Begin with a Mythical Christ?* (Ottawa: Canadian Humanist Publications, 1999), Chapter 2, "A Conspiracy of Silence," pp. 23-30.

before, for polemical reasons, church authorities posited a recent historical Jesus who had provided their teachings and thus guaranteed their truth. Had there been a historical Jesus, a near-contemporary of Paul, an itinerant teacher and miracle-worker, surely we should see some evidence of it in his writings. And we don't. When we do run across parallels between the teachings of epistles and gospels, radical critics hold, it seems more likely that Christians chose favorite passages from the epistles and credited them to Jesus, once they had come to believe there *was* such a person. In effect, that is what the conservative apologists are doing when they ascribe sayings from Romans 12 (or the Letter of James) to Jesus. But this is preposterous: who would try to drive home a point by quoting the Son of God—and then leave out his name?

Paul and the Powers

In Chapter 13 we have a warning aimed at Gentile Christians not to allow their vaunted "freedom from the law" to spill over into a license to cheat on their taxes or to do whatever else they may think they can get away with. But biblical law and secular, civil law are not the same thing.

Okay, but how can Paul say that God has appointed the secular powers, given the light in which they are portrayed elsewhere in the New Testament, e.g., Revelation chapter 13? Actually, it is not that much of a stretch. He presupposes the contemporary belief in the Principalities and Powers, the old "sons of God" from Genesis 6:1-4 and Psalm 82, fallen angels who, their self-aggrandizement and malicious mischief notwithstanding, rule the nations from behind the thrones. Like African religions as well as the Yezidis of Syria, who believe the Creator has withdrawn from the annoying affairs of humans and left them in the hands of subordinate deities, Jewish apocalyptic belief held that one must make the best of the unfair and incompetent government of the Powers, which after all, must be better than sheer chaos.

Now Accepting Implications

Paul gets down to brass tacks in 14:1-15:13, dealing with issues of controversy between the Jewish and Gentile factions in the Roman churches. Specifically, he addresses the observance of dietary laws and sacred calendars. Paul appears to take the side of the Torah-free faction but adopts a remarkably tolerant stance: let each side recognize that the other side's preferred practice is intended, and experienced, as a way to serve God and that God accepts it as such and will uphold each sincere individual, whichever way he or she leans. The Torah-Christian must stop worrying that, without the Law, the Gentile will fall into sin. Let God take care of it! Likewise, the Gentile must be considerate; he mustn't offend the Jew by flaunting things offensive to him, inviting him over for a nice ham sandwich. Live and let live, for Pete's sake!

On the other hand, let not the "weaker brother" (the one, as we should say, neurotically afraid God will smite him should he relax his strict Torah-observance) adopt freer behavior until he is genuinely convinced he'd be justified in doing so. Otherwise, he will be sinning insofar as he is violating his conscience, brushing his qualms aside rather than resolving them.

By the way, Paul puts the discussion in terms, not of kosher versus nonkosher food, but rather of vegetables versus meat. Why? Judaism was not vegetarian. True, but Jews living among the Gentiles in the Diaspora could not in every case determine if meat available at the market had been slaughtered according to Levitical protocol; in that case, they'd have to stick to salad[45]—poor devils!

Wish Me Luck

Romans 15:14-33 deals explicitly with Paul's plans to visit Rome once he stops by Jerusalem to deliver the funds he has collected from the Gentile congregations. He seems anxious that the gift (tribute?) may not be gracefully received, though he does not say why. Acts 21 indicates his fears were well-founded. Now he is attempting to raise new funds for his trip to Rome, assuming he would have to pay his own way rather than traveling under guard and in chains as Acts depicts the events.

---

[45] Watson, *Paul, Judaism and the Gentiles*, p. 95.

Give my Regards to the Appian Way

Chapter 16 is mainly a list of shout-outs to various members of the congregations. At first this chapter might seem as tedious as a Chronicles genealogy, but on a closer look it becomes quite interesting. Many scholars understand it as an originally separate letter of recommendation for the deaconess (actually "deacon") Phoebe, arriving from the church at Cenchreae to serve in some capacity in the church at Ephesus. For one thing, Romans seems to want to conclude with the doxology at the end of chapter 15.[46] For another, it seems distinctly odd that Paul should know dozens of members of a congregation he has never visited! That would be the case if Chapter 16 is really addressed to Rome, but not if it was originally aimed at Ephesus where he had carried on an extensive ministry (Acts 19).

Several women are listed in the chapter, seemingly important leaders in the church. We hear of Mary (verse 6), some kind of Christian worker, Tryphaena and Tryphosa, "workers in the Lord" (verse 12), and Prisca (verse 3), the wife of Aquila, both teachers in Ephesus (Acts 19). But the most fascinating of all is Junia (verse 7), who is called "noteworthy among the apostles." The King James Version got this right, but until recently most translations gratuitously rendered the Greek "Junian" as a male name, "Junius." You see, "Junian" has an accusative ending because it is the direct object of the sentence. But it would come out like this whether the nominative form were the male Junius or the female Junia. And it so happens that ancient Greek literature provides no example of a (hypothetical) name "Junius," whereas the name "Junia" is quite common. Translators just could not imagine that there might have been female apostles, so they posited a contraction of the male name, "Juniatus," for what they figured must be a male apostle.[47]

---

[46] A similar wrap-up doxology appears at 11:33-36, implying that an earlier edition of Romans ended right there, before someone added the subsequent material.
[47] Eldon J. Epp: *Junia: The First Woman Apostle* (Minneapolis: Augsburg Fortress, 2005).

15

The First Epistle to the Corinthians
Now Concerning Corinth

An Overview

Paul's letters to Corinth reach us in a bit of a mess. It appears no one in the Corinthian church(s) took especial care of the now-precious autograph manuscripts until sometime after they were initially read. Perhaps latent hostility toward Paul nursed by some in the congregation (he rebukes plenty of people in those letters!) resulted in neglect of the writings till long afterward when things cooled down and a new generation arose that knew not Paul or his controversies, and when they chanced upon the ill-preserved letters (or fragments of letters), they recognized the same value in them that subsequent readers have. Someone then did his best to assemble the literary remains in what looked to be the most likely order. Even so, in the present texts of 1 and 2 Corinthians we find surprising, even mystifying, reversals and contradictions suggesting that they had some trouble putting Humpty back together again. Walter Schmithals[48] performs what some would call micro-surgery on the text, dividing the two canonical epistles into snippets representing several short Pauline letters to Corinth. (One thinks of the team of Dead Sea Scrolls scholars with their magnifying glasses and pinchers, trying to assemble a jigsaw puzzle from a pile of postage-stamp-size papyrus fragments.) Other scholars slice the Corinthian pie differently, and I follow their simpler approach in what follows.[49]

The Sitz-im-Leben

Paul starts the Corinthian church in 51 C.E., residing there for eighteen months. He returns to Ephesus to resume work there.

---

[48] Walter Schmithals, *Gnosticism in Corinth*. Trans. John E. Steely (New York: Abingdon Press, 1971), pp. 87-101. As distinct from Schmithals's division of the epistle into source fragments, I have here embraced his comprehensive understanding of 1 Corinthians as responding to Corinthian Gnosticism.

[49] I take a more radical critical approach in my book *The Amazing Colossal Apostle: The Search for the Historical Paul* (Salt Lake City: Signature Books, 2012), Chapter 10, pp. 299-375.

Meanwhile a scandal is brewing in Corinth: a man is sleeping with his step-mother after the death of his father. Paul hears about it somehow, perhaps not in detail. He fires off a letter, directing the Corinthians to shun the offender. Second Corinthians 6:14-7:1, which is obviously in the wrong place any way you cut it, may be a surviving fragment of this letter, which need not have been much longer. (Ancient letters were usually very brief.)

The letter has no effect. It may be that the offender and his supporters are rejecting Paul's command with a *reductio ad absurdum*: why not go the whole way and shield oneself from contaminating contact with sinners *period* (cf., Matt. 13:24-30.)? Paul rejects such reasoning in 1 Corinthians 5:9-13, explaining that there is a valid distinction to be made.

Next Paul is visited by two different groups of Corinthian church members. Some of Chloe's people (possibly slaves or relatives), perhaps visiting Ephesus on business (cf., Matt. 25:14-19), treat Paul to gossip about dissention, immorality, etc. Then he receives an official delegation from the church, three members of Stephanas' household, namely Stephanas himself and his sons Fortunatus and Achaicus. They present him with a letter from the congregation containing a list of questions. Paul writes 1 Corinthians to address both groups' concerns. Specifically, he lowers the boom on the immoral person, who is by some definitions committing adultery.[50] Paul orders the congregation to kick him out. Paul is amazed that this man is being tolerated.[51] I suspect it was this case that led to Paul's initial letter, though now, having learned more specifics, he is all the more outraged. Chloe's associates have also informed him of sectarian strife in the congregation(s). There are factions dedicated to Paul, Cephas, Apollos, and Christ. Paul seems to regard Apollos as a close colleague (1 Cor. 3:5-6; 4:6; 16:12), but the other two present real puzzles. I consider the Christ party to be Gnostics who (like Paul

---

[50] We might compare the situation with Woody Allen casting aside his domestic partner, Mia Farrow, to take up with Mia's adopted daughter Soon-Yi Previn, whom he then married. (He had not married Mia.) This is kind of disgusting, granted, but not as absolutely loathsome as if he had married his own biological daughter, or if, and of course this is my point, the Corinthian offender had actually been having intercourse with his own mother.

[51] Once the minister of a socially very liberal church down the block from mine returned from a European vacation only to find a man on the sidewalk handing out leaflets accusing the Reverend of cuckolding him while away. Stepping up to the pulpit, the pastor freely admitted it, and the congregation broke into applause. Things haven't changed much, I guess.

himself in Galatians 1:1, 11-12) eschewed all dependence on any mortal teacher or apostle, claiming revelations direct from the heavenly Christ himself. The party of Cephas (if Cephas is indeed to be identified with Peter)[52] must have been Jewish Torah-Christians (whether extreme or moderate) who appealed to Peter for their beliefs and practices. It seems like this last group's travelling "apostles" had shown up in Corinth (as also in Galatians) and were trying to discredit Paul. He deals with the Gnostic Christ party in 1 Corinthians[53] and with the Judaizing Cephas party in the Severe Letter, 2 Corinthians 10-13.

The situation with Paul's opponents (I think especially the Cephas faction) escalates, with these outsiders (and their fans in Corinth) badmouthing Paul. I would guess the Cephas party was taking advantage of the controversy over the incestuous man in order to denigrate Paul's authority, pointing to the culprit's behavior as a result of Pauline "libertine" teaching. "Paul is to blame for the very scandal he condemns! Had he stuck with the Torah, this sort of thing would never have happened!" Of course, Paul cannot let this carping go unanswered lest anyone think he *has* no defense. So he sends a rebuttal, and a substantial portion of it meets us in 2 Corinthians 2:14-7:4.

During his next circuit-riding tour, Paul visits Corinth again ("the painful visit," 2 Cor. 2:1) and has a public confrontation with the immoral man. But it is a stalemate: the man will not leave, and no one backs Paul up (cf., Paul's being left to twist in the wind in Galatians 2:11-14). The apostle is duly outraged, needless to say. He leaves in a huff and continues his travels. He had planned to drop in on the Corinthians again on his way home, but now he skips them, not relishing the prospect of further friction with "his" church. Wouldn't you know it, some in Corinth take offense at this, so once he learns of it he fires off "the severe letter" (2 Cor. 2:4-5) which we now find as 2 Corinthians chapters 10-13. He sends it by way of his colleague Titus, whom he also wants to take up a collection[54] for the relief of the Jerusalem church. Titus returns with the news that the Corinthians have finally decided to obey Paul, reaffirming their loyalty

---

[52] Samuel Sandmel, *The Genius of Paul: A Study in History* (New York: Schocken Books, 1970), pp. 182-184.

[53] Again, see Schmithals's brilliant analysis in his *Gnosticism in Corinth*.

[54] Dieter Georgi, *Remembering the Poor: The History of Paul's Collection for Jerusalem*. Trans. Ingrid Racz (Nashville: Abingdon Press, 1992); Keith F. Nickle, *The Collection: A Study in Paul's Strategy*. Studies in Biblical Theology No. 48 (London: SCM Press, 1966).

to him and severely punishing the offender. Paul, greatly relieved, writes them "the joyful letter" (2 Cor. 1-2:13; 7:5-16). Chapters 8 and 9 look like a pair of fundraising letters sent before Titus' visit, urging the Corinthians to be ready for it.[55]

A Little Flattery Never Hurt Anybody

Paul gets right into a theme that will occupy him throughout the letter: spiritual gifts and inspired speech (1:4-7). The subject surfaces in some places but is only thinly veiled throughout, providing a unifying theme. The Corinthians (or at least *some* of them) have been, as they themselves do not tire of boasting, richly endowed with "speech," i.e., speaking in tongues and prophecy, and "knowledge," i.e., *gnosis*: the "word of gnosis" and the "word of Sophia" ("wisdom"), esoteric revelation. As will become abundantly clear, many or all of the problems plaguing the Corinthian church are occasioned by tensions between a charismatically endowed Gnostic elite and the ordinary "pew potatoes" who both envy and resent them. Paul is buttering up the charismatics before he turns to chastise them for insensitivity, condescension, and disdain toward their "weaker brethren." We do not know if they actually exhibited these traits or if, like later anti-heretical writers, Paul merely inferred such attitudes from the fact of their grand claims. After all, Jewish-Christian legalists did the same thing to him, assuming that Paul saw the same implications of his Torah-free gospel as they did: a recipe for amoral antinomianism. Just as Paul repudiates their inferences in Romans, for all we know, the Corinthian Gnostics may well have shaken their heads at his misunderstandings (as they viewed it) of their position.

Wisdom versus Wisdom

After noting with displeasure the reported party strife, and listing the factional totems, including himself, Paul *seems* to pivot and to abandon the topic to go on to a discussion of divine versus worldly wisdom. But has he in fact changed the subject? No. Because the

---

[55] Dieter Georgi, *The Opponents of Paul in Second Corinthians*. Trans. Harold Attridge, Isabel and Thomas Best, Bernadette Brooten, Ron Cameron, Frank Fallon, Stephen Gero, Renate Rose, Herman Wartjen, and Michael Williams (Philadelphia: Fortress Press, 1986), p. 17. (That's nearly as many translators as worked on the Septuagint!)

THE FIRST EPISTLE TO THE CORINTHIANS

Corinthian personality cults in general and the Gnostic "Christ party" in particular presuppose that the important thing is human wisdom: "My guru's better than your guru!" But the cross of Christ negates such vanity, to say nothing of Gnostic elitism. Here Paul is applying the doctrine of justification by grace through faith to the area of knowledge, just as he applies it to that of works of the Law in Galatians. Grace is antipodal to any sort of self-sufficiency ("boasting"), whether of perfect ritual performance or of intellectual mastery. If one regards religious orthopraxy as required for salvation, one credits oneself with the achievement. If one must master a conceptual theology in order to be saved, salvation is no longer a free gift from a loving God but rather an awarded prize. And Paul will have none of that.

We find a classic statement of the paradox of divine revelation in 1:17-2:5. Human wisdom is highly vaunted as the treasury of accumulated insight enriching the lives of all who will humble themselves to take instruction from it. The Book of Proverbs certainly views it this way. Don't we all? And yet an arbitrary factor has been introduced. A monkey-wrench of an *event* has been thrown into the works—by God. All philosophies are static rational systems, theoretical structures of coherent principles. From them the wise deduce their proper courses of action. But now the gospel has been revealed, and it is the report of an event, something produced by the free act of God, not predictable or derivable from any set of philosophical axioms. This makes it impossible for wisdom to lead one to accept the gospel. The only way to accept it is by faith in the proclamation, the preaching of the word. Someone says that something happened. Do you believe it? "Who has believed our report?" (Isa. 53:1a).

No wonder intellectuals (Matt. 11:25-26) and jurists (Luke 7:29-30) alike dismiss it (1Cor. 1:20). In 1 Corinthians 2:1-5 Paul explains that, when first preaching in Corinth, he had made it his policy not to try to win converts by means of rhetorical legerdemain. Why? Because such intellectual persuasion does not sink its anchor very deep (cf., Mark 4:5-6). As soon as Paul went on to the next town, some other sophist or guru would likely come along with his own dazzling spiel, and Paul's converts would flock to him instead, being blown this way and that by every wind of doctrine (Eph. 4:14), with ears itching to hear the latest teaching (2 Tim. 4:3). No, real conviction comes by way of the Spirit. In non-theological terms, I think this means that when people come to faith through an emotional experience, no "mere" rational argument can budge them from it.[56]

But suddenly Paul seems to be singing a very different tune (2:6-16). Now we learn that Paul in fact did and does preach a species of esoteric wisdom to selected converts able to handle it. It is the revelation of the mystery of salvation, that which philosophical reasoning could never have guessed: Christ descended into the sub-lunar world of matter, clothing himself in the semblance of mortal flesh in order to slip past the watchful eyes of the demonic Archons who patrol the concentric heavenly spheres nabbing souls who seek to wend their way to God after death. For Christ was on a secret mission to subvert and to destroy the Archons and their reign of oppression. They recognized him once he appeared and thought to stop him, engineering his crucifixion, little suspecting that in doing so they would be ensuring the very victory they sought to prevent!

But is not this pretty much the essence of Gnostic doctrine? Has Paul suddenly switched sides? No, because he considers these malevolent entities responsible for the worldly wisdom that prevents the intellectuals from embracing his gospel (and, as we will see in Galatians and Colossians, for the delusions of prideful religious legalism). As will also become evident in chapter 15, Paul may not be so far from his Gnostic rivals.[57] This should be no surprise at all, since the Nag Hammadi texts make it clear that the numerous Gnostic sects polemicized against one another in just the same (sometimes hair-splitting) way Paul disputes with the Corinthian Gnostics.[58] It is worth noting that Paul makes the same sort of polemical move in 2 Corinthians 12:1-10. There he is trying to deflate the grand claims of the Judaizing apostles who bragged about their visions from God. He says that if such things impress the Corinthians (which they shouldn't!), he, too, can entertain them with tales of celestial

---

[56] James Barr, *Fundamentalism* (Philadelphia: Westminster Press, 1977), p. 38: "just as a personal conversion is normal as an entry into fundamentalist religion, something not far short of another conversion may be needed before one can get out of it."

[57] Ernst Käsemann, *Perspectives on Paul*. Trans. Margaret Kohl (Philadelphia: Fortress Press, 1971), Chapter I, "On Paul's Anthropology," p. 2; James D.G. Dunn, in his great book, *Unity and Diversity in the New Testament: An Inquiry into the Character of Earliest Christianity* (Philadelphia: Westminster Press, 1977), p. 289: "at several points *Paul is plainly in sympathy with the views of the Corinthian gnostics;*" Hyam Maccoby, *Paul and Hellenism* (London: SCM Press/Philadelphia: Trinity Press International, 1991), p. 37: "it may be useful to consider Paul's views as a kind of moderate Gnosticism." Richard Reitzenstein, *Hellenistic Mystery Religions: Their Basic Ideas and Significance*. Trans. John E. Steely. Pittsburgh Theological Monograph Series Number 15 (Pittsburgh: Pickwick Press, 1978), p. 443: "Paul is a gnostic."

[58] Maccoby, *Paul and Hellenism*, pp. 38, 47.

adventures. But the ironic punch-line of the vision he describes is that all such self-glorifying is worthless because the real glory is that which is discovered amid one's suffering for Christ. (Ouch!)

In 1 Corinthians 3:4-15 Paul appears willing to regard the other figureheads as fellow-workers in tending God's (mission) field (cf., John 4:35-38) and in laying the foundation of his house (the Christian community, cf., Matt. 13:24-30; 1 Pet. 2:4-6), but they will not reciprocate. In 2 Corinthians 10:13-16, Paul takes off the gloves in dealing with the Judaizing Cephas party because they dare to trespass onto Paul's *field*, and in Romans 15:18-20, where he says they are presuming to build upon his *foundation*. But for now, he only goes so far as to admit (3:10-15) that, theoretically, some apostle's work might turn out, on the Day of Judgment, to have been shoddy and unsound (cf., Matt. 7:24-27). But even if this were to occur, the failed apostle in question would still not succumb to the flames along with the mess he has made (verse 15). Does he have anyone in particular in mind? Cephas? Apollos? It doesn't matter. His point is that the one who really needs to worry about possible damnation is anyone who dares destroy the harmony of the Christian community by fomenting the very sort of internecine strife now brewing among the Corinthians (verses 16-17).

In 4:1-5 Paul claims immunity from criticism for himself, Apollos, and Cephas. Again, theoretically, one or all of them might err, even Paul, for all he knows, but that is for God to decide at the Judgment, not troublemaking church members before that time. Any church pastor knows the headaches his or her parishioners may gratuitously cause. But what Paul says is nonetheless a bit unsettling: is it not open to dangerous abuse? Any Jim Jones, David Koresh, or Charles Manson[59] might point to this verse (especially *in context!*) to squelch dissent from their congregations. It may seem untoward for a minister to sleep with women in the church, but have some faith! Sure, it may not seem wise to *you*, but God's seeming foolishness is *like* that. Don't risk blaspheming the Holy Spirit!

The argument moves on (verses 6-8) to tackle an underlying issue: the arrogance of the Gnostic party is rooted in what theologians call "over-realized eschatology" or "enthusiasm" (Ernst Käsemann).[60] This is the belief that the Eschaton, the kingdom of God, has already dawned in its fullness, albeit invisibly to those lacking the eye of faith.

---

[59] Or any of the cult demagogues scrutinized in Colin Wilson's *Rogue Messiahs: Tales of Self-Proclaimed Saviors* (Charlottesville, VA: Hampton Roads Publishing, 2000).
[60] Käsemann, *Perspectives on Paul*, e.g., pp. 2, 38, 55, 57, 67, 120, 124-125, 130, 137.

"His disciples say to him, 'When will the kingdom come?' Jesus says, 'It will not come in a way you expect; they will not be able to say, "Look, here!" or "See, there!" Rather, the kingdom of the Father is spread out over the earth without people recognizing it'" (Thomas 113). "Jesus said to her, 'Your brother will rise again.' Martha said to him, 'I know that he will rise again in the resurrection at the last day.' Jesus said to her, 'I am the resurrection'" (John 11:23-25a). "Truly, truly, I say to you, the hour is coming, and now is, when the dead will hear the voice of the Son of God, and those who hear will live" (John 5:25). Paul seems to have espoused what some call "inaugurated (but not yet consummated) eschatology"[61] or "eschatology that is in the process of realizing itself."[62] The kingdom of God, the era of salvation, had dawned with Jesus, but it had not yet been consummated. That must await the Second Coming of Christ, and in the meantime the kingdom of God is experienced by believers only as an inner transformation.

But the Gnostics believed, as we have seen, that the whole thing has happened in baptism. There will be no apocalyptic fireworks, no Antichrist, no Armageddon. Naturally, they expected a great deal from present spiritual experience, including visions, revelations, prophecies, healing miracles, speaking in tongues, etc. It is a safe bet that the Corinthians outside of the "I am of Christ" party experienced none of these things, hence the envy (and condescension) evident in chapters 12 and 14. The same pattern has, not surprisingly, been repeated in the modern Charismatic Movement in mainstream churches. And the Prosperity Gospel preached by televangelists like Kenneth Copeland, Creflow Dollar, and others is clearly the same sort of "enthusiasm."[63] "Already you are filled! [contra Matt. 5:6] Already you have become rich! [contra Matt. 19:29; but parallel to Rev. 3:17] Without us, you have become kings! And would that you did reign so that we might share the reign with you! [contra Matt. 19:28; Rev. 20:4]" (1 Cor. 4:8). By contrast, Paul rejects this "theology of glory" as

---

[61] A.M. Hunter, *Introducing New Testament Theology* (Philadelphia: Westminster Press, 1957), p. 27.

[62] Norman Perrin, *The Kingdom of God in the Teaching of Jesus.* New Testament Library (London: SCM Press, 1963), pp. 87-89; Günther Bornkamm, *Jesus of Nazareth.* Trans. Irene and Fraser McLuskey with James M. Robinson (New York: Harper & Row, 1960), Chapter IV, "The Dawn of the Kingdom of God," pp. 64-95; George Eldon Ladd, *The Presence of the Future: The Eschatology of Biblical Realism* (Grand Rapids: Eerdmans, 1974).

[63] Gordon D. Fee, *The Disease of the Health & Wealth Gospels* (Costa Mesa: The Word for Today, 1979).

premature. For him, the surpassing glory and power of Christ are indeed a present possession but are revealed, yet hidden, in the Christ-like sufferings of those who follow in Christ's footsteps on the way to the cross (2 Cor. 12: 9-10). Paul warns that, on his next visit (which some think he hasn't the guts to make), he will take the Gnostic braggarts in hand and show them the error of their ways (4:18-20)! Now *that* would be something to see.

Beelzebub, Bailiff

Back in 1:13, Paul repudiated any fan-worship directed to him with a *reduction ad absurdum*: "Was Paul crucified for you? Or were you baptized in the name of Paul?" They are holding Paul, Cephas, and Apollos in a reverence that can be appropriate only for Jesus Christ. But in 5:3-5 Paul speaks of himself in a manner that practically makes him a second Christ. Jesus says, "Where two or three are gathered in my name, there am I in the midst of them" (Matt. 18:20). The saying comes at the end of a section on excommunication. First Corinthians 5:3-5 deals with the same question and in much the same terms, only this time the divine spirit hovering invisibly over the judicial proceedings is not that of Jesus but of Paul himself!

> For though absent in body I am present in spirit, and as if present, I have already pronounced judgment in the name of the Lord Jesus on the man who has done such a thing. When you are assembled, and my spirit is present, with the power of our Lord Jesus, you are to deliver this man to Satan for the destruction of the flesh, that his spirit may be saved in the day of the Lord Jesus.[64]

Just as "the Satan" appears in both Testaments as God's prosecutor and chief of sting operations, here he has become the bailiff to whom the condemned is handed over to be delivered to punishment (cf., Luke 12:58). We also seem to hear echoes of Job, where God grants the Satan leave to afflict Job's flesh with boils and sores. This might well be what Paul means by "the destruction of the flesh." Or he just might mean that Satan will kill the poor slob. But if he does, at least the sinner will have gotten his punishment over with in this life (the

---

[64] This piece of early Christian jurisprudence is a prime candidate for a bit of text from an epistle subsequently winding up ascribed to a historical Jesus in the gospels.

end of it!) instead of facing something worse post mortem. In either case, however, the point would seem the same as in Mark 9:43-48: better to lose some skin now than to have your shapely butt tossed into Gehenna.

Paul has let it be known that he is outraged at the failure of the Corinthian church to take action against the notorious sinner in their midst, but it is only the tip of a larger iceberg. Though the congregation as a whole is too chicken (or "broad-minded") to take action against a flagrant sinner whose mere presence must vitiate any claim that Christians, like Jews, stand for higher moral standards (5:7-8), individual congregants don't seem to mind suing each other in the public courts (6:1, 4-5). This Paul decidedly does not like. It is a public relations nightmare: they are airing the church's dirty linen, which it would be better to launder privately. Does this mean that Paul prefers to conceal the church's genuine faults and create a false front? Not necessarily, since he does believe their disputes can be mediated within the congregation without binding legal authority. If they can do that successfully, then they will *deserve* the better public image they are cultivating. What he is proposing has a direct parallel in the establishment of local Jewish courts where Jews might settle their issues instead of taking them to official Roman courts. If they did the latter, Jews would likely invite social ostracism.[65]

Strangely, in arguing his case, Paul seems to lean for a moment in the direction of the "realized eschatology" he opposes elsewhere. He expects that one day in the sweet bye-and-bye, Christian believers will pass judgment on the fallen angels and rule the world (6:2-3)! If such weighty judicial responsibilities are one day to rest on their (winged) shoulders, should they not be able to scrape up at least a few guys with sense enough to mediate the trivial affairs of the here and now? Does he mean to call into the present the Solomonic wisdom promised to the righteous in the Eschaton? Heck, if they had gotten to that point, there wouldn't *be* any of these lawsuits.

Actually, he says, it would be better simply to suck it up: to turn the other cheek and let your misbehaving brother get away with it. Let his guilty conscience rule against him. But then what are Christians doing defrauding each other (or anyone else, for that matter) in the first place? You just can't expect to act that way and still be welcomed into the kingdom of God. Paul then lists some major offenses that exclude from salvation any who commit them. Most are

---

[65] J. Duncan M. Derrett, "Law in the New Testament: The Parable of the Unjust Judge." *New Testament Studies* 18 (1971-1972), pp. 178-191.

pretty obvious as well as clear in meaning. However, it is worth pointing out that "homosexuals" (verse 9) is a misleading translation. Paul does seem to issue a blanket condemnation of male homosexuality in Romans 1:27,[66] but here he is more specific. He uses two rare Greek words (i.e., they happen to occur so seldom in extant Greek texts that it is hard, from the context, to be certain what they mean). The first, *malakoi*, "soft ones" or "effeminate," seems to denote powdered, perfumed, and coiffed call-boys, catamites. The second, *arsenokoitai*, is more difficult, meaning either "men who have sex" or "those who have sex with men." (Of course, women would qualify, but that would not be condemned as a moral perversion.) No, according to John Boswell, the word seems to denote either gay male prostitutes or their customers.[67] These nuances would imply condemnation of specific homosexual sins, not homosexuality in general, though that is probably presupposed. On the other hand, Robin Scroggs[68] plausibly suggests that *arsenokoitai* just translates the Old Testament Hebrew for one who "lie[s] with a male" (as with a woman) from Leviticus 18:22. And Derrick Sherwin Bailey thinks *malakoi* denotes the passive role in gay sex, while *arsenokoitai* would denote those on the giving end.[69] So who knows?

Is Gnosis Carnal Knowledge?

The transition to verses 12-20 seems arbitrary and abrupt—unless we are to understand that the offenses the Corinthians are committing against one another, and especially the evil deeds just listed, are supposed to stem from a theological antinomianism on the part of some. And the finger must point to the Gnostics, (implicitly) depicted as libertines. We know that early church heresiologists (heresy experts) accused the Gnostics of sexual abandon based on their belief that they were exempt from the laws issued by the Demiurge (Jehovah, the

---

[66] I think that Romans 1:26b refers to bestiality, not lesbianism, and that it and the homosexuality business in verse 27 reflect Leviticus 18:22-23.

[67] John Boswell, *Christianity, Social Tolerance, and Homosexuality: Gay People in Western Europe from the Beginning of the Christian Era to the Fourteenth Century* (Chicago: University of Chicago Press, 1980), pp. 106-107.

[68] Robin Scroggs, *The New Testament and Homosexuality: Contextual Background for Contemporary Debate* (Philadelphia: Fortress Press, 1983), pp. 107-108.

[69] Derrick Sherwin Bailey, *Homosexuality in the Western Christian Tradition* (London: Longmans, Green, 1955), p. 38.

subordinate God). Though the various Gnostics who wrote the Nag Hammadi texts appear to have been ascetics, we do know of at least one libertine Gnostic sect, the Phibionites, described by Epiphanius, fourth-century bishop of Salamis, who says he had, in his youth, attended one of their meetings.

> Their women, they share in common; and when anyone arrives who might be alien to their doctrine, the men and women have a sign by which they make themselves known to each other. . . when they have so assured themselves, they address themselves immediately to the feast, serving up a lavish bounty of meats and wines, even though they may be poor. And when they have thus banqueted. . . they proceed to the work of mutual incitement. Husbands separate from wives, and a man will say to his own spouse: "Arise and celebrate the 'love feast' with thy brother." And the wretches mingle with each other, and although I am verily mortified to tell of the infamies they perpetrate, I shall not hesitate. . .
>
> For after they have consorted together in a passionate debauch, they do not stop there in their blasphemy of Heaven. The women and the men take the man's ejaculation into their hands, stand up, throw back their heads in self-denial towards Heaven and, even with that impurity on their palms, pretend to pray as so-called Soldiers of God and Gnostics, offering to the Father, the Primal Being of All Nature, what is on their hands, with the words: "We bring to Thee this oblation, which is the very Body of Christ." Whereupon, without further ado, they consume it, take hold of their shame and say: "This is the Body of Christ, the Paschal Sacrifice through which our bodies suffer and are forced to confess the sufferings of Christ." And when the woman is in her period, they do likewise with her menstruation. The unclean flow of blood, which they garner, is taken up in the same way and eaten together. And that, they say, is Christ's Blood. For when they read in Revelation, "I saw the tree of life with its twelve kinds of fruit, yielding its fruit each month" (Rev 22:2), they interpret this as an allusion to the monthly incidence of the female period. (*Panarion* 26.4.1)

Unless our goal is to clean up the image of the ancient Gnostics, there is no reason to deny that some of them embraced such antinomianism. And it is then no surprise that Paul at once locks horns with them. Verses 12-13 has Paul grant the Gnostic claim to a higher knowledge transcending human law (specifically the Jewish Torah) but then challenge their application of it: yes, yes, we know (Paul, too, claims the gnosis) that "all things are lawful for me," but that doesn't mean everything is just as *advisable* as everything else. Some things you might do, you would regret because they will harm you. I think Paul is really (to borrow Kant's terms) arguing that even if we jettison any "categorical imperative" (an absolute duty to obey God's commands), we still must take seriously "hypothetical imperatives," the prudential considerations that dictate that certain behaviors will bring about certain results we may not like, and it would be just stupid to behave heedless of these likely results. Lawful? Yes, certainly. Expedient? No. Don't be a child!

These Gnostics must have been justifying their visits to the Red Light District on the basis that the flesh is morally irrelevant, and that since it is the creation of the ignorant Demiurge, one might as well give it what it wants. If the stomach is hungry, by all means feed it. Why not? And if one is feeling randy, heck, it's just a hormonal thing—so what? Paul rejects this thinking in no uncertain terms. He cannot bring himself to write off the body this way. What the body wants to do in this case is evil, a product of unsanctified lusts, and one cannot prevent oneself (one's soul) being tainted with that evil.

The Gnostics probably shared some form of yogic/Tantric detachment: the belief that the enlightened person henceforth lived out his earthly existence in a state of "mere witness" in which no worldly deed accrues karma, good or bad, therefore attracting no reward or judgment.[70] As opportunities to experience spiritual transcendence, such ordinarily "sinful" acts may actually contribute to salvation. A Tantric maxim runs: "By the same acts that cause some men to boil in hell for a hundred thousand eons, the yogi gains his eternal salvation."[71]

Needless to say, Paul takes a different view of the matter. He understands it along anthropological lines. All taboos on things entering the body (food, sex, etc.) mirror and symbolize the rules protecting the body politic, the community. This is why Ezra and

---

[70] Mircea Eliade, *Yoga: Immortality and Freedom*. Trans. Willard R. Trask. Bollingen Series LVI (Princeton: Princeton University Press, 1970), pp. 33-34.

[71] Eliade, *Yoga*, p. 263; Agehananda Bharati, *The Tantric Tradition* (Garden City: Doubleday Anchor Books, 1970), p. 290.

Nehemiah insisted that Jews divorce their non-Jewish spouses. This was the reason for kosher laws and rituals like circumcision: they constituted high walls to turn away those who might seek entry to the community, bringing heathen ways with them. It is why even today Jewish leaders oppose interfaith marriage, since such unions will swiftly erode Jewish identity. If, Paul says, you as a Christian feel free to patronize prostitutes, you are degrading the Christian community, contributing to the relaxation of its standards. It is the same danger the church faced by accommodating the incestuous behavior of the man Paul insisted they excommunicate. The Christian whoremaster is sinning against the Body of Christ (one's physical body = one's Christian "body politic") by joining it with a prostitute.

We can see the danger Paul describes in the recent statistics on youth pre-marital sex: Evangelicals are now neck-and-neck with their "unsaved" contemporaries. Whether pre-marital sex is morally wrong or right is not the issue. This *is*: precious little is left to distinguish fornicating Christian youth from the "sinners" they are supposed to be "witnessing to." The Evangelical teen urges the non-Christian teen to jump ship and swim on over. But the latter is confused: "What are you talking about? You're standing on the same deck with me!"

Everything You Always Wanted to Know About Celibacy but Were Afraid to Ask

Chapter 7 is where Paul begins to address the questions sent him via the household of Stephanas. Up to this point he has been reacting to the oral reports from Chloe's people. But there may be less discontinuity between chapters 6 and 7 than this might suggest, for he continues to talk about Christian sexuality. In chapter 7, the issue is celibacy, or, to borrow and generalize a second-century term, "encratism" (from the Greek *encrateo*, "self-control," implying sexual continence). Is this not the opposite end of the spectrum from Gnostic libertinism? It is more like the opposite side of the same coin, for both represent the characteristic sectarian transformation of conventional sex ethics and definitions of marriage. When radical religious communes say they have renounced worldly marriage bonds, some mean they have embraced free love instead, while others, like the modern Shaker sect, swear off sex completely. Some will repudiate marriage but not sex, while others will renounce sex but not marriage, as we will shortly see.

In verses 1-7 Paul endorses celibacy (and not just for clergy, of whom there were none yet), though he cautions his readers about some inherent dangers. "It is good for a man not to touch a woman" is a solid endorsement of celibacy, since "to touch" was a contemporary euphemism for "to have sex with." But it may go farther still, in view of the fact that the word *aner* means both "man" and "husband," and the word *gune* means both "woman" and "wife." In view of what immediately follows, it is probable that Paul means to say, "It is good for a husband to refrain from sex with his wife." But one would be foolish not to reckon with the live possibility that one spouse will prove unable to hold out for the long haul (just as Jerry, Kramer, Elaine, and George had to drop out of their masturbation moratorium on *Seinfeld*) and will seek satisfaction outside the marriage. (Maybe he is too embarrassed to admit his weakness to his wife, or maybe she has locked the bedroom door against him, as Scarlet does to Rhett in *Gone with the Wind*.)

So Paul suggests only temporary abstinence for days or weeks, while pious husband and wife devote themselves to prayer instead. Given this proviso, "Let each husband have his wife" ("to have," in such a context, is another euphemism for sex, as it still is today). And he suggests that single men and women intending a career in celibacy might want to think again; he prescribes marriage as a "concession," seeing that at least it is preferable to what may happen if one is driven crazy by sexual desire.

Some in the congregation have already divorced, believing that sex even within marriage is unclean (verses 10-11). Of course, Paul has come pretty close to saying the same thing himself when he advises deferring sex for a period of prayer, as if sexuality and spirituality are incompatible.[72] But this is not the sole reason for divorce in Corinth. Plutarch urged new brides not to stray from their husbands' traditional gods in favor of exotic Mystery Cult deities.[73]

---

[72] Dietrich Bonhoeffer quipped, "But, speaking frankly, to long for the transcendent when you are in your wife's arms is, to put it mildly, a lack of taste." (*Letters and Papers from Prison*. Trans. Reginald H. Fuller [New York: Macmillan, 1953], p. 113). Bonhoeffer, in the German original, was spelled "Bonhöffer." A teacher of mine, Robert F. Streetman, a bit too enamored of German umlauts, used to pronounce the theologian's name "Bernherffer."

[73] Plutarch, "Marriage Counsel." In *On Love, the Family, and the Good Life: Selected Essays of Plutarch*. Trans. Moses Hadas (New York: New American Library/Mentor Books, 1957), p. 83.

> A wife ought not to acquire friends of her own, but share in her husband's friends. First and greatest of friends are the gods, and hence it becomes the wife to worship the gods her husband believes in and to recognize none other. Her house door should be closed to exotic rites and alien superstitions. No god can be pleased with clandestine and surreptitious rituals performed by a woman.

That would constitute religious cheating (a metaphor familiar from the Old Testament). Apparently, some of the pagan husbands of Christian women in Corinth agreed, and had sent their insubordinate wives packing (verses 10-11). Needless to say, it does not occur to Paul to suggest that the wife drop her new faith in order to restore domestic harmony (cf., Luke 14:26). Paul tells such women they are free to marry a new husband so long as he is a Christian.

Or the situation may be identical to that described in the Apocryphal Acts of the Apostles: it is not merely the woman's conversion to the Christian sect that is the problem, but rather that the wife refuses to have sex with her heathen husband! It is pretty easy to see such a husband divorcing such a wife. But Paul doesn't think Christian wives should initiate divorce because, they imagine, a mixed marriage is no marriage in the eyes of God. In answer to a follow-up question, Paul (verse 12) assures Christian wives who are still married to non-Christians that they need not worry that any children they may have with an unbelieving husband will be illegitimate in God's eyes (verse 14). No, the fact that the mother is a Christian makes the child automatically legitimate ("clean"). (This is exactly the same as the contemporary Jewish policy toward the children of mixed marriages.) Nor are they "living in sin" with a non-Christian mate. The union is sanctified anyway in God's eyes.

What about widows? Should they remarry? In verses 39-40, Paul advises against it, though they are free to do as they wish. But they would do better to join the stipended Order of Widows and Virgins (the precursors of nuns) and henceforth consecrate themselves to prayer. Domestic duties and sexual-spousal duties, though quite legitimate, do not allow for single-minded devotion to Christ (e.g., contemplative prayer and ministries of charity).

Much scholarly debate has centered on Paul's strange-sounding advice in verses 36-38. What kind of people is he talking about? Engaged couples? Father, daughter, and fiancé? Or something else entirely? I think the New English Bible gets this right.

> If a man has a partner in celibacy and feels that he is not behaving properly towards her, if, that is, his instincts are too strong for him, and something must be done, he may do as he pleases; there is nothing wrong in it; let them marry. But if a man is steadfast in his purpose, being under no compulsion, and has complete control of his own choice; and if he has decided in his own mind to preserve his partner in her virginity, he will do well. Thus, he who marries his partner does well, and he who does not will do better.

There is much discussion in second- and third-century sources about the *virgines subintroductae* or *agapetae*, consecrated women who lived and travelled with celibate Christian men, something like today's Catholic priests and their housekeepers living under the same roof in the rectory. Some praised the arrangement, while others thought it invited scandal, real or imagined. In any case, I think 1 Corinthians 7:36-38 attests the practice.

Who were these encratite Corinthians? I would have to include them among the Gnostics. They were venturing to bring the post-sexual state of the resurrection (Mark 12:25, "when they rise from the dead, they neither marry nor are given in marriage, but are like angels in heaven.") into the present on the assumption of fully realized eschatology.

One last note on this chapter. In verse 10, Paul declares, "To the married, I give charge, not I but the Lord," etc. A bit later on, he admits, "Now concerning the unmarried, I have no command of the Lord, but I give my opinion as one who by the Lord's mercy is trustworthy" (verse 25). I believe that some read way too much into these verses when they say Paul is drawing a clear line between actual teachings/sayings of the historical Jesus (in this case, Mark 10:11-12) and his own opinions.[74] I think it much sounder to interpret these passages in light of another from the same epistle, 1 Corinthians 14:37, "If any one thinks that he is a prophet, or spiritual, he should acknowledge that what I am writing to you is a command of the Lord." In other words, Paul differentiates between revealed commands vouchsafed him by the heavenly Christ on the one hand and his own studied opinions on the other. If there is any relation between 1 Corinthians 7:10 and its Markan counterpart, I should deem it more likely that a saying of Paul has been credited to Jesus rather than the

---

[74] E.g., F.F. Bruce, *The New Testament Documents: Are They Reliable?* (Grand Rapids: Eerdmans, 1960), p. 46.

other way around.

Why Does He Eat with Idolaters and Diabolists?

Chapters 8-10 deal with a theologically laden question of etiquette. Suppose a non-Christian friend, say a worshipper of the traditional Olympian deities or of the savior gods of the Mystery Cults, invites you to a dinner party, and he has rented out the dining hall of a local temple for the event. Or maybe he is hosting it at his home, but the steaks he grills up were purchased at the public meat market, and chances are good the steaks were left-overs from temple sacrifices. Should you go? Hmmm... Well, it is clear that Gnostics in the Corinthian congregation felt no qualms about it, but that others in the church were scandalized; hence the question submitted to Paul. As we will see, he seems to give two somewhat inconsistent replies, one he thinks will make sense to each of two factions: Gnostics and Judaizers.

You can tell he is addressing Gnostics as soon as he grants their premise, "We know that all of us possess knowledge (*gnosis*)." In this case, knowledge of *what*? That there is but one single God and one single Lord, namely the Creator and his Son through whom he made all things. This way of putting it echoes the language of the Mystery Cults, [75] each with its top-tier deities like Zeus, and its second-tier saviors like Hercules and Asclepius. The former were called *theoi* ("gods"), while the latter were called *kurioi* ("lords"). He assumes that no one in the Corinthian church will dispute Christian exclusivity (though some "weaker brethren" may have a less than secure hold on the idea, as we will soon see). And since we know this, it follows that the worshippers of these fictional gods are just wasting their breath: no one is on the other end of the phone (like Atheist Dial-a-Prayer). Think of 1 Kings 18:26-29. And this in turn means that one need not worry if the meat one is invited to eat had been offered in sacrifice to Apollo or Serapis; it might as well have been offered by a little girl to her dolly. So the Gnostics are quite right—so far.

But, as the Gnostics themselves are fond of pointing out, not everybody in the congregation is quite as clued in as they are. There

---

[75] Paul thus admits that his religion is structured the same way, Jesus being analogous to Hercules, etc. See Wilhelm Bousset, *Kyrios Christos: A History of the Belief in Christ from the Beginnings of Christianity to Irenaeus*. Trans. John E. Steely (New York: Abingdon Press, 1970).

must be some who spot their oh-so-sophisticated brethren strolling into a heathen temple with their pagan buddies and infer (wrongly) that the Gnostic brethren are not exclusive monotheists after all. And this would be quite natural given that in that milieu an individual might belong to several religions simultaneously in order to cover all bets.[76] The "weaker brother" might figure, "*Huh!* I guess *I* can split my worship between several religions, too!" Thus the Gnostic might easily be (albeit unwittingly) leading his weaker brother astray. Surely he can't want that? His goal must be to uplift the ungifted to heights of greater knowledge such as the Gnostic himself already occupies. Don't lead the poor guy into greater confusion! So, pal Gnostic, you're right, but you're wrong.

Chapter 9 has a pretty tenuous connection with its context and might have been placed here by the later editor assembling the textual jigsaw puzzle. But it may simply be a digression. The discussion does start with Paul using himself as an example of yielding one's rights for the good of others, the thing he is asking the stronger brethren to do for the sake of the weaker. But from there, the argument seems to take a pretty circuitous route.

Paul makes a strong case that, as an apostle[77] (an authoritative missionary pioneer, like Barnabas, not one of the Twelve but on the same level),[78] he has every right to refrain from secular work, being subsidized by his churches so he can devote his full attention to preaching the gospel (cf., Acts 6:2). And he certainly has the right to take a Christian woman along with him (cf., Luke 8:3) to assist him, as do other apostles (here again, the *agapetae*). But he does neither. Why?

---

[76] They realized what Pascal, with his famous "wager," did not: it's not simply a question of whether God exists or he doesn't. No, you have a whole slate of gods, like the variety of horses on the race track. Which one will pay off? To play it safe, many people in the Hellenistic world placed at least a modest bet on several of the divine nags. See Rodney Stark, *The Rise of Christianity: A Sociologist Reconsiders History* (Princeton: Princeton University Press, 1996), pp. 203-206.

[77] "Am I not an apostle? Have I not seen the Lord?" (9:1). This equation implies that having had a resurrection appearance vouchsafed one was a necessary credential if one were to be recognized as an apostle. See Reginald H. Fuller, *The Formation of the Resurrection Narratives* (New York: Macmillan, 1971), pp. 45-48; Rudolf Bultmann, *Theology of the New Testament*. Complete in One Volume. Trans. Kendrick Grobel. Scribner Studies in Contemporary Theology (New York: Scribners, 1951, 1955), Vol. 1, p. 60.

[78] Günther Bornkamm, *Paul*. Trans. D.M.G. Stalker (New York: Harper & Row, 1971), pp. 74-75; Walter Schmithals, *The Office of Apostle in the Early Church*. Trans. John E. Steely (New York: Abingdon Press, 1969); Günter Klein, *Die zwölf Apostel: Ursprung und Gehalt einer Idee* (Göttingen: Vandenhoeck & Ruprecht, 1961).

He does not want people to get the wrong idea (just like he doesn't want the weaker brethren to get the wrong idea about the stronger eating at Chock Full o' Gods). One can well imagine what many would think: Paul is exploiting and swindling the poor rubes he recruits, and, like Simon Magus, he is travelling with a prostitute. No, it is a point of pride with him that he does work for a living (like the rabbis) and that he eschews female companionship (just as Billy Graham always made it a policy to keep the door open whenever he was in his office counseling a female parishioner). It is all for the success of the evangelistic mission. Indeed he will adapt himself to the point of Torah-observance when among Jews, dropping it when among Gentiles. When in Rome...

It seems odd for Paul to veer so far off the track on such a slight pretext. One suspects that he is taking the opportunity to answer a criticism from opponents in Corinth. As Gerd Theissen observes,[79] it appears that some were calling Paul's (supposed) bluff: real apostles do not hesitate to welcome financial support from the congregations where they speak (cf., Matt. 10:9-10). If Paul refuses to do this, it only shows he knows he does not really qualify. This charge would have been made by Cephas or Apollos (or their representatives), who had recruited partisans for themselves during stopovers in Corinth, planting the seeds of the factional strife discussed in 1:11-17; 3:1-22.

The difference in approach when he returns to the question of food offered to idols in chapter 10 provides a great example of his chameleon-like approach to what theologians call "contextualization." Now he reverses himself on whether idols are just grotesque statues. Now it seems they are the ventriloquist dummies of living demons! (This was the common Jewish opinion of pagan gods.) You don't, he warns the Corinthians, want to be caught worshipping demons, because that's just what you are *doing* if you partake of their sacrifices (even via the secular after-market). Have you forgotten how God laid waste no less than 23,000 Israelites in the wake of the Baal-Peor fiasco in Numbers chapter 25?[80] He's still got an itchy trigger finger.

This is an argument designed to appeal to Jewish Torah-Christians in Corinth. The notion that Gentile gods are really demons is attested in Deuteronomy 32:17, and the bizarre business about a

---

[79] Gerd Theissen, *The Social Setting of Pauline Christianity: Essays on Corinth.* Trans. John H. Schütz (Edinburgh: T&T Clark, 1982), p. 53.

[80] Numbers 25:9 puts the number of the slain at 24,000. Where'd Paul get the extra 500? Collateral damage?

rock following Israel through the desert (10:1-4) is a widely known midrashic invention to connect Exodus 17:6 and Numbers 20:11, two versions of the story where water springs from a rock to slake the thirst of the parched Israelites. The first takes place in Rephidim, the second in Kadesh. Was it the same rock, a portable water source? In any case, the same story appears in the Greek *Biblical Antiquities of Pseudo-Philo*.[81]

Paul circles back to the Gnostics in verses 23-24, then moves from theory to specifics. He knows his readers will be exasperated, asking, "Well, what am I supposed to *do* then? Go vegetarian, just to be on the safe side? Not likely! Make a jerk of myself by asking the guy who invites me over for a steak, 'Uh, do you happen to know if the butcher you bought the beef from got it from the temple? Because if you don't, I'm gonna have to have a soyburger!'?" Don't worry, Paul has a reasonable compromise: if you don't want to hear the answer, don't ask the question! But suppose your host happens to volunteer, "Y'know, I got a great deal on these steaks! They were discounted because they came from the Isis temple!" Then you're going to have to spit it out and excuse yourself. Sorry.

You can imagine your host's puzzled expression, and your chagrinned explanation: "Yeah... y'see, I can't eat it because some idiot in my church might have seen you buy the meat, and he might know where it came from, and then he might think my coming here means I'm a damn polytheist. Yeah, I know it's crazy." I think it a safe bet that no one obeyed the apostle on this one. Would you?[82]

From Adam's Rib to Women's Lib

In 1 Corinthians 10:2-16 Paul tries to resolve a congregational row over whether women should be allowed to pray and prophesy in public and without a veil over the head. It is plain he doesn't want them to, and he uses every argument he can think of. Yet even he cannot carry it off with a straight face. Bequeathing theologians a Christological migraine, Paul subordinates Christ to God in the Great

---

[81] Westminster Abbey claims to have this rock, the Stone of Scone, which sits beneath the coronation throne used by numerous kings of Scotland and England. An old gent pointed it out to me when I visited London in 1973. The legend circulated among Diaspora Jews, as Hyam Maccoby shows in *Paul and Hellenism*, p. 153.

[82] Need I add that today's equivalent might be, "Look, I'm sorry I can't attend Fiesta Night at the frat house this evening. Some hyper-sensitive PC nut on campus might accuse me of friggin' 'cultural appropriation.'"

Chain of Being: God is the head of (i.e., chief over) Christ, Christ is head over every husband, and the husband is head over the wife. Good luck squaring *that* with the Athanasian Creed, huh?

Anyway, given this hierarchical order, Paul says that men, directly reflecting the glory of God,[83] must not appear at worship with heads covered, but women are only designed to reflect the glory of *men*. They find themselves at one remove from God and thus are obliged to cover their heads in God's presence (i.e., in public worship) and to *unveil* them before their husbands at home. Obviously, this is meant as synecdoche (a part standing for the whole) for the wife being naked in front of her husband. Women were created for the benefit of men, a la Genesis 2, not men for women. And Paul extends his reference to the Eden story as currently interpreted: Eve was created for Adam and was, like him, naked, and this attracted the lascivious attentions of the Archons (the sons of God from Genesis 6:1-4), who proceeded to rape her. (*The Hypostasis of the Archons*, one of the Nag Hammadi documents, spells all this out, with its own Gnostic spin.) Corinthian church ladies, Paul suggests, should beware the danger that frisky angels observing their worship might notice a pretty face if it went unveiled, and one might find herself molested by an incubus!

On second thought, though, as Christians, men and women are interdependent (on the same level after all?), and, too, even though the first woman was made from the first man, all the subsequent men have come from women, so, what the heck, maybe the whole thing evens out in the end. Talk about an uncertain sound from the bugle (1 Cor. 14:8)!

Notice, however, that Paul does *not* challenge the propriety of women publicly praying and prophesying. Some point to an apparent contradiction in 14:34-35:

> the women should keep silence in the churches. For they are not permitted to speak, but should be subordinate, as even the law says. If there is anything they desire to know, let them ask their husbands at home. For it is shameful for a woman to speak in church.

This seems to contradict what Paul says in chapter 11 about *wives* prophesying: it is ultimately because she belongs to her husband that a woman must display his authority on her head via her veil. Yet in

---

[83] Especially the bald ones?

14:34-35 Paul explicitly says wives must keep mum in church. I think there is a missing puzzle piece here, though it is not hard to discern its outline. Paul's informants may not have been entirely clear describing the situation, ignoring the fact (as I see it) that the women publicly praying/prophesying were *consecrated virgins* as described in 7:34: "the unmarried woman or girl [literally, "virgin"] is anxious about the affairs of the Lord, how to be holy in body and spirit; but the married woman is anxious about worldly affairs, how to please her husband." It is this exemption from domestic, wifely duties and status that absolves her (or *should* absolve her) of the requirement of wearing a veil.[84] After all, doesn't Paul say to the Corinthians elsewhere (2 Cor. 3:18), "And *we all, with unveiled face*, behold... the glory of the Lord," etc.?

Table Manners

Pursuing the general topic of church decorum, Paul deals next with the Agape Feast (11:17-34). This was, we think, the larger meal within which the Eucharist (Holy Communion) was celebrated. In verses 17-22, he rebukes the Corinthians for shaming the poorer members, probably slaves, who can't get off work till late and miss the community meal. Before they get there, the more well-to-do members (no doubt including the household of Stephanas!) treat the meal like an all-you-can-eat buffet, and there are but slim pickings when the rest show up. But it is an easy problem to fix: those better off should eat a big lunch before they arrive and eat light once they get there, to make sure there's plenty left for everybody.

It is not clear how the preceding leads to verses 23-26, Paul's version of the Words of Institution from the Last Supper. This version doesn't match any of the Synoptic versions exactly.[85] You have to wonder (though that's all you can do) whether this section is a later

---

[84] Peter Brown, *The Body and Society: Men, Women, and Sexual Renunciation in Early Christianity*. Lectures on the History of Religions, new series no. 13 (New York: Columbia University Press, 1988), pp. 80-81.

[85] For detailed comparisons, see Joachim Jeremias, *The Eucharistic Words of Jesus*. Trans. Arnold Ehrhardt (Oxford: Basil Blackwell, 1955); Albert Schweitzer, *The Problem of the Lord's Supper according to the Scholarly Research of the Nineteenth Century and the Historical Accounts. Volume I: The Lord's Supper in Relationship to the Life of Jesus and the History of the Early Church.* Trans. A.J. Mattill, Jr. (Macon: Mercer University Press, 1982).

interpolation.[86] Verses 27-34 would make sense as the original, direct continuation to verses 17-22. Especially in view of verses 33-34, verse 27 need not refer back to verses 23-26, where the "body of Christ" refers to the sacramental bread. Rather, verse 27 would be the first mention of the body and blood of Christ, and the reference would be to the corporate body of Christ as the church community. "Not to discern the body" (verse 29) would refer to the casual, cavalier attitude of those who stuff themselves without a thought for the poor Lazaruses of the congregation, not to anyone's disregard of the Real Presence of Christ in the elements. The crime for which God is smiting some of the Corinthians (verse 30) is not some lack of sacramental mindfulness but rather the lack of consideration for poorer members at the meal, just as in verses 33-34. In short, nothing after the Words of Institution section needs to be read as referring back to it.[87]

But perhaps Paul did write verses 23-26. In that case, where did he get this liturgical material (a ceremonial etiology for the Eucharist)? Most have assumed Paul "received" (verse 23) the material from the other apostles or generally from Christians before him. But, as Maccoby points out, the terminology might very well mean that Paul "received" the information from the heavenly Christ in a vision, just as Moses received the Ten Commandments direct from God on the mountaintop before he delivered them to Israel.[88] In other words, Paul would stand at the beginning of the tradition, not somewhere down the line. However, this theory seems to be ruled out by the fact that the 1 Corinthians version evidences signs of having evolved from an earlier form of the Words of Institution as preserved in Mark. Thus it cannot be a *de novo* revelation to Paul.

---

[86] Jean Magne, *From Christianity to Gnosis and From Gnosis to Christianity: An Itinerary through the Texts To and From the Tree of Paradise.* Trans. A.F.W. Armstrong. Brown Judaic Studies, 286 (Atlanta: Scholars Press, 1993), p. 33.

[87] Another reason for suspecting verses 23-26 to be an interpolation is that otherwise it would be the only instance of Paul narrating an episode from the life of an earthly Jesus.

[88] Maccoby, *Paul and Hellenism.* p. 92; Dunn, *Unity and Diversity in the New Testament,* p. 67: "he specifically designates the source of the Last Supper tradition as 'the Lord'. This seems to mean not so much that the earthly Jesus was the source of the tradition, but rather that Paul understood the present, exalted Jesus to be the immediate source of the historical formula."

THE FIRST EPISTLE TO THE CORINTHIANS

Pneumatics, You Know the Drill

With chapters 12-13 we finally get to the root of most of the problems in Corinth, the *pneumatikoi*. How to translate this? It just means "spirituals," but spiritual *whats*? Usually we think of the *charismata* (charismatic gifts) discussed at length in these chapters, but I think the intended reference is to "spiritual ones," those endowed with the Spirit (as in 1 Corinthians 2:13, 15; 3:1). Paul, like the Valentinian Gnostics of the second century, who claimed him as their "grandfounder,"[89] divided mankind into three categories. First came the pneumatics who possessed a spark of the divine. Second were the *psuchikoi* ("psychics," implying "natural ones" or "soulish ones," setting aside the modern meaning of the term as those with telepathy, etc.). They were bereft of true divinity but were devotees of conventional religion, whether Jewish or Christian. Third came the irreligious drones, two-legged animals, the riff-raff. These they called the *sarkikoi* ("carnal ones") or the *hylikoi* ("wooden-heads"). Not very flattering, but certainly inductively based on observation. Paul's "weaker brethren" were the psychics, what I like to call the "pew-potatoes." The sarkics were just the profane, the "sinners." It seems to me that throughout 1 Corinthians Paul is trying to find a platform for co-existence between the pneumatics (the "stronger brethren," among whom he includes himself, perhaps at times a mite disingenuously) and the psychics, who are both envious and suspicious of the pneumatics.[90] Paul, as we have seen, tries to persuade the pneumatics to treat the psychics with compassionate consideration, to give them a hand up, or at least not to scandalize them.

Surely the most startling verse of the whole Bible must be 1 Corinthians 12:3, "I want you to understand that no one speaking by the Spirit of God ever says 'Jesus be cursed!' and no one can say 'Jesus is Lord' except by the Holy Spirit." Who does Paul have in mind here?

---

[89] Paul taught Theodas, who taught Valentinus.

[90] Much the same division, though with more severe tensions, is manifest in 1 John. Anyone familiar with the Charismatic Movement in the mainstream Protestant denominations and the Roman Catholic Church will immediately recognize the same pattern. See Ralph Martin (Roman Catholic), *Unless the Lord Build the House... The Church and the New Pentecost* (Notre Dame: Ave Maria Press, 1972); Kevin Ranaghan (Roman Catholic), *Catholic Pentecostals* (Rahway: Paulist Press, 1969); J. Rodman Williams (Presbyterian), *The Era of the Spirit* (Plainfield: Logos International, 1971); Dennis J. Bennett (Episcopalian), *Nine O'Clock in the Morning* (Plainfield: Logos International, 1970); Harald Bredesen (Lutheran), *Need a Miracle?* (Praise Books, 1979).

It must be somebody; as a purely hypothetical proposition it is just ludicrous, like announcing, "An amoeba cannot be elected President of the United States." Uh, *yeah*, but so *what?* Paul must be addressing a real issue, no matter how bizarre it sounds outside its original context. But I am convinced we know what that context was. Some in the Corinthian congregation are standing up to prophesy, eyes rolled back to show the whites, and saying, "Jesus be damned!" Sometimes you hear people blurting out things like this in the middle of a church service, but of course, it's only the mentally impaired.[91] That's not in view here, because it is a question about ostensibly inspired bulletins from God, which some are inclined to take seriously. It is a doctrinal proposal, exactly like 1 John 4:1-3, and indeed it concerns pretty much the same issue: Gnostic Christology.

Surely it was (at least some among) the pneumatics who disparaged the incarnation of Jesus. Third-century theologian Origen of Alexandria mentions this practice as still alive in his own day. He bemoans the fact that the Ophite Gnostics "do not admit anyone into their meeting unless he has first pronounced curses against Jesus" (*Contra Celsum* VI:28) "There is a certain sect which does not admit a convert unless he pronounces anathemas on Jesus; and that sect is worthy of the name which it has chosen; for it is the sect of the so-called Ophites, who utter blasphemous words in praise of the serpent" (*Catena fragm. 47 on I Corinthians xii.3*).

Still, we have to ask: why would any co-called Christians say such a thing? The answer: they did not believe in a unitary "Jesus Christ," but instead believed that the human Jesus was but the temporary "channeler" for the Christ Spirit who had descended to meet him at his baptism ("he saw the heavens opened and the Spirit descending *into* him[92] like a dove.") and departed from him on the cross ("My God, my God, why have you forsaken me?"). It does seem a bit odd that they would anathematize the human Jesus, but the point must have been to reject the worship of Jesus in his own right, which would make him into an idol. Thus these Corinthian pneumatic Gnostics could and did say *both* "I belong to Christ!" *and* "Jesus be cursed!" It was theology, not Tourette's Syndrome.

Verses 4-11 list the charismatic gifts which Paul says have been distributed among the congregants. He first stipulates the spectacular

---

[91] My beloved father-in-law, Carl Selby, was a stroke victim, and he used to let go with some beauties!

[92] This is the literal translation of Mark 1:10. Matthew 3:16 and Luke 3:22 use a different preposition, "upon."

powers claimed by the pneumatics[93] (the word of *sophia*, the word of *gnosis*; mountain-moving faith, as in 13:2; miraculous healing; prophecy; the detection of lying spirits, as in 12:3; speaking in tongues and their oracular interpretation). Verse 13 assures the Corinthians, both pneumatics and psychics, that they all possess the divine Spirit, obviously an attempt to reconcile the two parties. Perhaps this convinced the psychics and caused them to glow with new self-esteem, but it is very hard to imagine any of the pneumatics buying it. Instead, I suspect, they were now convinced that Paul was no real pneumatic, no matter what he might claim for himself, or he could never have said this.

The analogies in verses 14-26 admit that some spiritual endowments are flashier than others while explaining that even the unspectacular gifts are equally necessary and not to be despised, whether in oneself or in others. The pedestrian foot shouldn't envy the multi-tasking hand and say, "I might as well head home—who's gonna miss me?" Same with the bummed-out ear versus the keen eye. (Wouldn't you rather be deaf than blind?) And the conceited eye would be foolish to give the blind hand a pink slip: "Your services are no longer required." Or imagine the so-brainy head telling the stinky foot, "Take a walk, pal!" Well, I hope you guys get along better with the prostheses you're going to be needing! We don't amputate the less presentable parts of our anatomy; we disguise them. We put lipstick on the pig. (This seems to me a rather poor argument, damning the psychics with faint praise. And Paul thought the *pneumatics* were condescending?)

Verses 27-31 repeat the list of spiritual gifts, this time inserting the humdrum "powers" of "administration" and "helping." This is like enumerating Superman's abilities as invulnerability, flying, X-Ray vision, superhuman strength, super-hearing, and winning at checkers. You can see how little Paul himself is convinced of his pretended egalitarianism when he goes on at once to rate apostleship and prophecy at the head of the list—and even urges his readers to seek these "greater gifts." Some interpreters think these greater gifts turn out to be faith, hope, and love (13:13), but 14:1 rules this out, contrasting prophesying with glossolalia as the higher with the lower.

---

[93] Analogous to the superhuman powers (*siddhis*) claimed by Hindu yogis. See Eliade, *Yoga*, p. 130.

All You Need Is Love

Chapter 13, a masterpiece of world literature, religious or secular, opens with yet another list of spiritual gifts. This one is especially interesting as it implies that mountain-moving faith, the courage of martyrdom, and voluntary poverty are viewed here as special empowerments from God for the few. This is not the impression we get from the pronouncements on these topics in the gospels, where all Christians are expected to give away all wealth to the poor and live hand-to-mouth; all Christians are to be ready for martyrdom, carrying their own crosses. But if Paul regards them as specialties of a spiritual elite, we must wonder if the gospel sayings, before being placed in their present narrative contexts, were intended for a similar minority, the itinerant radicals who were special envoys of the Son of Man.[94]

First Corinthians 13:8-13 touches on Paul's expectation that the revelatory gifts of the pneumatics are only temporary stop-gaps until we need no more hints and glimpses because we see God face to face at the Parousia of Christ. On the other hand, faith, hope, and love will continue. Why is love the greatest of that triad? Because the other two will become just as superfluous as tongue-speaking on the day when we shall know as we are known. "We walk by faith, not by sight" (2 Cor. 5:7). "Who hopes for what he sees?" (Rom. 8:24). When we *do* see, faith and hope will be moot. But love will be perfected.

Chapter 14 must have had the pneumatics shaking their heads with skepticism. Would Paul, if he were really a pneumatic, fail to grasp the edifying character of ecstatic speech, speaking in the languages of angels? Paul contends that only that speech from which one may take away some rational lesson is edifying. Such thinking has placed the pulpit at the center of the platform in non-liturgical Protestant churches. Their churches are essentially schoolrooms with a choir loft. Pentecostals know better, or at least think differently, as do those who miss the Latin Mass. Speaking in tongues, whether glossolalia or Latin, brings home the numinous sense of an opening to the unseen celestial sphere. Like the Dead Sea Scrolls community, the Corinthians apparently believed that the angels stood by, invisibly sharing their worship (remember the danger of unveiled Corinthian females arousing the lusts of angels looking down at them from the

---

[94] Gerd Theissen, "The Wandering Radicals: Light Shed by the Sociology of Literature on the Early Transmission of Jesus Sayings," in Theissen, *Social Reality and the Early Christians: Theology, Ethics, and the New Testament*. Trans. Margaret Kohl (Minneapolis: Fortress Press, 1992), pp. 33-59.

ceiling, 11:10).

Paul's insistence that every public tongues-utterance be converted into an intelligible message betrays his tilt toward rationalism in religion. His true heirs today are the Calvinists who want to redefine "prophecy" as "preaching the gospel." And worse yet, he stipulates that each prophet wait his turn and that the Spirit must be quenched after the first two or three in line have prophesied. He seems to view Spirit-inspired prophets as so many stand-up comics waiting in the wings of a comedy club. Does this man really have any sense of what is going on in a charismatic worship service? I imagine the Gnostic Corinthians were already making plans for separate worship meetings,[95] which is the way they functioned in Irenaeus' day. And one wonders if this might just be what Paul intended.

I have to wonder if Paul's boast that he speaks in tongues more than any of the Corinthians do (14:18) is more of his chameleon strategy, being all things to all men (9:20-22), i.e., *pretending* to all men to be all things.

When They Rise from the Dead

Remember, Paul has not discussed these issues with the Corinthians in person. He is dependent on what Chloe's representatives told him and what was said in the letter from the household of Stephanas. The last thing we can suppose is that Paul's informants really understood the issues they wanted him to address. It seems probable that those who wrote the letter to Paul were worried about teachings and prophecies that seemed alarming to them. And experience has shown that those who recoil at some new idea may not have given it a fair hearing. And chapter 15 reads like Paul's response to a confused report of the doctrine of the pneumatics.

The listing of witnesses to the resurrection of Jesus (verses 3-11) may imply that Paul is arguing against some who denied that Jesus rose from the dead.[96] *If this is what I and the other apostles preached, how can some of you say Jesus didn't rise* (verse 12)? But the subsequent discussion implies that these doubters *did* believe in *Jesus'* resurrection. It was the future resurrection of believers that they rejected, apparently

---

[95] Brown, *Body and Society*, pp. 120, 244; Elaine Pagels, *The Gnostic Gospels*, (New York: Random House, 1979), Chapter V, "Whose Church Is the 'True Church?'" pp. 102-118.

[96] Bultmann, *Theology of the New Testament*. Vol. I, p. 295.

believing that their baptismal participation in that resurrection obviated the need for a future fleshly resurrection. But Paul doesn't seem to see the issue. To him it is puzzling that anyone could accept Jesus' resurrection and yet reject the notion of resurrection in principle. Acts 4:1-2; 23:6; 24:20-21; 26:8 portray Paul preaching the resurrection of Jesus as a test case of the reality of resurrection, speaking to Sadducees who rejected the whole idea (Mark 12:18). He wonders why the Corinthian pneumatics are not similarly consistent. Somebody who didn't understand their position has unwittingly misrepresented it to Paul.

Verses 20-28 raise a number of fascinating theological points. Verse 20 repeats the Adam-Christ comparison we saw in Romans chapter 5, but with a different end in view. First we read that Christ's resurrection is like the first-fruits of a harvest, the first portion of the crop to come ripe, whereupon it is offered to God as a token of gratitude to ensure the rest of the harvest will be successful. The implication is that the general resurrection of believers cannot be far off. If it were, then the analogy would be spoiled. Remember Mark 13:28-29, "From the fig tree learn its lesson: as soon as its branch becomes tender and puts forth its leaves, you know that summer is near. So also, when you see these things taking place, you know that he is near, at the very gates."

Next (verse 22) we read that, just as the sin of the original Adam brought death to the entire human race, the latter-day Adam, Christ, brings resurrection to all. *All?* If you mean just "all Christians," this is an odd way to say it. This verse is, of course, one of the foundation stones of Christian Universalism.[97] The very next verse sets out a timetable for the eschatological resurrection: Stage One, Christ himself on Easter. Stage Two, when he returns from heaven, raising "those who belong to him." The most natural (non-forced)

---

[97] Charles Chauncy, *The Mystery Hid from Ages and Generations, Made Manifest by the Gospel-Revelation: Or, The Salvation of All Men, The Great Thing Aimed at in the Scheme of God, as Opened in the New-Testament Writings, and Entrusted with Jesus Christ to Bring into Effect* (London: Charles Dilly, 1784), p. 201; Thomas Baldwin Thayer, *Theology of Universalism: Being an Exposition of its Doctrines and Teachings, in their Logical and Moral Relations; including a Criticism of the Texts, Cited in Proof of the Trinity, Vicarious Atonement, Natural Depravity, a General Judgment and Endless Punishment* (Boston: Universalist Publishing House, 1862), pp. 223-224, 226; Hosea Ballou, A Treatise on Atonement; in Which the Finite Nature of Sin is Argued, Its Cause and Consequences as Such; the Necessity and Nature of Atonement; and Its Glorious Consequences, in the Reconciliation of All Men to Holiness and Happiness (Hallowell: C. Spaulding, 3rd. ed., 1828), pp. 211-212.

reading of this phrase would imply that there are also some who do *not* belong to him. What happens to *them*? Apparently nothing: they're dead and they stay that way. There is nothing here about a resurrection of the unrighteous to face judgment (contra Acts 24:15; Rev. 20:11-15). Nor are we to infer, on the basis of verse 22, that now *all* belong to him.[98] That is another *ad hoc* harmonization, this time on behalf of Universalism. It's just inconsistent. Who knows what this writer really thought? (If this stuff were actually an inerrant revelation from God, you'd think it would at least be intelligible.)

Verses 29-34 seem to be a reply to people who believe there is no life after death, as if that is what the Corinthian deniers of resurrection believed. But of course it is not. Don't blame Paul. He was only working from the fragmentary information he had received. But one of his arguments against this imagined position is his rhetorical question, "If the dead are not raised, then why are some baptized for them?" (verse 29). Not much of an argument, the answer being, "Because they *think* there *is* life after death, though they're wrong and wasting their time."

But that seems so stupid, it is hard to imagine Paul offering such an argument. Thus he may well be asking why *the Corinthian Gnostics*, whom he has been *told* deny any life after death, are getting baptized on behalf of friends and family who never heard the gospel. And we do hear that Marcionites and Cerinthians baptized for the dead. John Chrysostom described the ritual of the Marcionites.

> For if one of their catechumens dies, they conceal a living person beneath the bier of the departed, approach the corpse, talk with the dead person, and ask him whether he intended to receive baptism. Thereupon the person who is concealed, speaking from beneath for the other who does not answer, avers that he did indeed plan to be baptized, and then they baptize him for the departed one.[99]

Epiphanius of Salamis explains the practice of the Cerinthians:

> when some of them die before being baptized, others are baptized in place of them, in their name, so that when they rise in the resurrection they may not have to pay the penalty of not having received baptism and become subject to the

---

[98] That is the view put forth by Thayer, pp. 225-226.
[99] Quoted in Schmithals, *Gnosticism in Corinth*, p. 256.

authority of the one who made the world.[100]

These sects did not reject postmortem salvation, and neither did the Gnostic pneumatics of Corinth.

Paul next (verses 35-57) tries to deflect a serious argument against the idea of resurrection, as Jesus does in Mark 12:24-27, but Paul's argument is better, though perhaps equally a product of off-the-cuff quick thinking.[101] What happens after you've been resurrected for a few decades? Do you start getting old and infirm again? Isn't that just the sort of nuisance you're hoping to be delivered *from*? That wouldn't be too far-fetched as an implication of Mark 9:43-48, which envisions the possibility of "entering into life maimed." Just as Jesus weaseled out of the Sadducees' trap by declaring that there will be no polyandry in heaven because marriage of any kind will be a thing of the past, Paul's reply is that the resurrection "body" will be an organism not of flesh and blood, but of pure spirit, just like the body of the risen Christ (contra Luke 24:36-43). The mortal, the corruptible, shall not inherit the kingdom of God.

Hmmm... that's kind of what the Gnostics thought: "when viewed from a second-century perspective, *Paul's teaching on the resurrection body in I Cor. 15 and II Cor. 5 seems to be more Gnostic than orthodox.*"[102] Gnostics didn't abandon hope for life after death; when they said "Goodbye, cruel world!" they expected to go to a better, non-material one. So did Paul. The only respect in which he appears to differ from the pneumatics is that of timing: Paul speaks here as if he still believes there will be a specific Resurrection Day in the near future, coinciding with the Parousia of Christ, whereas Gnostics believed their privileged knowledge would enable their disincarnate selves to ascend directly to the heavenly Pleroma immediately upon death. They would have to make it past the Archons seeking to bar the

---

[100] *The* Panarion *of St. Epiphanius, Bishop of Salamis: Selected Passages.* Trans. Philip R. Amidon (New York: Oxford University Press, 1990), p. 88.

[101] Dunn, *Unity and Diversity in the New Testament*, pp. 30, 59, ventures that theological contradictions are the result of creative attempts at solving theological problems arising from specific situations, hence are spontaneous creations, not simply revealed dogmas. Winging it, in other words. Similarly, Georgi, *Opponents of Paul*, p. 342: "it is impossible to take Paul as a representative for theology as the combination of doctrine and *Weltanschauung*. Arguments and statements by Paul cannot be read as if they were informative pieces to be projected into a system of thought. Even less can Paul be seen as somebody who had a finished theological theory of which he used individual fixed parts on individual occasions, going to his bookshelf as it were, and pulling a particular volume necessary to deal with the question at hand."

[102] Dunn, *Unity and Diversity in the New Testament*, p. 290.

way, but they knew the passwords. Paul *ought* to believe this, too, given what he said (2:6-8) about Christ's secret infiltration of the sub-lunar world to defeat these same Archons. My guess would be that he is combining elements of the eschatologies of the psychics (the "orthodox") and the pneumatics (the Gnostics) to create a compromise on paper, something hardly unknown in the subsequent history of theology.

In the inevitably anticlimactic chapter 16, Paul reminds his readers to be ready with their money for the relief of the Jerusalem church; he outlines travel plans for himself, Timothy, and Apollos; sends greetings to his colleagues Aquila and Prisca; and gives his endorsement to Stephanas and his sons Fortunatus and Achaicus. They are the leaders of the Corinthian church community because of their priority as the first Pauline converts in the province of Achaia (and no doubt because they owned a large enough home to accommodate the weekly church services). It is they who carried the letter of questions to Paul and are now returning with his reply, the present letter from him, 1 Corinthians.

.

16
The Second Epistle to the Corinthians
Jigsaw Scripture

Oh for a Couple of She-Bears! (2:14-7:4)

This section looks like a separate letter (or what's *left* of one) in which Paul rebuts the criticisms of opponents and rivals in Corinth,[103] whom I would identify with the Judaeo-Christian Cephas party. As Günther Bornkamm suggests,[104] this letter fits best between 1 Corinthians and the "Severe Letter" (2 Cor. chapters 10-13). Things are heating up between Paul and the representatives (and the partisans) of Cephas, but it is not yet clear that the Corinthians have deserted Paul *en masse*, as it will be in the Severe Letter.

Paul offers a spirited defense/explanation of his "boasted" authority versus his weaknesses and sufferings. Chapter 2, verse 14 compares the apostolic-evangelistic mission to a triumphal procession given for a victorious Roman general leading his chained prisoners in his train amid cheering crowds and clouds of incense. Verses 15-16 follow up the implied incense reference, suggesting that, depending on whether you are one of the saved or one of the lost, you will find the scent of the gospel a fragrant perfume or a sickening stench.[105] (The contrast is much the same as that drawn in 1 Corinthians 1:18, 23-24—some get it, some don't.) Is Paul boasting when he speaks so highly of his ministry (2 Cor. 2:16b)? No, for it is God who has chosen him for the job. He is no con artist like some he could name and as some accuse him of being (v. 17). By contrast, "We speak in Christ." Naturally, we can be sure his rivals would have said the same thing, so

---

[103] Dieter Georgi, in *The Opponents of Paul in Second Corinthians*. Trans. Harold Attridge, Isabel and Thomas Best, Bernadette Brooten, Ron Cameron, Frank Fallon, Stephen Gero, Renate Rose, Herman Wartjen, and Michael Williams (Philadelphia: Fortress Press, 1986), pp. 13-14. In the present book I am operating within the paradigm of mainstream New Testament critics, whereas, in my book *The Amazing Colossal Apostle*, I analyze 2 Corinthians a la the Dutch Radical Criticism (though not necessarily adhering to the particular exegeses of Van Manen, Bruno Bauer, or others of that persuasion).

[104] Günther Bornkamm, *Paul*. Trans. D.M.G. Stalker (New York: Harper & Row, 1971), p. 245.

[105] Richard Reitzenstein, *The Hellenistic Mystery Religions: Their Basic Ideas and Significance*. Trans. John E. Steely. Pittsburgh Theological Monograph Series Number 15 (Pittsburgh: Pickwick Press, 1978), p. 79.

how is one to know who is the genuine article? Paul will get to that in short order.

Paul is quite aware that he seems to be bragging, but he says he disdains all human credentials. This is a direct swipe at the Cephas agents whom he sarcastically dubs the "superapostles" (*huperlion apostoloi*); they show the Corinthians glowing letters of recommendation from the churches they have previously visited, and they then ask for similar endorsements from the Corinthians to add to their dossier.[106] But Paul is so proud of his Corinthian protégés that he knows the church and its very existence and spiritual welfare are themselves a living testimony to his ministry. In short, it is God who has made him competent for the apostolic task, and *that* is why he can "boast" (cf., 16b).

The reference in verses 5-18 to letters inscribed not on stone tablets but on the fleshy walls of human hearts combines allusions to both the ten commandments and to the prophecy of a new covenant (Jer. 31:31-34; Ezek. 11:19-20), and this leads Paul to explain the difference between the old covenant with its mediator Moses and the new one mediated by Paul.

Verse 6 gives us the famous "spirit versus letter" dichotomy. The contrast is not one between literal and allegorical interpretation of scripture,[107] but rather between law and grace, written code and Spirit. Paul explains (defends) his controversial "boldness" with a text-twisting exegesis of the Exodus 34 story of Moses' visits to the Tent of

---

[106] As Georgi, *The Opponents of Paul*, pp. 244-245, suggests, these letters would have included testimonies of miracles they claimed to have performed. Cf., Luke 4:23b, "what we have heard you did at Capernaum, do here also in your own country." See also Stevan L. Davies, *The Revolt of the Widows: The Social World of the Apocryphal Acts* (Carbondale: University of Southern Illinois Press, 1980), pp. 30-32: "The apocryphal Acts are hyperbolic collections of the 'proofs' reportedly offered by charismatic apostles and of reports that people found those 'proofs' convincing."

[107] This is not to say that Paul was particularly literalistic in his use of scripture. The ensuing discussion of Exodus 34:34 proves he wasn't. "Paul had a mystical experience which he interpreted in such a way that it shattered the traditional authority... A purely mystical exegesis of the old words replaced the original frame and provided the foundation of the new authority which he felt called upon to establish... In a manner of speaking, Paul read the Old Testament 'against the grain.' The incredible violence with which he did so shows not only how incompatible his experience was with the meaning of the old books, but also how determined he was to preserve, if only by purely mystical exegeses, his bond with the sacred text... Having found a new source, it breaks away from the authority constituted in Judaism, but continues in part to clothe itself in the images of the old authority, which has now been reinterpreted in purely spiritual terms." Gershom Scholem, *On the Kabbalah and its Symbolism*. Trans. Ralph Manheim (New York: Schocken Books, 1969), pp. 14-15.

Meeting. Why did Moses veil his face upon exiting the mediumistic tent? Paul says it was to conceal the *fading* of the divine radiance he had absorbed while talking face to face with Yahweh. (Did Paul realize he was characterizing Moses as a charlatan who was trying to give the Israelites the wrong impression? He doesn't go all the way to suggesting that Moses' face really *did not shine at all* and that he was just *telling* them it did. The veil made it impossible to tell whether it glowed or not! You'd just have to take his word for it.[108]) If you look up the Exodus text, it is quite clear that Moses covered his face because it was *still* glowing, and he didn't want to *frighten* the Israelites. When he doffed it, it was to *show* them it *was* normal. In contrast to Moses' humility (or shame), Paul is very bold (bold-faced, one might say) because he has nothing to be ashamed of: the splendor of the new covenant is unfading.

He carries the contrast further in verses 14-18, a parenthetical statement about the new covenant as freedom in the Spirit, freedom from obligation to keep the Torah (at least if you're a Gentile Christian). Jews (or, as I think more likely, Torah-Christians) are prevented ("veiled," get it?) from seeing the truth when they read scripture (specifically, Exodus 34). What does the text "really" mean? In verse 16 Paul paraphrases Exodus 34:34: "but whenever Moses went in before the Lord to speak with him he took the veil off." From this Paul takes away that, in the same way, "when anyone turns to the Lord," i.e., converts to Christianity, the veil blinding him to the real import of scripture is stripped away, and the new Christian enters the freedom from Torah regulations. When Paul says, "Now the Lord is the Spirit," he is not making a Christological statement, that the Lord Jesus is identical with the Spirit (not inherently implausible, given 1 Corinthians 15:45) but means that "the Lord" in Exodus 34:34 really denotes "the Spirit" which/who brings renewal and freedom.[109] This freedom is the same that Moses enjoyed in the Tent of Meeting: face-to-face communion with God: "And we all, with unveiled face, beholding the glory of the Lord, are being changed into his likeness from one degree of glory to another; for this comes from the Lord who is the Spirit." Though Paul finds all this in Exodus 34, the spiritual idiom seems to derive from prevalent Hellenistic Mystery Religions,[110] which promised an inner metamorphosis from mere

---

[108] "Pay no attention to the man [with his face] behind the curtain!"
[109] C.K. Barrett, *The Second Epistle to the Corinthians.* Harper's New Testament Commentaries (Harper & Row, 1973), pp. 122-123.
[110] Reitzenstein, *Hellenistic Mystery Religions*, pp. 63-64, 454-455.

humanity to divinity via mystical contemplation. Note that in 1 Corinthians 13:12 Paul looks forward to an eschatological face-to-face encounter with God.

Who exactly was it whom Paul envisioned blinding/veiling people to the true meaning of scripture? It depends on whether Paul is referring to the same spiritual blindness he mentions in 2 Corinthians 4:3-4. There we are told it is "the god of this world" who has "blinded the minds of the unbelievers, to keep them from seeing the light of the gospel of the glory of Christ, who is the likeness of God." In both cases, I think, it makes the best sense if we understand "the god of this world" in a Marcionite sense as the Demiurge, Jehovah, the Old Testament Creator, who was a different deity from the Father of Jesus. He had revealed the Torah and used it to gain the obedience of his Jewish worshippers. Whether he was blinding (indoctrinating) Jewish Torah-Christians or non-Christian Jews, it would be the Demiurge who prevented people from seeing the open door of gospel freedom, *freedom from the Jewish Law.*[111]

The Prize in the Crackerjack Box

Paul's opponents had been running him down as a miserable sad sack conspicuously devoid of the glory one should expect from a genuine apostle. Paul is not embarrassed by his various vicissitudes and in fact hangs them out on the clothesline for all to see (6:4-10). What the flashy superapostles do not seem to grasp is only the first and fundamental thing about being an apostle. The treasure of Christ's power is purposely (and inevitably) deposited in the humblest, most fragile containers in order to make its glory clear by contrast. What keeps Paul going? Not his own resources! It must be something else: the power of Christ.

For a would-be apostle to magnify his own glory (Reverend Ike style) is like Helal, son of Shahar, making himself "like the Most High" (Isa. 14:14), as if little Venus could outshine the rising sun. Or one might compare apostleship to placing a beautiful picture in a simple frame; if you put it in a gaudy frame, it will only distract from the canvas, not enhance it. Right now, Christ's resurrected life is thus

---

[111] Otherwise, the reference would be to Satan who would be understood as the *de facto* "god" whom "worldly" humanity inadvertently worships. Some, however, think the reference is to the Christian God and his mysterious "hardening" of the reprobate. Who knows?

manifested through our weakness, but soon it will transform our weakness. The argument is parallel to that in Philippians 3:10-11. Like that passage, the argument here in 2 Corinthians leads straight to the End-Time resurrection. The triumphalism of the Cadillac-driving superapostles is another piece of realized eschatology: claiming heavenly glory, rule, and riches here and now. (And this implies Paul is also answering the sniping of the Corinthian Gnostics again.)

Back in 1 Corinthians 15:35, Paul asked rhetorically, "How are the dead raised? With what kind of body do they come?" He returns to the question here. Paul does not relish the prospect of a postmortem half-existence as either a disembodied spirit or a dead corpse. The word "naked" in 5:3 could refer to either, in view of 1 Corinthians 15:37 which describes the dead body as a "naked kernel" planted in the ground to blossom into the "pneumatic body" of the resurrection. Here he says that the alternative to either oblivion or being another Jacob Marley is donning the heavenly body ("dwelling," 5:1-2; cf., 2 Pet. 1:13-14). Some see a contradiction here with the similar discussion in 1 Corinthian 15:42-54 on the grounds that 1 Corinthians 15 envisions a transformation of the mortal body into an immortal one as it rises out of the grave (or the urn or the lion's belly or whatever), while 2 Corinthians 5 seems to picture a celestial parking lot where your immortal body already exists and lies idle waiting for you (cf., 1 Pet. 1:4-5).[112] I confess I don't see the problem. Both passages speak of "putting on" the new body. And "heavenly dwelling" (body) in 2 Corinthians 5:2 need mean only that one's risen body will be fit for heaven, just as in 1 Corinthians 15:49-50.

How is the Spirit an "earnest"[113] (down payment, guarantee) of the future resurrection (verse 5)? The experience of it transforming your life is described, e.g., in 4:16, as something of a resurrection in its own right. Of course, this is rather close to the view of the Corinthian Gnostics, with the key difference that Paul does not, like them, reject an eschatological resurrection as superfluous. And since the transformation of the moral life by the Spirit is actual empirical evidence (the whole point of viewing it as a down payment) for the future bodily resurrection, it is also something of a mitigation of 5:7, "We walk by faith, not by sight."

What on earth can it mean in verse 9 for Paul to "aim to please him" "whether we are at home or away" from the body? Good behavior in heaven? That's kind of a given, isn't it? Of course, he only

---

[112] Reitzenstein, *Hellenistic Mystery Religions*, pp. 45-46, 451-452.
[113] For Hellenistic parallels see Reitzenstein, *Hellentistic Mystery Religions*, p. 453.

means that we want to make God proud by good behavior while alive on earth or, if it comes to that, by martyrdom (cf., Phil. 1:20, "it is my eager expectation and hope that I shall not at all be ashamed, but that with full courage now as always Christ will be honored in my body, whether by life or by death.")

Whence the gravity of this resolve? Because otherwise there will be hell to pay: "For we must all appear before the judgment seat of Christ, so that each one may receive good or evil, according to what he has done in the body. Therefore, knowing the fear of the Lord, we persuade men" (5:10-11a; cf., Rev. 20:12). Three things bear noting here. First, we see again that the "works" for which Paul says we are no longer responsible are not "good deeds" but rather ceremonial "works of the Law."[114] He does not speak here of "believers" but of the *righteous*.

Second, these verses speak of a postmortem assize of the wicked and of some grave punishment that awaits them, which is not what 1 Corinthians 15:23 would lead us to believe. There, the idea is of the wicked simply missing out on resurrection and remaining dead as a door nail.

Third, Paul says his urgency in fulfilling his evangelistic task is motivated by "the fear of the Lord," which could possibly mean he is concerned to rescue sinners from the fearful wrath of the Day of Judgment, but which, in view of 1 Corinthians 9:16b ("Woe to me if I do not preach the gospel!") probably means he knows he will get his head handed to him if he fails!

Were You There When They Crucified my Lord?

Second Corinthians 5:14-21 offers some "red meat" for theologians! For one thing, these verses form the basis for Karl Barth's "identification" theory of the atonement. We are used to hearing that "Christ died for us," in our place or on our behalf. And though verse 15 does feature such terminology, there is a distinctive difference. As Barth pointed out, this passage says that, when Christ died, *we* died. This is not to say what he said in Romans 6:3-5, that, subsequent to his death we patched into that death sacramentally, by being baptized.

---

[114] Francis Watson, *Paul, Judaism and the Gentiles: A Sociological Approach*. Society for New Testament Monograph Series 56 (New York: Cambridge University Press, 1986), pp. 64, 66, 78, 140; E.P. Sanders, *Paul, the Law, and the Jewish People* (Minneapolis: Fortress Press, 1983, pp. 46.

We usually receive the impression that, because Christ died, we escaped or evaded death. But not here. *We died on the cross.*[115] In fact, it says *everyone* died there. This means all things are (or ought to be) very different. One may even say that all who are "in Christ" (verse 17) constitute a "new creation" and accordingly no longer view anyone "according to the flesh" (verse 16). We can never see people the way we used to.[116]

Verse 21 ("For our sake he made him to be sin who knew no sin, so that in him we might become the righteousness of God.") is foundational to the Penal Substitution theory of the atonement, which sees Jesus Christ as having paid for our crimes against God, whereupon God transfers Christ's righteousness (his sinless record) over to our account. That is, I think, a fair interpretation of the passage, but it does not match it exactly. This is no criticism since the verse is somewhat enigmatic. But I think that Barth's interpretation is pretty compelling: Christ never sinned but became sin for us, receiving the judgment due us, and that, since we all died with him on the cross of that judgment, we come away from Golgotha having gained God's righteousness since Christ had/has it, and we were integrated into him. It may be reading too much into the text to infer, as Protestant theology has done, that this "becoming the righteousness of God" is in the nature of a legal fiction ("'justified' means 'just *as if* I'd never sinned.'"). Barth, with Catholic theology, insists that God in Christ has not merely *declared* us righteous ("on paper," as it were) but has actually *made* us righteous. I should say that is sticking closer to the text, though, again, who knows?

You have no doubt noticed the implicit universalism in verses 14-15. We see more of it, and again, Barth spotted it a long time ago, in verse 19-20: through Christ's death God has healed the breach that had yawned between him and the human race. It's settled.[117] And so what is the point of evangelism? This question is often pressed upon Christian Universalists. Paul seems to be saying that the role of the

---

[115] G.C. Berkouwer, *The Triumph of Grace in the Theology of Karl Barth.* Trans. Harry R. Boer (London: Paternoster Press, 1956), p. 135.

[116] If you'll forgive an ironic analogy, I think of the "paradigm shift" I underwent when I exited fundamentalism/evangelicalism: no longer did I divide up everyone around me as either "saved" or "unsaved," but as just "people," interesting people from whom I could learn and to whom I could relate. The world was a new place for me.

[117] Herbert Hartwell, *The Theology of Karl Barth: An Introduction* (Philadelphia: Westminster Press, 1964), p. 138; Colin Brown, *Karl Barth and the Christian Message* (Chicago: Inter-Varsity Press, 1967), pp. 132-133.

missionary or evangelist is to spread the news that the war is over. Hostilities have ceased! Put down your guns! Come out of that cave! When I was a boy in the early 1960s one used to hear of isolated Japanese soldiers on this or that Pacific atoll, cleaning their rifles and awaiting orders from Tojo. Once contacted, they realized how much time they had lost and returned to their homes and families, though it took some convincing. Even so, God has reconciled the human race to himself, but some haven't heard the news, so we have to tell them.[118] They may remain unreconciled to God, but God has been reconciled to them for a very long time.

Then there is Christology. Does verse 19 refer to the divine incarnation? That is not clear. For one thing, even if Paul intended to say, "God was in Christ," that leaves a lot unexplained. It could even be taken in a Gnostic "channeler" direction. But it is just as possible that Paul intended to say, "In Christ [i.e., *by means of* Christ], God was reconciling the world to himself." For another, does verse 16 imply that Paul or other apostles were contemporaries of a historical Jesus? Morton Smith reads the phrase "we once knew Christ according to the flesh" as meaning "we knew Christ in person."[119] On this basis, Smith thinks it likely that Paul is saying that he was personally acquainted with the earthly Jesus, just as the disciples were, though Paul himself would not have been a sympathizer at that time. He could have been listening to Jesus from the sidelines, just as Acts places him in Stephen's audience (Acts 7:58).

But others think that "we" really means "some," the point being that Paul's opponents (especially if, as C.K. Barrett thought, following F.C. Baur,[120] the "superapostles" should be identified with Peter, James the Just, and John) did, unlike Paul, know the historical Jesus, but that the fact is simply not relevant. What counts now is the ascended Christ who occasionally issues revelations from heaven, as he has to Paul.[121] These are exactly the terms of the debate between Simon Peter and Paul ("Simon Magus") in the Pseudo-Clementines.[122]

---

[118] Cf., William E. Hordern, A *Layman's Guide to Protestant Theology* (New York: Macmillan, 1962), Chapter 6, "Karl Barth," pp. 141-142.

[119] Morton Smith, *Jesus the Magician* (New York: Harper & Row, 1981), p. 3.

[120] C.K. Barrett, *The Signs of an Apostle*. The Cato Lecture, 1969 (Philadelphia: Fortress Press, 1972), p. 37.

[121] Reitzenstein, *Hellenistic Mystery Religions*, p. 477.

[122] F.C. Baur, *Paul the Apostle of Jesus Christ: His Life and Works, His Epistles and Teachings. A Contribution to a Critical History of Primitive Christianity.* 2 vols. Trans. Eduard Zeller (London: Williams & Norgate, 1873-1875; rpt. Peabody: Hendrickson Publishers, 2003), vol. I, pp. 88, 95, 135; Hans-Joachim Schoeps, *Jewish Christianity:*

Peter demands to know how his opponent dares claim to be an apostle of Christ and yet contradicts Peter's doctrine since Peter got it directly from Jesus when he was walking the earth. Simon's (Paul's) teaching is instead based on subjective visions, notoriously unreliable.

Still others (like the RSV translators) think that "regarding Christ according to the flesh" denotes "viewing Christ from a worldly, unregenerate perspective" (as in 11:4). If this is the case, no one in the dispute is necessarily claiming to have shaken hands with the Messiah. As the verse in question passes directly into the business about a new creation in which everything suddenly looks different, and this experience is shared by all the baptized, it seems to rule out the notion of having known Jesus personally, since most Christians, e.g., those in Corinth, cannot have seen Jesus in the flesh (cf., 1 Pet. 1:8).

Interpolated Interlude (6:14-7:1)

Most scholars consider 6:14-7:1 to be a later addition to the text, or rather a misplaced fragment (perhaps of Paul's very first letter to the Corinthians, the one *before* our "First" Corinthians). The material does not seem to fit the train of thought in the context. And notice how smoothly the surrounding text flows if you bracket this portion. "Our mouth is open to you, Corinthians; our heart is wide. You are not restricted by us, but you are restricted in your own affections. In return—I speak as to children—widen your hearts also" (6:11-13). "Open your hearts to us; we have wronged no one, we have corrupted no one, we have taken advantage of no one" (7:2). Chapter 7, verses 2-4a (ending with "I have great pride in you") form the end of what, borrowing from Justin Martyr, we might call Paul's First Apology. Now for the Second Apology, the Severe Letter...

Lord, Do You Want Us to Call Down Fire from Heaven?

The Severe Letter (2 Cor. 10-13) is an angry attempt to get the Corinthian congregation, lately wavering in their loyalty to Paul, to fall back in line. On the one hand, a significant portion of the congregation refuses to heed Paul's demand that they excommunicate

---

Factional Disputes in the Early Church. Trans. Douglas R.A. Hare (Philadelphia: Fortress Press, 1969), pp. 47-58.

the incestuous man. On the other hand, the Torah-Christian Cephas party is seizing on the case to flog Paul: had he taught the Corinthians they must keep Levitical law, this abomination could never have occurred in the first place. His rejoinder is not merely personal defensiveness, however much modern readers may like to think so; he is concerned with certain important underlying issues ill-understood by these recent converts.

Paul's rivals/critics claim he is a big talker but a wimp in person (10:1, 9-11), but Paul replies that it is just a matter of his exercising proper humility. Specifically, the charge seems to be that he had humbly declined financial support from the Corinthians, thus proving himself no real apostle, since *real* apostles have the right to be compensated by their flocks (11:7-11). This issue had already come up when Paul touched on it in 1 Corinthians chapter 9. At any rate, Paul now explains that he simply did not want to burden the congregation, though he does accept remuneration from other congregations. But his defense here does not seem to square with 1 Corinthians; there he sure sounds like he is defending a general policy of refusing payment in order to head off any suspicions that he is only preaching the gospel as a money-making scheme.

In what did his "big talk" consist? In his letters, the opponents say, he boasts of his authority (10:8). Well, *that's* certainly true: just *read* any of them! Or at least he assumes an authoritative stance because he has reason to assume his readers think of him as an authority. In reply, Paul turns the tables on his critics. He says that what matters is the use to which one's authority is *put*. And he uses it to build up (to edify), not to tear down (10:8; 11:21a). But his critics? They are the ones guilty of hollow boasting. Since it was Paul, not these interlopers, who started the church at Corinth, he *does* have authority there. Guess who doesn't? (10:13-16). As Jewish Torah-Christians, aren't they violating the terms of the agreement Paul made with the Jerusalem Pillars (Gal. 2:7-9), mapping out the separate Pauline and Torah-Christian spheres of interest? Remember?

When they saw that I had been entrusted with the gospel to the uncircumcised, just as Peter had been entrusted with the gospel to the circumcised (for he who worked through Peter for the mission to the circumcised worked through me also for the Gentiles), and when they perceived the grace that was given to me, James and Cephas and John, who were reputed to be pillars, gave to me and Barnabas the right hand of fellowship, that we should go to the Gentiles and they to the circumcised.

The opponents claim Paul is secretly guided by "worldly"

motives, that he is a hypocrite (10:2-5). He makes a show of refusing their money only to ingratiate himself (12:16). Paul denies this, claiming rather that he attacks futile, worldly sophism, fighting for belief in the gospel (as in 1 Corinthians 1:18-31). No, Paul counters, *they* are the worldly ones (11:18) since they boast of purely human credentials that count for nothing in God's eyes, notably religious and national backgrounds (11:21b-22; cf., Phil. 3:3-6). Here Paul, in effect, echoes John the Baptist rebuking those who were confident and complacent, resting on their laurels: "Do not presume to say to yourselves, 'We have Abraham as our father'; for I tell you, God is able from these stones to raise up children to Abraham" (Matt. 3:9). Specifically, they boast of their Jewish Christianity as if that were an advantage, and that Paul will never admit. In fact, he rejects their version of Christianity as a false gospel (11:1-6, 13-15, 22; cf., Gal.1:7-9).[123]

Paul rejects his rivals' flashy triumphalism (bragging of past successes and miracles) as a false model of Christian apostleship. The true apostle is the one who goes the way of the cross. To reinforce his disdain, Paul embarks upon his own boasting rant (not unlike that of the Pharisee in Luke 18:11-12, but Paul *knows* he is playing the fool). Paul possessed all the "required" Jewish credentials (11:21b-22), the visions and revelations (12:1-10), and the miracles (12:11-12), but he renounces any confidence based on them. These things are "of the flesh," but the power of Christ appears only when false confidence in the flesh has evaporated (12:9-10). It is this power which gives him the apostolic authority he will use to discipline them next time he sees them.

Paul doesn't take refuge in externals like these to impress the Corinthians but instead relies on a tested and proven character which they may observe for themselves (12:6). After all, who can really know whether impressive-sounding miracle claims are even true?

But let us pause for a moment to take a closer look at the story of Paul's visionary journey to the Third Heaven. Why is Paul

---

[123] How interesting that in 11:2-3 Paul alludes to the contemporary Jewish belief that Satan sexually seduced Eve in Eden, begetting Cain. See also 1 John 3:12; 4 Macc. 18:7-8 ("I was a pure virgin and did not go outside my father's house; but I guarded the rib from which woman was made. No seducer corrupted me on a desert plain, nor did the destroyer, the deceitful serpent, defile the purity of my virginity"). Also it is curious that in 11:14 he says Satan merely *disguises* himself as an angel of light, implying he is actually something else. Does this imply he did not know or did not accept the identification of Satan with Helal (Lucifer, the "light-bearer") from Isaiah 14?

ambiguous as to whether it was his own adventure or that of another (12:2-5)? At first he seems clearly to distinguish himself from the visionary ("I'm happy to boast about this man, but not about myself"). But immediately he slips into first-person narrative. Why? My guess is that he is winking to the reader to let him know the story is fictional.

Paul says he was afflicted with a "thorn in the flesh." I am convinced Paul is not telling of some chronic but mundane affliction God plagued him with to keep him humble. He does not mean his prayers for relief went unanswered till he was assured his frailty was an advantage, opening a conduit for Christ's charismatic power to flow into him. No, though the lesson is the same, I believe we are reading an account of an ascension to the throne of God (the Merkavah). Paul's elation ("knowledge puffing up," 1 Corinthians 8:1) invited a chastising assault by one of the angels serving the Accuser Satan. Paul's pride made him suspect, like Job, and God allowed Satan to have him pummeled, as he had once tormented Job. Paul begged the enthroned Lord Jesus to call off the pugnacious angel three times in rapid succession (like Jesus' own threefold petition for deliverance in Mark 14:36, 39, 41). In the end he submitted to the punishing, because he learned from his Lord's answer that it was for his own good: "My grace is sufficient for you, for my power is perfected in weakness" (2 Cor. 12:9).

This reading of the story may seem far-fetched, but it certainly conforms to accounts of the visionary ascents of Jewish Merkavah mystics:

> As the journey progresses, the dangers become progressively greater. Angels and archons storm against the traveler "in order to drive him out." [quoting *Hagigah* 15b] "But if one was unworthy to see the King in his beauty, the angels at the gates disturbed his senses and confused him... And he does not go until they strike his head with iron bars and wound him." [quoting the Munich ms of the Hekhaloth texts][124]

See You Soon (12:14-21)

Paul wants to avoid another "painful visit" like the last one, when he

---

[124] Gershom G. Scholem, *Major Trends in Jewish Mysticism*. Trans. George Lichtheim (New York: Schocken Books, 1973), Second Lecture, "Merkabah Mysticism and Jewish Gnosticism," pp. 52-53 and 51.

confronted certain immoral persons but was not supported by the church. One wonders if perhaps Stephanas was a friend or business associate of the immoral man and was unwilling to back up Paul's demand for his excommunication. Remember, Paul had been informed of the scandal via oral gossip from Chloe's people. There had been no mention of the mess in Stephanas' letter of questions.

He warns them to shape up before he arrives and not to be misled by his rivals to think he won't take stern measures. Paul wants to avoid a nasty scene in which the "conceited" and "selfish" superapostles, "jealous" of Paul's apostolic authority, might circulate more "slander" and "gossip" about him to discredit him. Let them back up any such charge, as the Law says, with two or three witnesses to the improprieties they accuse Paul of. He is confident they will not find any.

What could Paul have done to carry out his threats? Excommunication, even without congregational backing? Handing them over to Satan, like God consigning Job to Satan's tender loving care? But how seriously would his enemies take his threats of excommunication if they rejected his authority to do it? Did he plan to smite them down with a word like Peter did with Ananias and Sapphira (Acts 5:4-5, 9-10)? One hates to think he thought he could, because then he would sound like some Voodoo sorcerer.[125]

Whew! (1:1-2:13; 7:5-16)

The Letter of Rejoicing represents a sigh of relief at the news that the Severe Letter had done its work. Paul's word had not returned unto him void. The Corinthians finally rallied around Paul and turned a deaf ear to the Cephas (and presumably Gnostic) agitators. They have apparently excommunicated the notorious sinner at last, and this act seems to have put the fear of God into the man and brought him to his senses. He must have terminated his illicit relationship with his widowed stepmother, and now Paul urges forgiveness and leniency in any penance assigned him. Paul speaks of personal offense against himself as well as the offense to the church. This implies that the excommunicated man had previously (during the "painful visit") told off Paul in public (as Paul had once told off Cephas in front of the

---

[125] And that would be another reason to regard the whole letter as a fictive pseudepigraph.

whole church at Antioch, Galatians 2:11-14).

The Quest for the Historical Titus

Paul begins by letting his hair down with the Corinthians now that he once again feels at ease with them. He has very recently experienced a close brush with the Grim Reaper and counts this close call as part of his sharing in the sufferings of his Lord. He is glad for such experiences because they further equip him for comforting others when they find themselves similarly squeezed by adversity. (It is rather like the discussion in Hebrews 4:14-5:9, where we read that Christ's trials and tribulations prepared him to empathize with poor mortals.)

From there, Paul launches into an explanation of his failure to make an anticipated stopover among the Corinthians on his way back home after visiting Macedonia. Some thought he had just left them in the lurch, but in fact his previous visit with them on his way *to* Macedonia had been such a disaster (the "painful visit") that he didn't want to chance an encore. So instead he sent Titus to them carrying the Severe Letter, hoping to patch things up. Good thing, too; it worked.

He was recently commencing what promised to be a fruitful evangelistic mission in Troas, where he was supposed to meet his colleague Titus, but Titus was nowhere to be seen. Worried about his friend, Paul cut short his mission and went looking for Titus. The story breaks off there to continue over in 7:5-16, where we learn that Paul's surmise had proved correct: Titus was up in Macedonia. Somewhere along the line signals got crossed. Titus had delivered the Severe Letter, reading the riot act to the naughty Corinthians, with good success, but for some reason he had gone from Achaia (the province where Corinth was located) up to Macedonia, the site of Paul's own recent work, instead of heading for Troas, across the Dardanelles, where he was to have rejoined Paul. But once they did meet up in Macedonia, Paul was absolutely thrilled with the news from Corinth, hence this letter.

Now Let Us Pay (2 Cor. 8 and 9)

Each of these chapters appears to be a separate letter in which Paul, reconciled to the Corinthians, directs them to prepare for the upcoming visit of Paul, Titus, and others to receive their contribution toward the relief fund for the Jerusalem church. You can tell they are separate letters because the opening of each chapter seems to *introduce* the subject of the collection. The first of the pair of letters (chapter 8) seeks discretely to shame any tight-fisted Corinthians by praising the great generosity of the Macedonians despite their abject poverty. They must be worse off than the Corinthians, so one can expect the latter will be even bigger givers. If not, they are going to look pretty bad! The second letter (chapter 9) takes a different tack, informing them that Paul has actually told the Macedonians (whose representatives will be coming to Corinth *with* Paul) that the Corinthians have long been ready with their contribution! They mustn't embarrass themselves, to say nothing of Paul, by having to rush to get everything together once Paul's group gets there!

There is an interesting bit of Christology hidden in 8:9, where the example of Christ is invoked as a paragon of generosity: "Though he was rich, yet for your sake he became poor, so that by his poverty you might become rich." Some cite this verse as evidence for Paul's knowledge of the character of the historical Jesus, as if, like Prince Siddhartha, he had been born to wealth but renounced it to undertake his saving mission. But this is to misunderstand (or to misrepresent) it. The point is instead equivalent to Philippians 2:6-11; it speaks of the condescension of a heavenly being to leave behind celestial glory for an earthly mission to save mankind.

17
The Epistle to the Galatians
Another Gospel

Overview

Paul has learned that Jewish Torah-observant Christians claiming the authority of the Jerusalem apostles (the "Pillars") have appeared in his churches (presumably Iconium, Derbe, Lystra, etc., as listed in Acts chapters 13-14). They are "correcting" Paul's teaching, informing his converts that, if they wish to become followers of the Jewish Messiah, they must convert not only to the Messiah but also to the Messiah's religion, Judaism. The Gentile Galatians must therefore be circumcised and keep the Torah.

These counter-missionaries, "Judaizers," claim that Paul is a (disobedient) subordinate of the Jerusalem apostles; thus their teaching takes priority over his. Paul, they aver, has cheapened the gospel by omitting the requirement of Torah-observation in order to make Christian conversion from paganism (or from being Gentile God-fearers) a more attractive option (1:10).[126] Obviously, Paul's version of Christianity *would* be more attractive to non-Jews who must be daunted by the prospect of embracing cultural mores completely alien to them.

Paul will argue that the Judaizers are being stricter than God himself! They are placing a false stumbling block in the path of potential converts. Jewish scribes and rabbis multiplied restrictions not explicitly mandated in the written Torah in order to make it more difficult for people to break the commandments that *are* written in the Torah. If you refrain from any physical effort on the Sabbath (a course of action not actually stipulated in the Law), you will be playing it safe re the commandment not to "work" on the Sabbath. If you never pronounce the divine name Yahweh at all, you are in no danger of taking that name in vain, whatever that means. This strategy they called "building a fence around the Torah." Paul is saying, in essence, that the Judaizers are making the Torah into a "fence around the gospel"—barring access, not to transgression but to salvation! By

---

[126] Francis Watson, *Paul, Judaism and the Gentiles: A Sociological Approach*. Society for New Testament Studies Monograph Series 56 (New York: Cambridge University Press, 1986), admits this was so. See pp. 34, 38, 177.

making circumcision and all it logically entails a prerequisite for Christian conversion, they are causing the "little ones who believe in me" to "stumble" (Mark 9:42).[127] They are making Torah-legalism more important than Christ. They are "shutting the kingdom of God in people's faces" (Matt. 23:13; Luke 11:46). The issue does not arise for faithful Jews who wish to embrace Christ. They're already acclimated to Judaism. So they are converting to Christ from square one. But Gentiles are being asked to make two big leaps: first Judaism (holy days, kosher laws, etc.), then Christ. Salvation instantly becomes "salvation by works," works *of the Law.*

How does Paul respond to the charges of his critics? He maintains that, on the one hand, he owes no allegiance to the Jerusalem apostles but is responsible only to Christ, having been called by Christ himself. He is no hireling of the Pillars. On the other, Paul had reached an arrangement with them, establishing peaceful co-existence with them, and they are now violating it by sending their representatives around to Paul's churches to enforce Torah-observance after all. Paul then deals with the central theological issue, explaining that the Torah was only a provisional measure, never intended as a path to salvation, but only as a preparation for the (Pauline) gospel. The truth of this should be evident from two considerations. First, faith predates the Law by centuries, as God's promise to Abraham[128] was predicated on his *believing* God when nobody had ever heard of the Jewish Law. Thus, in principle, Law-observance *cannot* be necessary to acceptance by God.

Second, the Mosaic Law *was given not by God but by angels.* This astonishing claim (reminiscent of Marcionism and Gnosticism)[129]

---

[127] Helmut Koester, "Mark 9.43-47 and Quintilian 8.3.75." *Harvard Theological Review* 71, 1978, p. 153.

[128] I cannot help noticing how Paul himself, as a biblical character, parallels Abraham at many points. Paul surpasses his contemporaries in his zeal for Judaism, recalling the traditional tale of Abraham, having converted to monotheism, smashing his father Terah's idols (See Robert Graves and Raphael Patai, *Hebrew Myths: The Book of Genesis* (New York: Greenwich House, 1983], Chapter 25, "Abraham and the Idols," pp. 140-142.). Just as Abraham heeded God's call to follow him into lands unknown, Paul heeds Christ's call to ministry on the Damascus Road, then off to Arabia. Yahweh several times appears to Abraham in his travels with a promise or a word of guidance; Christ occasionally appears to Paul to guide and encourage him. Abraham meets the venerable priest-king Melchizedek in Salem, as Paul meets his elder apostles in Jerusalem. Peter and Paul divide the world mission field between them as Lot and Abraham divided the grazing lands. Peter's city, Jerusalem, is destroyed, as is Lot's adopted city of Sodom. Parallelomania? Probably. Still, it makes you wonder...

[129] Lloyd Gaston, *Paul and the Torah* (Vancouver: University of British Columbia Press,

leads to another: The dispensation of Law was actually the reign over mankind by evil angels (the fallen sons of God from Genesis 6:1-4 (cf., Deut. 32:8; Ps. 82). These angels are still at work, seeking to prolong their superannuated rule, using the Judaizers as their stooges. God formerly tolerated their rule, until the advent of the gospel, but no more. Thus anyone who fails to "get with the program" and commits himself to keep the Torah is severing any and all connection with Christ. One cannot have both Christ and the Torah.

Why not? The problem is that legalism assumes and fosters the belief that human beings possess the natural ability to obey the commandments and so to please God. But this betokens an unwarranted confidence in "the flesh" (understood here not so much as the seat of sensuality and lust as the negligible strength of mere humans as creatures and the accompanying delusion of self-sufficiency). So the only course of action, Paul says, is to have done with the Law and one's futile efforts at self-salvation. Then one can open oneself to the Spirit, a new source of power enabling one to keep God's standards in grateful acknowledgment that he provides the obedience he requires.

Paul's account of crucial events in this letter is partially paralleled by the account in the Book of Acts, but the two versions diverge at very important points. This is the result of Acts' much later tendency to minimize conflicts in the early years of Christianity in order to fabricate a "golden age" of apostolic unity for propaganda purposes.[130]

Salvation and Salutation (1:1-17)

Paul cannot restrain himself and begins his defense in the very first verses (1-5) of the letter. He will have it understood at the very outset that his commission as an apostle comes straight from God with no human mediators, certainly not senior apostles from Jerusalem. Not every preacher propagates the same gospel he does, and that means they preach a spurious gospel (verses 6-7) and are damned (verses 8-9). Of course he refers to the Judaizers. I think these are the same as the

---

1987), pp. 35-37; Hyam Maccoby, *Paul and Hellenism* (Philadelphia: Trinity Press International / London: SCM Press, 1991), pp. 9, 40-42, 160.

[130] Robert L. Wilkin, *The Myth of Christian Beginnings: History's Impact on Belief* (Garden City: Doubleday Anchor Books, 1972), Chapter I, "The Use of the Past," pp. 1-26; Chapter II, "The Older the Better," pp. 27-51.

Cephas party that caused Paul so much trouble in Corinth (he said the same things about them in 2 Corinthians 11:4-5). We can see this because of the subsequent references to Cephas as a hypocrite, a Judaizer, and a backstabber. Their pestiferous subversion in the Galatian congregations denoted the violation of Paul's now defunct compact with Cephas. If, as some would like to think, the Judaizers appealed to Cephas without his knowledge or agreement (cf., 1 John 2:19), then Paul knows nothing about this, since he clearly blames Cephas (and James) for the Judaizers' efforts.

In verse 8 Paul anticipates his argument in 3:19-20; 4:8-10: the Torah gospel is a revelation, all right, but a revelation from the fallen angels who seek to continue their rule thereby (cf., Col. 2:15-18). The Jewish Law and the Jewish gospel are cut from the same cloth and by the same tailors.

Paul, the Seal of the Prophets

When Paul warns his readers not to believe any other gospel even if it should be brought by an angel, he raises a fascinating larger issue. In the biblical tradition it is commonly alleged that this or that revelation has been brought to earth by an angel. The archangel Gabriel delivers revelations to Daniel (Dan. 8:15-17; chapters 10-12). Angels tell Joseph (Matt. 1:20-21), Mary (Luke 1:26-38), and the shepherds (Luke 2:9-14) of the conception and birth of Jesus. Jesus sends his angel to John on Patmos to impart the Book of Revelation (Rev. 1:1). The angel Uriel vouchsafes heavenly secrets to Ezra (2 Esdras/4 Ezra 2:43, etc.). Angels contact Baruch (3 Bar. 1:3, etc.) and other Old Testament heroes in the Pseudepigrapha. Angels bearing new revelations appear to Elchasai and to Muhammad.[131] Nor let us forget Joseph Smith. Paul seems to know either the fact or the likelihood that the Judaizing superapostles make such claims. But not him. The Risen Christ did not bother sending messenger boys but appeared to Paul in person.

What we see Paul doing here is a classic maneuver used throughout the long history of revealed religions. Each faith announces it has transcended (and "fulfilled") its parent tradition by virtue of a new revelation (Heb. 1:1-2). Then the newly revealed faith,

---

[131] Tor Andrae, *Mohammed: The Man and his Faith*. Trans. Theophil Menzel (New York: Harper Torchbooks, Cloister Library, 1960), Chapter IV, "Mohammed's Doctrine of Revelation," pp. 94-113.

which one might naively expect to have shown itself forever receptive to new revelations, quickly retreats into dogmatism, barring the door to any *further* revelations. Now it has its own cherished orthodoxy and does not want anyone to rock the boat.

Hyrum Page received a revelation through a seer stone about the location of the New Jerusalem. Page was one of the eight witnesses of the Book of Mormon plates. Joseph Smith translated the Book of Mormon and received his early revelations through seer stones. Smith condemned Page's revelation as a revelation of Satan even though many Mormons believed it. In response to the challenge, Smith dictated a revelation (*Doctrines and Covenants* 28: 11-12) that clarified that "no one shall be appointed to Receive commandments & Revelations in this Church excepting my Servant Joseph." Page was convinced to denounce his own revelation. This was confirmed by unanimous vote in a meeting. Later, the stone was ground to powder and Page's revelation burned.[132]

Similarly, the brand-new Pentecostal movement was jolted when John G. Schaepe, during a camp meeting (April 1913), announced that he had received a revelation that there is no Trinity, just "Jesus only."[133] At once, the Assemblies of God formulated an inflexible doctrinal creed as a bulwark against heresy. And the beat goes on. We already see Paul squelching claims of new revelation superseding his own.

In verses 11-17, Paul recalls how his conversion was brought about by no human agency, nor was it followed by an apprenticeship to the Jerusalem apostles (though Acts paints a picture of Paul as a sub-apostolic protégé). Notice that three things often read in between these lines do not actually appear here. First, Paul says nothing about some shattering visionary encounter on the road to Damascus. It is not even clear whether he means God revealed his Son *to* him (objectively) or *in* him (subjectively, or even as expressing his resurrection power *through* Paul during his vicissitudes, a la 2 Corinthians 4:7-12). Let us not be too quick to read into this brief and

---

[132] E-mail from Mark D. Thomas, January 27, 2016. Cf., Steven L. Shields, *Divergent Paths of the Restoration: A History of the Latter Day Saint Movement* (Los Angeles: Restoration Research, 4th ed., 1990), pp. 21 ("The year 1831 saw another prophet, John Noah, making claims of divine calling. In accord with church procedure he was excommunicated for that claim"), 27 ("On March 7, 1842, Oliver H. Olney was removed from fellowship in the LDS Church on charges of having set himself up as a prophet."), etc.

[133] Walter J. Hollenweger, *The Pentecostals: The Charismatic Movement in the Churches.* Trans. R.A. Wilson (Minneapolis: Augsburg Publishing House, 1972), pp. 31-32.

enigmatic passage the Acts stories of Paul's conversion.

Second, Galatians never refers to "the twelve apostles," to whom Paul might or might not have been apprenticed, but only to "the apostles" and "the Pillars." This is important because we must not read the gospels into Galatians and assume that the Jerusalem leaders based their authority upon instruction from a historical Jesus, recently departed, or even that there were twelve of them.

Similarly, though it matters less, there is a third unfounded assumption, that, when Paul says that, immediately after his call to apostleship, he made a bee-line to Arabia, conspicuously skipping Jerusalem, he probably does not mean he retreated to the Arabian Desert like St. Anthony seeking solitude in the sands of Egypt, but rather that he ministered for three years in Romanized Nabatea, whose king, Aretas IV, defeated Herod Antipas in battle after Antipas cast off Aretas' daughter to take up with Herodias. Paul reports his narrow escape from Aretas' agents in 2 Corinthians 11:32.

In any event, we can't help noticing that this version of Paul's post-call actions clashes pretty flagrantly with the version told in Acts 9:19b-26. There we read that Paul at once began to preach Jesus in Damascus for "several days" and "many days" before he had to flee to Jerusalem, where Barnabas vouched for him to the apostles. Even if Aretas' domain included Damascus at this time (which is a matter of some dispute),[134] there is still a contradiction since Galatians 1:15-18 has Paul visit Jerusalem only after *three years*. It looks like Acts shortened the length of Paul's stay in Damascus/Arabia in order to bring him more directly to Jerusalem and into the orbit of its apostles.[135]

Ain't Paul

Verses 18-24 present special problems. There is pretty good reason to

---

[134] Ernst Haenchen, *The Acts of the Apostles: A Commentary* Trans. Bernard Noble, Gerald Shinn, and R. McL. Wilson (Philadelphia: Westminster Press, 1971), pp. 332-335.

[135] F.C. Baur, *Paul the Apostle of Jesus Christ: His Life and Works, his Epistles and Teachings. A Contribution to a Critical History of Primitive Christianity*, 2 vols. Trans. Eduard Zeller. Theological Translation Fund Library (London: Williams & Norgate, 1873-1875; rpt. Peabody: Hendrickson Publishers, 2003), vol. I, pp. 110-116; Edward Zeller, *The Contents and Origin of The Acts of the Apostles Critically Investigated*. 2 vols. Trans. Joseph Dare. Theological Translation Fund Library (London: Williams & Norgate, 1875; rpt: Eugene: Wipf & Stock Publishers, 2007), vol. I, p. 300 ; Haenchen, *Acts of the Apostles*, p. 335.

think the passage is a post-Pauline interpolation. In Tertullian's late second-century polemic against Marcion (which echoes strikingly the Acts/Galatians wrangling over the issue of Paul's independence from the Pillars) Tertullian argues that Paul was in fact a delegate of the Jerusalem apostles, receiving his gospel from them. His favorite passage to use as a weapon against the Marcionites, who insisted on (or even exaggerated) Paul's independence, was Galatians 2:1-2, which has Paul journeying to Jerusalem to submit his teaching to the Pillars for their approval, something we can hardly picture Paul doing given his protestations in Galatians chapter 1. Tertullian refers to this event simply as "Paul's visit to Jerusalem." Why not "Paul's *second* visit"? And why not appeal to that first visit in Galatians 1:18-24, especially since it already said Paul had sought out Cephas to consult with him.[136] One has to suspect that in Tertullian's day, the text of Galatians available to him did not include 1:18-24, and that a subsequent copyist added it in order to make the same point Tertullian was trying to make: "See? Paul knew he dared not disagree with Cephas and the Pillars!" How can Tertullian have skipped this passage had it been available to him? As it turns out, none of the Church Fathers who comment on the Marcionite text mention this passage.[137]

Acts chapter 15 has Paul and his colleagues visiting the Jerusalem apostles and elders seeking a ruling on the question of whether Gentile converts have to get circumcised and keep the Torah if they want to be saved. The story is a great example of Acts' agenda to settle an issue current in its own day (the second century) by pretending it had been resolved back in the shining time of apostolic unity and authority. The occasion: "some men came down from Judea and were teaching the brethren [in Antioch], 'Unless you are circumcised according to the custom of Moses, you cannot be saved'" (15:1). This is of course just what was happening in Galatia and prompted the epistle to that congregation.

Most think Acts 15 is another version of the Jerusalem meeting related in Galatians 2:1-10, but they are very different. The Acts version is clearly fictive, and not merely because it differs from

---

[136] James D.G. Dunn, *Jesus, Paul and the Law: Studies in Mark and Galatians* (Louisville: Westminster/John Knox Press, 1990), Chapter 5, "The Relationship between Paul and Jerusalem according to Galatians 1 and 2," pp. 108-128.

[137] Jason D. BeDuhn, *The First New Testament: Marcion's Scriptural Canon* (Salem, OR: Polebridge Press, 2013), p. 262. This is a wonderful book despite the author's weird translation of the Marcionite text, hampered by doctrinaire Political Correctness.

Galatians. Acts portrays Peter as simply seconding Paul's proposal that Gentile converts be excused from Torah-observance. This seems slightly suspicious in its own right, but Peter is also shown claiming to have been the one to initiate the mission to the Gentiles (as in Acts chapters 10-11), which ill-comports equally with the whole notion of Paul as *the* apostle to the Gentiles and that of Peter and his fellow Jewish apostles restricting their mission to the towns of Israel (Matt. 10:23) and governing the twelve tribes (Matt. 19:28; Luke 22:29-30).

Worse yet, Peter is made to voice the frustration of Gentile would-be proselytes to Judaism: "why do you make trial of God by putting a yoke upon the neck of the disciples *which neither our fathers nor we have been able to bear?*" Can we imagine a religious Jew voicing such sentiments? The Torah was a burden to Gentiles because to embrace it was to embrace a whole different set of cultural mores and practices. Now *that* is a burden! Imagine yourself converting from, say, Presbyterianism to Sunni Islam—yikes!

Circumspection and Circumcision

After all sides are heard, James the Just delivers a verdict, a compromise: Gentile Christians will not have to get circumcised but will have to keep a handful of regulations so as not to offend law-keeping Jewish neighbors. For instance, they must refrain from eating meat previously offered in sacrifice to pagan idols (gods) (Acts 15:19-21). As we have seen, Paul does urge his readers to avoid such meat (1 Cor. 8-9), but it is very significant that, though he marshals every argument he can think of, however mutually incompatible, one thing he does *not* mention is a decree from James bearing explicitly on the issue. It is just like the problem of Paul never citing a saying ascribed to Jesus in the gospels when presumably it would have settled any issue at once; he must not have known any such Jesus sayings because they had not yet been attributed to Jesus. Likewise, how could Paul *not* have invoked the so-called Jerusalem Decree on the issue of idol-meat? He didn't know of it because it didn't *exist* till Acts' author invented it.

In Galatians Paul admits that he did in fact go to Jerusalem (spurred by a revelation) to compare notes with the elder apostles, just to make sure he had not got it all wrong. And he was careful to do this in a closed-door meeting in order to prevent public humiliation before the larger church. Given what we read in chapter 1, it is almost inconceivable for Paul to have done this! Much less to admit it here! Is he not conceding the claim of the Judaizers that he was but a flunky of the Jerusalem apostles?

Now he is willing to admit an earlier submission to the approval of the Jerusalem Pillars for the simple reason that they did approve![138] Cephas, James, and John had heard him out and given their blessing to his mission. As long as he stayed out of the Jewish-Christian sphere of influence ("mission market"), it was all right for Paul to preach a Torah-free (circumcision-free) gospel among the Gentiles.[139] Oh yes, one more thing: Paul (to put it bluntly) would have to pay tribute[140] to Jerusalem (Gal. 2:10). This was the cost for the endorsement of Jerusalem's apostles. And he did. We have already seen how seriously Paul took the matter in 1 and 2 Corinthians.

It is obvious what Jerusalem got out of the deal: Paul represented a huge new constituency. Paul didn't need the Pillars; they needed him and the money he could bring in. But why *did* the Pillars' approval make any difference to Paul? He had his own thing going. In what way did it add credibility to his preaching? It's not as if the Stoics and the Priapus cultists, much less Gentile God-fearers, would already have either known or esteemed a small circle of Essene knock-offs far away in Jerusalem and would be less likely to take seriously the preaching of "this babbler" (Acts 17:18) named Paul if he couldn't display the Good Apostleship Seal of Approval.

Might Paul simply have figured that his handshake with Cephas, James, and John would have silenced his opponents on the ground in Corinth, Galatia, Colossae, Philippi, etc.? It seems clear that the Judaizers were sent by Cephas ("I belong to Cephas," 1 Corinthians 1:12) and James the Just ("certain men came from

---

[138] I suspect this is the origin of the pericope Mark 9:38-40. It might preserve an objection to Paul put forth by John, one of the three Pillars.

[139] Galatians 2:7-8 suddenly mentions "Peter" for the only time in the whole epistle. It looks like these two verses are an interpolation made by someone who assumed Cephas and Peter were the same man. There is also the oddity that it seems to put a single man, Peter, in charge of the whole task of evangelizing Jews. See Ernst Barnikol, "The Non-Pauline Origin of the Parallelism of the Apostles Peter and Paul. Galatians 2:7-8." Trans. Darrell J. Doughty and B. Keith Brewer. *Journal of Higher Criticism* 5/2 (Fall 1998), pp. 285-300. Also, William O. Walker, Jr., "Galatians 2:7b-8 as a Non-Pauline Interpolation." *Catholic Biblical Quarterly* 65/4 (October 2003), pp. 568-587. On the other hand, this might mean only that the mission to the circumcised was to be led by Peter, just as the Gentile Mission was headed up by Paul. Besides, can we be sure that these verses *are* identifying Peter with Cephas? Theoretically, Peter may have been appointed to the task by the Pillars, *Cephas*, James, and John.

[140] Sanders, *Paul, the Law, and the Jewish People*, p. 171.

James," Galatians 2:12) to tamper with Paul's converts.[141] Paul hoped to get the Pillars to call them off. That would be my guess, especially in view of the direction his argument takes next, namely that the activity of the Judaizers was a reneging on the Jerusalem agreement.

Galatians 2:11-12 records a public clash between Paul and Cephas on the occasion of the latter's visit to Antioch. In the beginning, everything was hunky-dory. Cephas happily shared the table with non-kosher Gentile Christians (cf., Luke 10:7-8). They were on Paul's turf, after all. When in Rome... But then a party sent from James joined him. Cephas suddenly had second thoughts and henceforth sat in the kosher section, along with the newcomers. Seeing this, Paul unloaded on him: "If you, though a Jew, behave ["live"] like a Gentile, not like a Jew, how can you Judaize the Gentiles?" (2:14).[142]

What was the "hypocrisy" of which Paul says he accused Cephas and Barnabas? What professed belief of Cephas was Cephas contradicting in practice? Was it that he was contradicting his actual belief in Jewish-Gentile Christian table fellowship by segregating himself, fearing the reaction of James' inspectors? Or was it that, once James' men arrived, Cephas reverted to his true colors and shunned the non-kosher rednecks? In that case, his free mixing with the Gentiles had been a betrayal of his real convictions. I suspect the latter. Barnabas' hypocrisy, by contrast, lay in his pretending to espouse James' position, fearing the disapproval of James' men. This seemed only logical to him in view of the importance Paul had obviously seen in the treaty with the holy trinity of Cephas, James, and John. Heck, weren't Cephas and Barnabas only "being all things to all men"? Sure, but it doesn't work when both groups are in the same room!

Paul regards this as a turning point, a betrayal of his accord with the Pillars. He traces his renewed troubles with Judaizers to this incident. This was just the sort of thing the whole Jerusalem accord was supposed to stop! He did continue to take up the collection for Jerusalem, which is surprising, but maybe his thought was that in this way he might shame the Pillars into keeping up their end of the deal after all. Remember, in Romans 15:30-31, he seems doubtful that they will accept the collection once he delivers it. And Acts 8:18-24;[143]

---

[141] Watson, *Paul, Judaism and the Gentiles*, p. 52.

[142] That's the literal translation. Cephas is the only one in the New Testament who is actually called a "Judaizer."

[143] Baur realized that Simon Magus' attempt to buy from Peter the prerogative of an

21:17-24 imply that they *didn't*.

"Those Galatians Should Have Listened to Saint Paul"[144]

Paul has to mount a theological argument (3:1-9) against the Judaizers (actually, to those Galatians who have accepted their line). He begins by appealing to the evidence of the Galatians' own experience. If one must be circumcised and keep the Mosaic Law to be saved, how is it that, back before the Judaizers appeared on the scene, the Galatians managed to receive the Spirit and its miracles *without law*? The Torah, then, would seem to be as needful as a fifth wheel. And wasn't it the same with the Patriarch Abraham? He was pronounced "saved" by *faith* long before the Law was given. If in principle Torah-keeping is necessary for salvation, how was Abraham's salvation possible? Did he have to mark time in Sheol for centuries till Moses could show up to bail him out?

But maybe the Law is *worse* than a superfluous fifth wheel. To rely on the Torah, Paul says (3:10-14), is actually to court damnation (cf., Gal. 1:8-9)! Why? Because the Law itself (scripture) prescribes death for any who fail to keep it. And everyone has![145] But, luckily, Christ has delivered us from that doom, taking the rap for us. In this way, the promise to Abraham, which extended to his posterity, is now seen to include all Christian believers. How does Paul know that? It follows that the same promise Abraham received would apply to all his descendants as long as you define "descendants" in figurative terms, as those who exercise the same sort of faith (i.e., apart from the Torah) that he did.

To back that up, Paul offers a piece of theo-grammatical legerdemain: didn't God promise great things to "your seed" (Gen. 12:7)? Hey, that's a singular, right? (Uh, no, it's clearly intended as a *collective* term.) *One* seed (descendant) then! And just who might *that* be? Gotta be Jesus, right? And this comes in handy in 3:19, when we learn that the promised blessing was finally awarded once Jesus, the designated heir ("the seed") arrived. Ironically, as the argument

---

apostle is a satirical version of Paul trying to "buy" recognition from the Pillars with the collection. F.C. Baur, *The Church History of the First Three Centuries*. Trans. Allan Menzies. Theological Translation Fund Library (London: Williams & Norgate, 1878), vol. I, pp. 94-98.

[144] Sam Malone.

[145] Sanders, *Paul, the Law, and the Jewish People*, pp. 25-27.

proceeds from there, it turns out that the "single seed," Jesus Christ, was a collective singular after all, for his appearance denotes the religious maturity of the human race, the point at which the "training wheels" of the Torah can be (and must be) cast aside (cf., 1 Cor. 13:10-11).

So what was the real purpose of the Torah? It was to keep us in line during the time of religious childhood and adolescence. Our tutors and schoolmasters were the angels who actually gave the Law to Moses. As school children, we had to keep in line, not to speak without being spoken to, not to eat between meals. Not anymore. Now it's up to us. In the same way, we no longer need holy days, kosher laws, etc. (4:10).

Who were these angels? They were "beings that by nature are no gods" (4:8-9), which implies that we thought they *were*. Here again we catch the distinctive scent of Gnosticism, the idea that the divine lawgiver was not the ultimate God, the Father, and that he (or in this passage, *they*) enslaved humanity by means of the laws. These beings are also called "weak and beggarly elemental spirits" (4:9), i.e., the angels in charge of rain, snow, etc. (cf., Eph. 2:2). God allowed their governance until humanity reached maturity with the coming of Christ. The idea may sound peculiar, but it is certainly biblical, harking back to Deuteronomy 32:8 which says God made sure he divided mankind into enough nations for each of the (seventy) sons of God to have one to rule, until, that is, the great day when God will retire them and assume direct control of the world (Ps. 82). All this means that the Galatians who have been won over by the Judaizers are, albeit unwittingly, going back to domination by angels (4:7-11).

In verses 12-20, Paul appeals to the Galatians to remember the good old days when they got along so famously, when Paul started the church, and to turn a cold shoulder to these insincere flatterers and exploiters. They're just counting scalps (Gal. 6:12-13), or foreskins (cf., 1 Sam. 18:25-27). What does Paul mean when he recalls the warm reception the Galatians once gave him: "You welcomed me as an angel of God, as Jesus Christ himself" (4:14)? (That sounds a bit odd, as Paul earlier disdained any angelic revelations he did not agree with, 1:8). In other words, they were responding in exactly the way hoped for in Matthew 10:40: "He who welcomes you welcomes me, and he who welcomes me welcomes him who sent me." They were treating Paul, despite his infirmity, as the righteous "sheep" treated Christ's afflicted emissaries in Matthew 25:34-40. And when they welcomed Paul "as an angel of God" they were following the example of Abraham who welcomed Yahweh's angels (whom he did not recognize at first) in Genesis 18:1-8 (cf., Heb. 13:2).

Paul resorts to allegory in verses 21-31. Torah-observant and Law-free Christians are both children of Abraham in a sense, but exactly in the sense that Abraham had two biological sons: Isaac and Ishmael, the first free, the second a slave. Accordingly, Paul's converts are free from the Torah, while the Judaizers and their converts are slaves to the Torah (and thus to the angels). The first two verses of chapter 5 contrast faith and the Law. Only the former brings the Spirit, while the latter eliminates the equality of access to God for Jews and Gentiles which the cross provides.

Verses 27-28 have become the charter of Christian feminism as they had earlier been the charter of Christian abolitionism. These verses probably incorporate a very early piece of baptismal liturgy,[146] either reflecting or anticipating the anti-sex spirituality of the encratites. They believed that the root of sin in Eden was God's splitting of the original androgynous human into the male Adam and the female Eve. Once these two began to copulate, humanity began to multiply, eventually dividing into various nationalities and classes, with all the strife between them. The key to salvation was therefore to undo the original sin, to abolish all ethnic, class, and gender distinctions through celibacy and baptism, which restores the primordial oneness of humanity, joining all the baptized together in/as the new Adam, the Son of Man.

Antidote for Antinomianism

Jews and Jewish Christians cannot help becoming alarmed whenever anyone talks about casting away the yoke of the Torah. Perhaps the chief objection to Paul's gospel was that it seemed to provide no safeguard against immorality. So in Galatians 5:13-6:10 Paul sets forth his antidote to antinomianism. It is the Spirit, energizing the believer from within, doing just what Jeremiah 31:33-34 said it would do: write the Law upon the heart so that obeying God's will becomes second nature. But of course it is up to the Galatians (like all Christians) to avail themselves of it. Paul doesn't want anyone to reject his gospel because they think it promotes libertinism. But neither does he want anyone *accepting* it because they think it promotes libertinism!

---

[146] Dennis Ronald MacDonald, *There Is No Male and Female: The Fate of a Dominical Saying in Paul and Gnosticism*. Harvard Dissertations in Religion Number 20 (Philadelphia: Fortress Press, 1987).

In 6:11-18, Paul turns the tables on the Judaizers: it is they who are shamelessly pandering—to human *vanity*, not to human laziness as they accuse Paul of doing. They seek to glory in the flesh, i.e., irrelevant human achievements (primarily the safeguarding of Jewish ethnic identity, the purpose of the ceremonial laws). So it is continued preaching of the Torah (to Gentiles) that promotes "cheap grace."[147] Torah-observance is not a viable way of salvation anyway (verse 13; cf., Heb. 10:1-10), but merely an excuse for boasting. As for Paul, he preaches the scandal of the cross, the total repudiation of worldly, fleshly achievements and qualifications. Through Christ's cross, Paul has died to all such puffery.

---

[147] Dietrich Bonhoeffer, *The Cost of Discipleship*. Trans. Reginald H. Fuller and Irmgard Booth (New York: Macmillan, 1963), p. 45.

18
The Epistle to the Ephesians
Pauline Pastiche

The (?) Epistle of Paul (?) to Ephesus (?)

The document we call "Ephesians" must have originated as a circular letter (an "encyclical") based on Colossians but more generalized, intended to introduce Paul and his teaching to congregations he had never personally visited, but which had been started by his associates (e.g., Tychicus, mentioned in 6:21). The letter would have been intended to strengthen Paul's ties with such Gentile churches. Actually, this already rules out Ephesus as the intended recipient, since Paul had stayed in Ephesus for no less than three years (Acts 20:31).[148] Is it possible he could say to the Ephesian Christians things like "I have *heard of* your faith in the Lord Jesus" (1:15) and "*assuming that you have heard of* the stewardship of God's grace that was given to me for you" (3:2)? Not unless his memory was even worse than mine. The capper is the fact that some of our early copies of the letter have no particular addressees. So why do other manuscripts specify "to the Ephesians"? Most likely because the eventual collector of the Pauline letters found a copy at Ephesus, and the memory of this circumstance led later copyists to supply "Ephesus" as the address.

But things get even stickier. Is this even a single epistle? It sure looks like the author was signing off in 3:20-21: a doxology followed by "Amen." And then someone decided to add more, maybe the original author, maybe somebody else.

Is Paul the author? Most critical scholars today think not, because of peculiarities of both style and vocabulary. The use of a number of words atypical for the Pauline letters[149] is not by itself decisive, true,[150] but, added to a couple of big stylistic considerations,

---

[148] George S. Duncan, *St. Paul's Ephesian Ministry: A Reconstruction with Special Reference to the Ephesian Origin of the Imprisonment Epistles* (London: Hodder and Stoughton, 1929).

[149] C. Leslie Mitton, *The Epistle to the Ephesians: Its Authorship, Origin and Purpose* (Oxford at the Clarendon Press, 1951), pp. 8-9. Mitton's discussion of all these points very valuably surveys previous scholarly discussion.

[150] Henry J. Cadbury, "The Dilemma of Ephesians." *New Testament Studies*, vol. 5, no. 2, 1959, p. 98.

it might be the straw that breaks the camel's back.[151] For one, there is the astonishing length of the sentences:[152] the whole of chapter 1 is comprised by a mere two sentences! Why would anyone write like this, Paul or anyone else? Consider this: as Edgar J. Goodspeed demonstrated,[153] virtually every line of Ephesians is closely paralleled in other Pauline epistles (not counting the later Pastoral Epistles, 1 and 2 Timothy and Titus), and the few *not* paralleled in Pauline sources are from the Septuagint. Now it begins to make sense: someone was trying to compose a "new" Pauline epistle, and, to make it sound "Pauline," he helped himself to bits and pieces from a collection of Pauline letters. (The lion's share of the Pauline parallels are with Colossians, the essential basis of Ephesians.)

And since the snippets had no original connection with each other, the writer just threaded them together as best he could, the result being that the Pauline pearls are simply hung together on a couple of very long strings. He was not composing sentences *de novo* but rather trying to get in as many bits and pieces as he could.

The evangelists used basically the same gimmick when they started with a jar full of individual pericopes (self-contained episodes, parables, aphorisms, miracle stories, etc.), lacking any context or implied sequence, and just glued them into place arbitrarily (sometimes topically). This is why Jesus is pictured as an itinerant. He did *this*, he went *there* and said *that*, he traveled *here* and predicted *this*, he journeyed *there* and exorcised *that*. Most of the time you see no particular logical sequence or plot line.[154] Ephesians reads a lot like that. "Here is a man who will often write several lines of a sentence before he has made up his mind how to finish it."[155] It is similar to the

---

[151] No actual camels were harmed in the use of this metaphor.

[152] Mitton, *Ephesians*, pp. 9-11.

[153] Edgar J. Goodspeed, *The Key to Ephesians: A Provocative Solution to a Problem in the Pauline Literature* (Chicago: University of Chicago Press, 1956).

[154] Karl Ludwig Schmidt, "Jesus Christ," Section 2, "The Gospels as Sources for the History of Jesus," pp. 98-99 of Jaroslav Pelikan, ed., *Twentieth Century Theology in the Making. Vol. 1: Themes of Biblical Theology.* Trans. R.A. Wilson. Fontana Library, Theology and Philosophy (London: Fontana Books / New York: Harper & Row, 1969); Schmidt, *The Place of the Gospels in the General History of Literature.* Trans. Byron R. McCane (Columbia: University of South Carolina Press, 2002), Chapter 6, "The Multiformity of the Framework of the Story of Jesus; *Chreia* Traditions," pp. 43-44.

[155] P.N. Harrison, "The Author of Ephesians." In F.L. Cross, ed., *Studia Evangelica Vol. II: Papers Presented to the Second International Congress on New Testament Studies Held at Christ Church, Oxford, 1961. Part I: The New Testament Scriptures.* Deutsche Akademie der Wissenschaften zu Berlin. Institut für Griechisch-Romische Altertumkunde Kommision für Spätantike Religionsgeschichte. Texte und Untersuchungen zur

apocryphal Letter of Paul to the Laodiceans, which incorporates verses from Philippians with a sprinkling of items from other Pauline and pseudo-Pauline letters:

> 1. Paul an Apostle, not of men, neither by man, but by Jesus Christ, to the brethren which are at Laodicea. 2. Grace be to you, and peace, from God the Father and our Lord Jesus Christ. 3. I thank Christ in every prayer of mine, that you may continue and persevere in good works, looking for that which is promised in the Day of Judgment. 4. Do not be troubled by the vain speeches of anyone who perverts the truth, that they may draw you aside from the truth of the Gospel which I have preached. 5. And now may God grant that my converts may attain to a perfect knowledge of the truth of the Gospel, be beneficent, and doing good works which accompany salvation. 6. And now my bonds, which I suffer in Christ, are manifest, in which I rejoice and am glad. 7. For I know that this shall turn to my salvation forever, which shall be through your prayer and the supply of the Holy Spirit. 8. Whether I live or die, to me to live shall be a life to Christ, to die will be joy. 9. And our Lord will grant us his mercy, that you may have the same love, and be like-minded. 10. Wherefore, my beloved, as you have heard of the coming of the Lord, so think and act reverently, and it shall be to you life eternal; 11. for it is God who is working in you; 12. and do all things without sin. 13. And what is best, my beloved; rejoice in the Lord Jesus Christ, and avoid all filthy lucre. 14. Let all your requests be made known to God, and be steady in the doctrine of Christ. 15. And whatever things are sound and true, and of good report, and chaste, and just, and lovely, these things do. 16. Those things which you have heard and received, think on these things, and peace shall be with you. 17. All the saints salute you. 18. The grace of our Lord Jesus Christ be with your spirit. Amen. 19. Cause this Epistle to be

---

Geschichte der Altchristlichen Literatur. Band 87 (Berlin: Akademie Verlag, 1964), p. 598.

read to the Colossians, and the Epistle of the Colossians to be read among you.

Equally odd is the use and overuse of a particular genitival construction,[156] "the this of that," phrases like: "the wish of his will" (1:11); "the praise of his glory" (1:12, 14); "the strength of his might" (1:19; 6:10). This kind of construction occasionally pops up in other Pauline letters, but Ephesians is *swarming* with them. Cadbury comments: "One could regard the letter as in some respects more Pauline than Paul."[157] The author is trying too hard to sound like Paul.

The same thing is often pointed out in the case of Morton Smith's Letter of Clement to Theodore containing a passage ascribed to a Secret Gospel of Mark. It sounds more like Clement than Clement does: too many of his favorite words that are, however, never so densely packed in his known writings.[158] Anyone familiar with pastiches of H.P. Lovecraft's fiction knows how his imitators use his distinctive vocabulary much more thickly than Lovecraft himself did. Gerard Genette notes that only a thin line separates pastiche from parody. He speaks of "the hyperbolic literalness of pastiche, which is always a little more ideolectical than the authentic text, as 'imitation' is always a *caricature* through accumulation and accentuation of specific characteristics."[159]

If Paul didn't write Ephesians, then who did? We cannot know,[160] but there is a very intriguing theory.[161] The use of the other epistles obviously means the writer had them available. How soon were the letters collected? It is reasonable to infer that the author of Ephesians was himself the collector of the Pauline canon, and Goodspeed ventured that the compiler wrote Ephesians as a cover

---

[156] Mitton, *Ephesians*, pp. 9, 11.

[157] Cadbury, "Dilemma of Ephesians," p. 99.

[158] Stephen C. Carlson, *The Gospel Hoax: Morton Smith's Invention of Secret Mark* (Waco: Baylor University Press, 2005), pp. 50-51.

[159] Gerard Genette, *Narrative Discourse: An Essay in Method*. Trans. Jane E. Lewin [Ithaca: Cornell University Press, 1980], p. 184.

[160] In *The Pre-Nicene New Testament* and *The Amazing Colossal Apostle*, I second the motion of R. Joseph Hoffmann, *Marcion: On the Restitution of Christianity: An Essay on the Development of Radical Paulinist Theology in the Second Century*. American Academy of Religion Academy Series 46 (Chico: Scholars Press, 1984), pp. 274-280, that Marcion wrote the epistle (which he called the Epistle to the *Laodiceans*). Here I am taking a more conventional approach, that of mainstream criticism, to see what sense may be made of the text when read through that lens.

[161] Goodspeed, *Key to Ephesians*, pp. xiv-xv.

letter, an introduction to the collection as a whole, an overture sounding and anticipating the major themes of the letters.[162] Ephesians 3:4 ("When you read this you can perceive my insight into the mystery of Christ," etc.) would make good sense as pointing forward to the collection of letters to follow.

Who would be motivated to collect the letters and to compose such an overture? Someone with a great interest in Paul, as if to repay a debt. Though there would doubtless have been many such, we do happen to know of one in particular, the runaway slave Onesimus, whom Paul persuaded to accept his gospel and to risk returning to his master Philemon. Onesimus carried with him Paul's plea on his behalf, our Letter to Philemon, in which he also asked Philemon to set Onesimus free and to send him back to Paul to serve as his assistant during his sojourn in the slammer. It must have worked, or we wouldn't be reading the Letter to Philemon today. It is difficult to imagine anyone else concerned to preserve that letter.[163]

Would Onesimus, after his apostolic patron died, have done all this work merely as a hobbyist? Possibly, but the scope and gravity of the task of editing and publishing (circulating) the collection would best befit someone with a position of authority in the church. And, what do you know? We read of a bishop of Ephesus *named Onesimus*, who, some sixty years after Paul's death, visited Ignatius of Antioch and was thereafter commended in the Ignatian Epistle to the Ephesians. That it was the very same Onesimus is strongly implied by what look like a whole series of echoes in that letter from Paul's Letter to Philemon.[164] Looks like the old apostle had quite an impact on his young convert's life.

Heaven! I'm in heaven!
And my heart beats so that I can hardly speak!

The first three chapters develop the theme of God's eternal plan, only recently accomplished through Christ: his predestination of

---

[162] Goodspeed, *Key to Ephesians*, pp. x-xi.

[163] Unless maybe Philemon *refused* Paul's request, crumpled up the letter and deep-sixed it, whereupon a Christian maid happened to notice it in the trashcan and retrieved it, like Constantine Tischendorf discovering discarded pages of the Codex Sinaiticus in the garbage can in his room at St. Catherine's monastery!

[164] John Knox, *Philemon Among the Letters of Paul: A New View of Its Place and Importance* (New York: Abingdon Press, 1935; rev. ed. 1959), pp. 98-108.

Christians to share the ascended glory of Christ. Christians form a new species uniting the long-separated ranks of Jews and Gentiles. This marks a momentous development wholly unsuspected in pre-Christian ages and now revealed to a stunned world through—Paul! *Not Christ, but Paul.* The author comes very close here to the nineteenth-twentieth-century Protestant Liberal view of Paul as "the second founder of Christianity,"[165] the transformation of "the religion *of* Jesus" into "the religion *about* Jesus,"[166] whose role then changed from "the proclaimer" to "the proclaimed."[167] I am reminded of the Ismail'i-Druze doctrine of the pairs of revealers who appear on earth to inaugurate every new period of revelation, first the "Proclaimer" who issues the public, exoteric version of the truth, then the "Foundation" who imparts the deeper, esoteric version among the elite.[168] The Gospel of John attests the same distinction, having Jesus preach straightforwardly to the crowds (John 18:19-21), to be followed shortly by the Paraclete, originally understood to be another flesh-and-blood human,[169] whom I would identify as the so-called Beloved Disciple, whose role is described in John 16:12-14.

By the way, the very notion of making the inclusion of uncircumcised Gentiles alongside Jews in the people of God a revelation of Paul's is by itself sufficient to render the gospels' "Great Commission" scenes (Matt. 28:18-20; Mark 16:9-20; Luke 24:47-49; John 20:21-23) theological fiction. Who would dare to steal credit from Jesus if he was known to have already ordered the Gentile

---

[165] William Wrede, *Paul.* Trans. Edward Lummis (London: Philip Green, 1907), pp. 179-180.

[166] Walter Kaufmann, *The Faith of a Heretic* (Garden City: Doubleday Anchor Books, 1963), p. 219; Jean Réville, *Liberal Christianity: Its Origin, Nature, and Mission.* Trans. Victor Leuliette. Crown Theological Library vol. IV (New York: G.P. Putnam's Sons / London: Williams & Norgate, 1903), p. 38; Cf., Adolf Harnack, *What Is Christianity?.* Trans. Thomas Bailey Saunders. Harper Torchbooks / Cloister Library (New York: Harper & Row, 1957), p. 143.

[167] Rudolf Bultmann, *Theology of the New Testament.* Complete in One Volume. Trans. Kendrick Grobel. Scribner Studies in Contemporary Theology (New York: Scribners, n.d.), vol. I, p. 33.

[168] Sami Nasib Makarem, *The Doctrine of the Ismail'is.* Islamic Series (Beirut: Arab Institute for Research and Publishing, 1972), pp. 28-34; Makarem, *The Druze Faith* (Delmar, NY: Caravan Books, 1974), pp. 71-72; Ignaz Goldziher, *Introduction to Islamic Theology and Law.* Trans. Andras and Ruth Hamori. Modern Classics in Near Eastern Studies (Princeton: Princeton University Press, 1981), p.220; Matti Moosa, *Extreme Shiites: The Ghulat Sects.* Contemporary Issues in the Middle East (Syracuse: Syracuse University Press, 1988), p. 313.

[169] Rudolf Bultmann, *The Gospel of John: A Commentary.* Trans. G.R. Beasley-Murray, R.W.N. Hoare, and J.K. Riches (Philadelphia: Westminster Press, 1971), p. 567.

Mission?

Parenthesis and Parousia

Strikingly, the same passage of Ephesians was taken up, and without distortion, by John Nelson Darby and the school of Dispensationalists descended from him, and forms the basis of their theology of salvation history. Darby, Cyrus I. Scofield, and others rejected the historic doctrine of supracessionism whereby Christians had replaced Jews in God's election, becoming the "new" or "true" Israel, while Jews were demoted to merely one more nation in need of Christian conversion. Darby was not by any stretch of the sanctified imagination an ecumenist, but if he was anything, he was a literalist. And he could not brook what seemed to him the allegorizing dismissal of the theocratic promises to Jews in the Old Testament.[170] So he rejected the Calvinist and Catholic notion that the Israelite prophets were "really" predicting the dawn of the Christian Church and the spiritual sovereignty of Jesus the crucified Savior, *not* the coming of the messianic, nationalistic Davidic kingdom.

Though Dispensationalists maintain that the Old Testament did predict Jesus' death, resurrection, and Second Coming, they insist that the period of the Church and the inclusion of Gentiles in a plan of salvation by grace through faith was utterly unanticipated, "a mystery hidden from ages and generations" till the Jewish rejection of Jesus as Davidic king "stopped the prophetic clock" and jogged things over to a different, temporary trajectory, the Dispensation of Grace, or the Church Age.[171] It began with the descent of the Spirit at Pentecost and will conclude with the Rapture of the Saints. At that point the prophetic clock starts up again. Then comes the Antichrist, inaugurating the Great Tribulation, a time of awful persecution for Jews until Jesus returns as both the Christian Savior and the Davidic monarch, ushering in the Millennial Kingdom, which he will rule from Jerusalem. Of course, Ephesians does not go nearly so far, but the Dispensationalist schema is squarely based upon the notion of the hidden mystery, an idea shared with the Dead Sea Scrolls sect who

---

[170] Ernest R. Sandeen, *The Origins of Fundamentalism: Toward a Historical Interpretation.* Facet Books. Historical Series 10 (Philadelphia: Fortress Press, 1968), p. 4.

[171] Harry A. Ironside, *The Great Parenthesis* (Grand Rapids: Zondervan, 1943); Ernest R. Sandeen, *The Roots of Fundamentalism: British and American Millenarianism, 1800-1930.* Twin Brooks Series (Grand Rapids: Baker Book House, 1978), p. 67.

"discovered" new Spirit-inspired bulletins between the lines of ancient scriptures.[172]

Predestination or Prestidigitation?

But wait—what is this about being *predestined?* "He chose us in him before the foundation of the world, that we should be holy and blameless before him. He destined us in love to be his sons through Jesus Christ, according to the purpose of his will... to unite all things in him, things in heaven and things on earth" (1:4-5, 10). This little phrase "in him" seems to push the meaning of predestination in a particular direction, away from the notion that God has picked out specific individuals for final salvation, as Calvinists believe. The idea seems to be rather that a great destiny awaits those who are somehow incorporated collectively "in Christ." Forster and Marston: "Perhaps the most important point to grasp about predestination is that it concerns man's future destiny. It does not concern who should, or should not, *become* Christians, but rather their destiny *as* Christians."[173] Arminians take this, not unreasonably, to mean that, while individuals have free choice in whether or not to embrace Christianity, once they *do* they are henceforth (happily) locked in to a particular course. As my old Baptist pastor, Charles W. Anderson,[174] used to put it, you can buy a ticket for any destination you want, but once you board the train, you are definitely headed toward that destination. Buying the ticket (your choice) is what predestines you, in this case to heavenly glory.[175]

But I do not think this interpretation is quite adequate. Ephesians 1:4 says "he chose us before the foundation of the world." If the Arminians were correct, shouldn't the verse say not "chose us in him," but rather "chose those who are in him," or some such? Doesn't

---

[172] Raymond E. Brown, *The Semitic Background of the Term "Mystery" in the New Testament.* Facet Books, Biblical Series 21 (Philadelphia: Fortress Press, 1968).

[173] Roger T. Forster and V. Paul Marston, *God's Strategy in Human History* (Wheaton: Tyndale House, 1974), p. 101.

[174] He said it in a sermon; who knows where he may have read it? I have the late Dr. Anderson's picture framed on my wall along with Tillich, Schleiermacher, Harnack, Bultmann, F.C. Baur, and Clark H. Pinnock. I guess you could say he's numbered among the transgressors.

[175] But can you hop off the train once you're on it? Strict Arminians say you can, though it would be a fatal, salvation-forfeiting mistake. Baptists like Dr. Anderson believe you can't. This latter is called the doctrine of "eternal security."

the "us" imply that God chose particular individuals, you, me, and Dr. Anderson? I think it does. But this still does not tip the scales in favor of Calvinism.

Mystical Body

I think the underlying concept is Gnostic, especially in light of Ephesians 4:10-16. "He who descended is he who also ascended far above all the heavens, that he might fill all things" (verse 10). This event began the process of "building up the body of Christ, until we all attain to the unity of the faith and knowledge of the Son of God, to mature manhood, to the measure of the stature of the fullness of Christ" (verses 12b-13). This all reflects the notion, found in Gnosticism, the Jewish Kabbalah, etc., of the *Anthropos*, the Primal Man, the Man of Light, the *Adam Kadmon*. He was the first emanation from the Godhead, each member of his gigantic humanoid body representing a different attribute of God. The Adam Kadmon (Heavenly Adam) was the living blueprint according to which the world was made. He was a vast, universe-filling Being of glorious light.[176] He contained all the souls of the human race latent within himself.[177]

Through a cosmic Fall, the divine Light streaming forth from him to fill the "shells" (*Kelipoth*), which had been designed to contain a celestial, non-material light-world, was lost and scattered among the murk of base matter.[178] Christian Gnostics said the Primal Adam was ripped to shreds (sparks) by the evil angels (Archons) who implanted them into the hitherto-inert material creation, including the fleshly Adam of Genesis chapters 2 and 3. According to the Lore of Creation passed down by Jewish Gnostics (Kabbalists), the Adam Kadmon was reduced in size to our present dimensions and wrapped in material

---

[176] Gershom Scholem, *On the Kabbalah and Its Symbolism*. Trans. Ralph Manheim (New York: Schocken Books, 1969), p 162; Hugh J. Schonfield, *Those Incredible Christians* (New York: Bantam Books, 1969), p. 249.

[177] Gershom G. Scholem, *Major Trends in Jewish Mysticism*. Trans. George Lichtheim.. Hilda Strook Lectures at the Jewish Institute of Religion (New York: Schocken Books, 1973), Seventh Lecture, "Isaac Luria and his School," p. 278; Scholem, *On the Kabbalah and Its Symbolism*, p. 115; Walter Schmithals, *The Office of Apostle in the Early Church*. Trans. John E. Steely (New York: Abingdon Press, 1969), p. 118.

[178] Scholem, *On the Kabbalah and Its Symbolism*, p. 114.

flesh ("coats of skin").[179] In both versions, the goal of salvation history was to gradually restore the integrity of the Man of Light, reassembling his sparks from the people in whom they were lodged (the Gnostic pneumatics themselves). It was but slightly different in Kabbalah: the scattered photons of the Shekinah (the glory cloud representing God's presence) must be regathered from the world of matter,[180] whereupon the Adam Kadmon would be restored to his lost glory.

This is what Ephesians seems to be describing: Christ is the Primal Man of Light who descended into the depth of the earth (i.e., came down into the material world, not somewhere below it). He appeared among men as one of them, the Adam Kadmon reduced in size and clothed in flesh. At his resurrection he returned to the Godhead (the Pleroma of the Gnostics, the *En-Sof* of the Kabbalah), figuratively reigning at God's right hand but actually regaining his gigantic cosmic stature.[181] His celestial body grows to its full stature bit by bit as more people share in his ascension by virtue of baptism,[182] enabling them to live simultaneously on the earthly plane (till the casting off of the "body of death") and in "the heavenlies." This is Gnosticism, so no wonder we have in Ephesians the idea of a spiritual resurrection already accomplished through baptism and sufficient unto itself.

"We" were "chosen in him before the creation of the world" in the sense of having been contained in the Primal Man, our souls being the photons comprising his celestial body. Our destiny (you're a Gnostic, too, right?) was to endure long imprisonment in a succession of perishing bodies (incarceration via [re]incarnation) till enlightenment frees the soul or spirit and enables it to return to its original home.

The Calvinist doctrine of election, predestination, and limited atonement is essentially Gnostic as well, but the focus is a bit different, being more concerned with the division between the pneumatics (spiritual ones, "the elect") who possess the imprisoned spark and the sarkics ("the reprobate") who are bereft of it. Only the former will return to the Pleroma, while the latter must ultimately sink back into the swampy void of matter once it loses its structure with the departure of all the divine photons whose presence had long held it together.

---

[179] Schonfield, *Incredible Christians*, pp. 249-250.
[180] Scholem, "Isaac Luria and his School," pp. 268, 279.
[181] Schonfield, *Incredible Christians*, pp. 250, 253.
[182] Schonfield, *Incredible Christians*, pp. 253-254.

Martin Luther's version of predestinarianism is not quite the same, lacking the notion of a limited atonement restricted in both intent and effect to the pre-chosen elect. It takes off from a different passage in Ephesians, chapter 2, verses 1-10. [183] In *The Bondage of the Will*, the great Reformer reasoned that, if we are *dead* in sin, spiritually as inert as a brick, we cannot possibly come alive under our own steam. If the metaphor is to mean anything, it has to imply our utter inability even to desire to repent. Lazarus didn't climb out of his tomb under his own steam. So if we do repent and accept the gospel, whose initiative must be responsible? God's. And then you're talking about predestination, right? Here "salvation by grace" demands predestination and indeed is equated with it.

Positional Truth

The unique spirituality of fundamentalism and evangelicalism stems from this Gnostic framework, though its origin is no longer recognized. All one needs to know is that, as a regenerated Christian, one invisibly occupies a "position" united to Christ in heaven. [184] This version of you is you as God sees you in Christ, justified and righteous. On the one hand, justification means your sins are forgiven and you stand acquitted before the Heavenly Judge. This is in one sense a kind of legal fiction, since God is treating you as the possessor of Christ's own righteousness, which he exchanged for the burden of your sin on the cross (2 Cor. 5:21). This is true even if your actual behavior ("the fruits of repentance," Matt. 3:8) is not yet much improved. On the other hand, you are still in the process of being sanctified here on earth below, taking up the slack between the version of you God sees when he looks at you through the blood-stained lens of Christ and the ordinary schmuck you see in the mirror.

---

[183] One commonly hears Ephesians 2:8-9 ("By grace you have been saved, through faith, and that not of yourselves. It is the gift of God, not of works, lest anyone should boast") invoked as attesting predestinarianism, as if the "that" referred back to "faith," which would imply that God gives faith to sinners who could not exercise it on their own initiative. Augustine viewed it this way, but Greek grammar rules it out. The Greek words for "faith" and "grace" are both feminine in gender, while the pronoun "that" is neuter. It wouldn't be if it referred directly to either of these nouns. Instead, it appears to refer to the whole process of salvation in the preceding verses. See Forster and Marston, *God's Strategy in Human History*, pp. 268-269.

[184] Harry A. Ironside, *In the Heavenlies: Practical Expository Addresses on the Epistle to the Ephesians* (Neptune, NJ: Loizeaux Brothers, 1937).

(This understanding comes awfully close to the Zoroastrian[185] and Gnostic concept of your having a heavenly spirit-double (a guardian angel that looks like you because he *is* you, Acts 12:13-15) already up there beholding the face of God (Matt. 18:10). At some point (the Gnostic sacrament of the Bridal Chamber[186] or the eschatological Marriage Supper of the Lamb) you and your heavenly alter ego will merge, and that will be full salvation.

And how do you become more and more sanctified? You must "appropriate" the "positional truth"[187] of what you are (or have) in heaven where you crowd in beside Christ enthroned with God. All the noble character traits ("the fruit of the Spirit," Gal. 5:22-23) you yearn to have are there, with Christ in heaven, in the "you" who is already in heaven "in him." How to experience them? You focus on them (Col. 3:1-3), reach out for them in imagination, and "appropriate" them here on earth. It is just like "claiming" one's (supposedly promised) physical healing from God. As Bultmann puts it, "The way the believer becomes what he already is consists therefore in the constant appropriation of grace by faith... The meaning is clear: the faith-bestowed possibility of 'living by the Spirit' must be explicitly laid hold of by 'walking by the Spirit.' The indicative is the foundation for the imperative."[188]

If and when this works for anybody, I think it can be understood along the lines of Claude Lévi-Strauss's essay, "The Effectiveness of Symbols." In discussing an African exorcism ritual based on a narrative of a magical victory by good spirits over evil ones, the latter symbolizing the pains of a prolonged pregnancy, Lévi-Strauss says,

> The cure would consist, therefore, in making explicit a situation originally existing on the emotional level and in rendering to the mind pains which the body refuses to

---

[185] R.C. Zaehner, *The Teachings of the Magi: A Compendium of Zoroastrian Beliefs* (New York: Oxford University Press /Galaxy Books, 1956), pp. 17, 41; Zaehner, *The Dawn and Twilight of Zoroastrianism*. History of Religion Series (New York: Phoenix Press, 1961), pp. 146-147.

[186] Gilles Quispell, "The Birth of the Child: Some Gnostic and Jewish Aspects." Trans. Ruth Horine. In *Eranos Lectures 3: Jewish and Gnostic Man* (Dallas: Spring Publications, 1986), p. 26.

[187] Miles J. Stanford, *The Green Letters: Principles of Spiritual Growth* (Grand Rapids: Zondervan, 1981); Stanford, *The Principle of Position: Foundations of Spiritual Growth* (Grand Rapids: Zondervan, 1976).

[188] Bultmann, *Theology of the New Testament*, vol. I, pp. 332-333.

tolerate. That the mythology of the shaman does not correspond to an objective reality does not matter. The sick woman believes in the myth and belongs to a society which believes in it. The tutelary spirits and malevolent spirits, the supernatural monsters and magical animals, are all part of a coherent system on which the native conception of the universe is founded.[189]

Obviously, the cases are not precisely the same, the one dealing with physical pain, the other with spiritual frustration, but I think the underlying principle is the same. The mythic framework, utilized as the program of a mind-game, enables the individual to get a handle on something otherwise too nebulous to know how to deal with.[190]

Bring Me a Higher Love

Ephesians 5:21-33 lists the duties of Christian wives and husbands. The section looks to have been developed from Colossians 3:18-4:1, which also stipulates rules of behavior for children and parents, slaves and masters. Martin Luther (or possibly some anonymous contemporary) called these sections (as well as 1 Peter 2:13-3:7) *Haustafeln* ("household tablets"). This is to compare these texts with wooden plaques posted in homes with mottos and rules for harmony among family members. John Howard Yoder[191] dismisses the possibility of literary dependence, i.e., that the similarities between the three passages are the result of various writers copying from one another. No, he says, the similarity must be understood via form criticism as three separate specimens of a kind of early Christian domestic exhortation formula. I cannot accept this. The dependence of Ephesians upon Colossians seems clear enough, and 1 Peter

---

[189] Claude Lévi-Strauss, "The Effectiveness of Symbols" in Lévi-Strauss, *Structural Anthropology*. Trans. Claire Jacobson and Brooke Grundfest Schoepf (Garden City: Doubleday Anchor Books, 1967), p. 192.

[190] There are equivalent devotional schemas that do not, however, employ the terms of Ephesians, such as the "let go and let God" model, the "let Christ live the Christian life through you" model, and the "rest/abide in Christ" model.

[191] John Howard Yoder, *The Politics of Jesus* (Grand Rapids: Eerdmans, 1972), p. 165, dependent upon the dissertation of David Schroeder, *Die Haustafel des Neues Testaments, Ihre Herrkunft und ihr theologische Sinn* (University of Hamburg, 1959).

appears to be partly based on Ephesians, as many scholars hold.[192]

This passage of Ephesians became the ground of intense debate in the 1970s when Evangelical Feminism came to the fore. How can one invoke the infallible scripture on behalf of male-female equality if it contains statements commanding female subordination to men? Some[193] drew attention to the fact that the passage starts out urging *mutual* submission between husband and wife. The key point is that verse 21 sets the tone: "Be subject to one another out of reverence for Christ." Note that "be subject" is not actually repeated in the next verse, despite the habit of most translations in supplying it. This implies that verse 22 tells the wife wherein her submission lies, while verse 25 ("Husbands, love your wives, as Christ loved the church and gave himself up for her") balances it out, specifying the nature of the husband's submission to his wife. So far, so good, but it seems hard to deny that the whole thing implies that, while the husband owes his wife any sacrifice on her behalf, the wife's responsibility is to obey him as the church is to obey Christ. Isn't this a perfect case of what Gerd Theissen, following Max Weber, called "a patriarchalism of love"?[194]

We are surprised to read in Ephesians 5:31-32, "'For this reason a man shall leave his father and mother and be joined to his wife, and the two shall become one flesh.' This is a great mystery, and I take it to mean Christ and the Church." The writer appears to be allegorizing the Genesis 2:24 text. Come to think of it, though, he supposes it is applicable to earthly, physical marriage, too. But what is this spiritual mystery, in which the writer seems more interested? I can't help thinking of Denis de Rougemont's great book, *Love in the Western World*.[195] He develops the astonishing thesis that the Western ideal of romantic love is a kind of secularized demythologization of the Gnostics' spurning of traditional marriage in favor of the ascetic's

---

[192] A similar view of their relation is that set forth in Winsome Munro, *Authority in Paul and Peter: The Identification of a Pastoral Stratum in the Pauline Corpus and I Peter.* Society for New Testament Studies Monograph Series 45 (New York: Cambridge University Press, 1983). She argues that these and similar passages are in fact part of a redactional layer added to these epistles by the same post-Pauline hand who wrote the Pastoral Epistles. The goal of this Pastoral Redactor was to tone down the original radicalism of the Pauline Epistles.

[193] I heard this interpretation from David M. Scholer who taught "The Role and Status of Women in the New Testament" at Gordon-Conwell Theological Seminary.

[194] Gerd Theissen, *Sociology of Early Palestinian Christianity.* Trans. John Bowden (Philadelphia: Fortress Press, 1978), p. 115.

[195] Denis de Rougemont, *Love in the Western World.* Trans. Montgomery Belgion (Garden City: Doubleday Anchor Books, 1957).

devotion to Dame Wisdom, the Gnostic Sophia, pretty much the "cognitive eros" of which Plato wrote. It is a love transcending domesticity (cf., 1 Cor. 7:32-35), child-rearing, and sexual responsibilities.

De Rougemont notes that the violent suppression of the neo-Manichean Catharist sect in the thirteenth century[196] closely coincided with the emergence of chivalric Courtly Love poetry which similarly avows deathless love for an unobtainable (married) woman. He infers that the Gnostic adoration for Dame Wisdom became a "love that dared not speak its name" and so continued under a pseudonym. Lancelot's love for Guinevere is a classic example. But doesn't that love finally collapse into sordid adultery? That is De Rougemont's point. The ascetic's transcendent love for Lady Wisdom gets translated into the adulterous romance of secret affairs and betrayals once it is petrified into earthly romantic love. The man who assures his mistress that he will soon leave his wife to marry his paramour never does it, for what he savors is the heady excitement of a love outside of humdrum domesticity. And if he *does* marry his girlfriend, he will soon be cheating on *her* with a *new* mistress. The spiritual love for an invisible, spiritual beloved, I think, was the sort of higher love the Ephesians writer found in Genesis 2:24. If so, we have yet more reason to detect a decidedly Gnostic flavor to Ephesians.

---

[196] Can you imagine such events occurring in the world of Disney's *Sleeping Beauty*, which is set somewhere in Western Europe in the same century?

19
The Epistle to the Philippians
Bible Bodhisattva

Overview

This is the first of Paul's Prison Epistles we will consider. Its occasion is clear: Paul is in prison, late in his career, probably at Rome, as tradition tells us. Paul could have written it during an earlier imprisonment in either Ephesus or Caesarea, but various factors favor Rome as the place of writing, notably the mentions of Caesar's household (1:32; 4:22) and of the Praetorian (i.e., Palace) Guard, Caesar's elite (though there was a detachment of them in Ephesus as well).

Philippians is essentially a thank-you note to this congregation, always a favorite of Paul's, and apparently one that has never caused him any trouble (note the several commendations and expressions of paternal pride). We read of the founding of this church in Acts 16. No doubt the earliest leader was Lydia, a wealthy seller of purple goods who hosted the house church. The Philippian jailor and his family would have been charter members, too, at least if these episodes have any historical core at all.[197]

Paul mentions the Macedonians (i.e., the Philippians and Thessalonians) in 2 Corinthians 8:1-5; 9:14; 11:9, praising them for their conspicuous generosity. Here he addresses his praise to the Philippians directly. They have sent their representative Epaphroditus with a large sum for Paul's needs. He stayed a good while to assist Paul, but he fell seriously ill, near death, but then made a dramatic recovery. Paul sent him back home, carrying this letter (2:25-30). Most of the letter is news and encouragement, thanks, and a bit of advice.

But is our Philippians a single letter? Günther Bornkamm[198] and Walter Schmithals[199] independently divided the text into three

---

[197] Gerd Lüdemann, *Early Christianity according to the Traditions in Acts: A Commentary.* Trans. John Bowden (Minneapolis: Fortress Press, 1989), pp. 183-184, thinks the story of Lydia's conversion and hospitality is basically historical, while that of the Philippian jailor is not. Take another look at my comments on Acts 16 in my chapter on Acts.

[198] Bornkamm, *Paul.* Trans. D.M.G. Stalker (New York: Harper & Row, 1971), pp. 246-247.

[199] Walter Schmithals, *Paul and the Gnostics.* Trans. John E. Steely (New York:

original letters or fragments of letters, a situation parallel to that of 2 Corinthians. Sounds good to me. I'm going with Schmithals's division.

First Philippians

The first (4:10-23) is a very brief note of thanks, the abiding highlight being Paul's famous statement of contentment:

> I have learned, in whatever state I am, to be content. I know how to be abased, and I know how to abound; in any and all circumstances I have learned the secret of facing plenty and hunger, abundance and want. I can do all things in him who strengthens me" (4:11-13).

Here Paul sounds like an Epicurean philosopher.[200] Epicurus named pleasure as the greatest good and the one to be sought above all others. But he hastened to define pleasure as "the absence of pain in the body and of trouble in the soul" (*Letter to Meneceus*). And he speaks of contentment in terms very similar to those in Philippians 4:11-13: "we regard independence of outward things as a great good, not so as in all cases to use little, but so as to be contented with little if we have not much, being honestly persuaded that they have the sweetest enjoyment of luxury who stand least in need of it (ibid.).[201]

Second Philippians

The second letter covers 1:1-3:1, 4:4-7. The very first verse ought to make an alarm go off: "bishops and deacons"? This seems anachronistic. We seem to be entering the realm of the late, pseudo-Pauline Pastorals here. In verses 3-11 Paul expresses pride and gratitude for the Philippians' "partnership" in the work of the gospel,

---

Abingdon Press, 1972), p. 79.

[200] Norman Wentworth DeWitt, *St. Paul and Epicurus* (Minneapolis: University of Minnesota Press, 1954), Chapter 10, "Paul's Knowledge of Epicureanism," pp. 167-184.

[201] Jason L. Saunders, ed. and trans. *Greek and Roman Philosophy after Aristotle*. Readings in the History of Philosophy (New York: Free Press / Macmillan, 1966), p. 51.

referring of course to their financial support (Matt. 10:42; 3 John 5-8). The more he has to engage in secular work (Acts 18:3-4), the less time he can devote to evangelism. So if you relieve Paul of the need for secular work, you multiply his evangelistic efforts. You are thus a "silent partner."

God has made a good start with the Philippians, and Paul fully expects their sanctification to be complete by the (imminent) coming of Christ (verses 6 and 10). John Wesley cited these verses in refutation of the typical Christian pessimism that none of them will "make it" to perfection in this life. Paul assumed we could, said Wesley. (But 3:12-13 may cause us to doubt this, since Paul himself disavows any notion that he himself has "arrived.")

Paul begs his friends (in verses 12-26) not to be discouraged by his imprisonment. One might think the progress of the gospel to have suffered a heavy blow, a serious setback, by this turn of events, but in fact the reverse is true. For one thing, Paul has managed to communicate the gospel to his rotating guards, who must be curious: "What are you in for, buddy?" If Roman soldiers were to become Christian converts they might prove instrumental in spreading the faith among family and friends at home when they returned there. After all, this is how Mithraism spread from the Parthian frontier all over Europe till it became the official religion of the Roman Empire.

For another, many of the brethren have decided to take up the slack, to get busy preaching since Paul's voice has gone silent. Paul even speaks of his *enemies* preaching Christ just to get him deeper into trouble, but he doesn't care *why* they do it as long as the gospel is in fact getting preached! This is very strange, though. It is pretty difficult to imagine anyone preaching precisely *because* it was dangerous—especially if they didn't actually believe what they were preaching. As Paul's enemies, they can scarcely have affirmed his beliefs. It seems more likely that he is impugning or caricaturing the motives of some colleagues with whom he has personal issues.

For yet a third thing, even if God *has* decided it is time for Paul to die, this, too, will glorify God, so the readers shouldn't fear that God's cause is in danger of being thwarted. Remember, Tertullian later remarked that "the blood of the martyrs is seed," the seed of the church. The spectacle of Christians willing to die for their faith does seem to have been a powerful advertisement for the worth of Christianity: if it's worth dying for, it must be worth living for.[202]

---

[202] E.R. Dodds, *Pagans and Christians in an Age of Anxiety: Some Aspects of Religious Experience from Marcus Aurelius to Constantine* (New York: Norton, 1970), pp. 132-133;

Besides, death would only be in Paul's interest! As a martyr, he would not need to wait for the End-Time resurrection along with everyone else, but would go straight to join Christ in heavenly glory (cf., Rev. 6:9-11; 20:4-6). You can't beat *that*! But Paul rather expects he will be released from prison (not executed) since there is further work that calls for his attention. Interestingly, these words portray Paul as a kind of Bodhisattva, an enlightened Buddhist adept who is fully entitled to enter the final bliss of Nirvana but defers it, lingering in this world of Samsara to assist in the spiritual advancement of others.

Perhaps Epaphroditus has informed Paul of chronic quarreling among some in the congregation. At any rate, Paul supplies a simple remedy for the ailment: everyone should stop thinking first of himself and submerge private matters in a common devotion to the evangelistic cause (1:27). In the next breath (1:28) he urges them not to be taken aback at eruptions of persecution; wasn't this what they signed on for? It's not an uninterrupted joy ride (as some triumphalistic Corinthians seemed to think). In fact, they should find the very fact of persecution encouraging! It only goes to show they are the real thing. Why would Satan bother them if they were no threat to him?

Might the congregation have been divided over how to respond to persecution? Some might have denied their Christian faith to get out of a tight spot, figuring that no harm would be done. After all, does not God look upon the heart (1 Samuel 16:7)? He knows you were just kidding. This was a significant issue in early Christianity,[203] as witness Mark 8:38, which must have originated in the early community to address this very issue.

Singing the Creed

Theologically, the most important piece of Philippians is the Kenosis

Rodney Stark, *The Rise of Christianity: A Sociologist Reconsiders History* (Princeton: Princeton University Press, 1996), Chapter 8, "The Martyrs: Sacrifice as a Rational Choice," pp. 163-189.

[203] Elaine Pagels, *The Gnostic Gospels* (New York: Random House, 1979), Chapter IV, "The Passion of Christ and the Persecution of Christians," pp. 70-101.

Hymn,[204] set forth in 2:6-11. ("Kenosis" means "emptying.") Paul quotes these lyrics from an early hymn about the incarnation. The imagery characterizes Christ as the pre-existent Wisdom personified as the Logos or Heavenly Adam, refusing to proudly exalt himself as the Edenic Adam did by usurping the prerogatives of God (the forbidden fruit of knowledge), but instead abasing himself via the incarnation, finally receiving the very divine honors he refused to seize for himself.[205] Let's take a look at the text piece by piece.

The phrase "though he was in the form of God" reflects Genesis 1:27, "God created man in his own image."[206] Thus this celestial entity was the prototype of the earthly Adam, Eve's husband. When the Adam Kadmon "did not count equality with God a thing to be grasped," he turned right where his earthly counterpart had long ago turned left. The latter had partaken of the fruit that should make him "like God, knowing good and evil," but the heavenly Adam did the opposite: he "emptied himself, taking the form of a servant." Much linguistic data attests that the Greek word *morphe* could mean (and was sometimes used to mean) "essence or nature," but that it could just as well (and often did) mean "form," exterior rather than interior.[207] Which does it mean in Philippians 2:6? In view of the recurrence of the word in verse 7, contrasting the original state of heavenly existence ("the form of God") with the earthly ("the form of a slave"),[208] I think it has to have an exterior reference in both cases. It seems to be precisely parallel to the Mahayana Buddhist Trikaya doctrine, according to which the Buddhas and Bodhisattvas recline in heavenly glory (the *Sambogkya*) until they descend to earth among

---

[204] I remember reading *Asimov's Guide to the Bible, Vol. 2: The New Testament* (New York: Avon Books, 1988) and discovering that his third-hand discussion of Philippians did not even mention this passage. *What the hell?*

[205] Ralph P. Martin, *Carmen Christi: Philippians ii.5-11 in Recent Interpretation and in the Setting of Early Christian Worship.* Society of New Testament Studies Monograph Series 4 (Cambridge at the University Press, 1967), pp. 116-133; James D.G. Dunn, *Christology in the Making: An Inquiry into the Origins of the Doctrine of the Incarnation* (London: SCM Press, 2nd ed., 1989), pp. 114-121.

[206] True, Genesis chapter one comes from the Priestly source, which regards "Adam" simply as the species name for the human race, while the rest of the Adam parallels in Philippians 2:6-11 are from chapters 2-3, part of the J source, which depicts Adam as a single individual, but by New Testament times the two had been harmonized and were both thought to refer to the Edenic Adam.

[207] Martin, *Carmen Christi*, pp. 100-110.

[208] Why a "slave"? Probably it denotes his subjection to "the thousand natural shocks that flesh is heir to," but it could very likely be a nod to the Eden story where Adam was created merely to serve Yahweh Elohim as his gardener.

mankind, whereupon they assume the outward form of mortals (the *Nirmankaya*, or "Transformation Body").[209]

This Transformation Body bears but the semblance of human flesh, and so, I take it, did the earthly "form" of the savior in Philippians 2:7: "being born in the *likeness* of men." This might mean full-scale Docetism, as in the Acts of John, where the hand reaching out to touch Jesus passes right through him, as if a three-dimensional holographic image. But it might be the same idea found in the Gnostic Hymn of the Pearl (in the Acts of Thomas): the Redeemer, his earthly mission accomplished, strips off his "filthy garment" of genuine flesh. It wasn't his true, defining self, more of a scuba-diving sheath of flesh. That is certainly the Kabbalistic notion of the Adam Kadmon, who, as of the Fall, gets reduced in size to the usual five or six feet and encased in a suit of sweaty flesh ("coats of skin"). He bears his treasure in a cheap earthen vessel.

The Kabbalistic story of the Adam Kadmon made him responsible for bungling his assigned task of regathering the divine photons scattered throughout the wrecked shards of the *Kelipoth* (the material world). His demotion and reduction to the flesh-clothed Adam of the earthly Eden was thus a punishment, but, as the Kenosis Hymn understands the heavenly Adam as undoing that primordial Fall, he must be depicted as undertaking the descent into matter as a voluntary sacrifice in order to initiate the saving process of regathering the divine sparks of the Shekinah all over again, successfully this time.[210]

"And being found in human form he humbled himself and became obedient unto death." This sentence is no mere poetic reiteration of the self-abnegation of a voluntary descent into the human condition (2 Cor. 8:9) but takes the humiliation one crucial step farther. Once he was here on earth, like Robinson Crusoe stranded on a desert island, he further submitted to death, something impossible during his original, cushy existence in heaven. (Paul has probably added "even death on a cross," which violates the poetic

---

[209] Paul J. Griffiths, *On Being Buddha: The Classical Doctrine of Buddhahood*. Toward a Comparative Philosophy of Religions Series (Albany: State University of New York Press, 1994), Chapter 4.2, "Bodies of Magical Transformation," pp. 90-97; Edward J. Thomas, *The History of Buddhist Thought* (London: Routledge & Kegan Paul, 1951), pp. 242-243; Thomas, *The Life of Buddha as Legend and History*. History of Civilizations (London: Routledge & Kegan Paul, 1975), pp. 215-216.
[210] Hugh J. Schonfield, *Those Incredible Christians* (New York: Bantam Books, 1969), pp. 249-251.

meter otherwise consistent throughout.)[211]

"Therefore God has highly exalted him and bestowed on him the name which is above every name, that at the name of Jesus every knee should bow, in heaven and on earth and under the earth, and every tongue confess that Jesus Christ is Lord, to the glory of God the Father." This passage is derived from another, Isaiah 45:23.

> By myself I have sworn,
> from my mouth has gone forth in righteousness
> a word that shall not return:[212]
> "To me every knee shall bow,
> every tongue shall swear."

In this Old Testament passage we hear Yahweh avowing that his enemies shall soon be groveling before him, swearing fealty despite themselves. The Kenosis Hymn transfers this scenario to the exaltation of the Heavenly Adam to his original glory (John 17:5). The implication might be that he thus attained the equality with God he had humbly declined before.

The poetic parallelism of the final section deserves closer scrutiny than it ordinarily receives. The savior goes unnamed till the end. "Therefore God has highly exalted him" parallels "bestowed on him the *name* which is above every *name*." The idea "that at the *name* of Jesus every knee should bow" corresponds to "every tongue [should] confess that *Jesus* Christ is Lord." Every knee throughout the universe bows when Jesus' name is announced, just as every pair of lips acknowledges his Lordship. The point is, as Paul Couchoud[213] alone seemed to notice, that it was not the *title* "Lord" (*Kurios*) that was bestowed upon the exalted savior but rather the throne-*name* "Jesus." Yes, he assumes the name Jesus only once he returns to heaven. What does this suggest as to whether Paul (or the author of the pre-Pauline hymn) believed there had been a man named Jesus already during an earthly sojourn, as in the gospels?

---

[211] Martin, *Carmen Christi*, pp. 314-315.

[212] Cf. Gilbert and Sullivan: "For he himself has said it, And it's greatly to his credit, That he is an Englishman!"

[213] Paul Louis Couchoud, *The Creation of the Christ: An Outline of the Beginnings of Christianity*. Trans. C. Bradlaugh Bonner (London: Watts & Co., 1939), p. 438.

THE EPISTLE TO THE PHILIPPIANS

Work out your Own Exegesis

If this weren't enough of a theological migraine, verses 12-13 speak of *synergism*, the idea that salvation requires our efforts precisely because God supplies the power (the Spirit) to make our efforts effective. This is no affront to Eastern Orthodox theology, which is openly synergistic, but Protestants have problems here because they follow the Lutheran (mis)interpretation of "salvation by grace through faith, not works" as a disavowal of moral good deeds rather than a rejection of "works of the law," ceremonial regulations defining Jewish ethnicity and cultural boundaries. (Of course, Protestants expect good deeds but make them the consequence of, not the requirement for, salvation.) Fundamentalists offer the exceedingly lame *ad hoc* interpretation that verse 12 means to let your inner regeneration "work itself outward" in good behavior. That would make it parallel to Matthew 5:16 ("Let your light so shine before men, that they may see your good works," etc.). And the desired point, not hiding one's light beneath a basket, is actually made in Philippians 2:15-16a ("that you may be blameless and innocent, children of God without blemish in the midst of a crooked and perverse generation, among whom you shine as lights in the world, holding fast the word of life"), but to force verse 12 to mean this is, I think, a clear attempt to avoid the plain sense of the text for theological reasons.

Paul seems to want to conclude as of 3:1, and Schmithals says he did, with what we now find in 4:4-7, an oft-quoted passage employed as a kind of mantra in Christian devotion: "Rejoice in the Lord always; again I will say, Rejoice. Let all men know your forbearance. The Lord is at hand. Have no anxiety about anything, but in everything by prayer and supplication with thanksgiving let your requests be made known to God. And the peace of God, which passes all understanding, will keep your hearts and your minds in Christ Jesus."

Third Philippians

We come to the third letter when we get to 3:2-4:3, 8-9. This one has much in common with the Severe Letter to Corinth (2 Cor. 10-13). Paul storms against the Judaizers. He sneers at their self-congratulation for being Jews (this carried a mystique of exotic "Orientalism" in the Hellenistic world): "Yeah? Me, *too!* So *what?*" Paul says he, too, was circumcised as an infant, hailing from the tribe of Benjamin, descended from real, ethnic Jews, not a proselyte in the bunch. He was trained as a Pharisee.[214] *Don't tell me I don't know what I'm talking about when it comes to Judaism!* But these are no longer weighty considerations, much less credentials for apostleship, and certainly not prerequisites for salvation! That he is once again talking about ritual, ceremonial markers of ethnicity, of belonging to God's chosen people, is evident from his characterizing these things as being "of the flesh," not in the sense of sensuality, but of material matters. He does not reject "salvation by good deeds," but "righteousness under the law" (3:6), "a righteousness of my own, based on law" (verse 9).[215] Paul has cast all this off as childish baubles (1 Cor. 13:11 plus Gal. 3:23-26). Once glorious in their own right, the sancta of Judaism are now overshadowed, outstripped to such an extent that, compared to the freedom of the gospel of Christ, they seem no better than a pile of manure ("if you'll forgive the disgusting imagery"[216]). One may ask: what is so much better about the Christian religion than the Jewish? I suspect that E.P. Sanders hits the crucifixion nail right on the head:

> He thus knows about two righteousnesses. The difference between them is not the distinction between merit and grace, but between two dispensations. There is a righteousness that comes by law, but it is now worth nothing because of a new dispensation. *Real* righteousness (the righteousness of or from God) is through Christ. It is this concrete fact of *Heilsgeschichte* [salvation history] which makes the other righteousness wrong, not the abstract superiority of grace to merit.[217]

---

[214] Hyam Maccoby, *Paul and Hellenism* (London: SCM Press / Philadelphia: Fortress Press, 1991), Chapter 5, "Paul and Pharisaism," pp. 129-154. Maccoby strongly repudiates the notion that Paul was ever educated as a Pharisee. If he was, he must have slept through his classes and flunked out because his exegesis of scripture sounds, if anything, more like that of the Gnostics on display in the Nag Hammadi texts. (*Gasp!* But what about W.D. Davies's venerable book, *Paul and Rabbinic Judaism?* It's a vast exercise in ecumenical text-twisting, if you ask me.)

[215] Cf., E.P. Sanders, *Paul, the Law, and the Jewish People* (Minneapolis: Fortress Press, 1983), p. 38: "'Their own righteousness,' in other words means, 'that righteousness which the Jews alone are privileged to obtain,' rather than 'self-righteousness which consists in individuals' presenting their merits as a claim upon God'" [Sanders's italics removed].

[216] Woody Allen, *Manhattan*. In Allen, *Four Films of Woody Allen: Annie Hall, Interiors, Manhattan, Stardust Memories* (New York: Random House, 1982), p. 223.

[217] Sanders, p. 140.

THE EPISTLE TO THE PHILIPPIANS

Philippians 3:10-16 speaks of the resurrection hope in decidedly Catholic terms, guarding against "presumption," pat confidence that one's salvation is a done deal. Evangelical Protestants delight in saying, "I know that, if I died tonight, I would go to heaven!" Are they foolish braggarts? Not at all. In fact their whole point is that, since no merit of theirs could decide the issue of salvation, they could never have confidence on that basis. Rather, they can be so sure of salvation because it is entirely predicated upon Christ's incomparable righteousness which has now been imputed to them. Roman Catholics gladly acknowledge the same thing, but they see that there's many a slip twixt the communion cup and the lip! Christ's atonement is admittedly sure and unshakeable, but can the same be said of our acceptance of it and endurance in it? Thus the need to watch one's step "with fear and trembling" (Phil. 2:12). A sobering prospect indeed.

As usual, Paul has enough ire to go around; he next warns against Christian libertines who degrade gospel liberty into a pathetic excuse for whooping it up (3:17-19). They in effect worship their stomach (possibly a euphemism, in such a context, for "penis").[218] They would not consider themselves no longer to be Christians, as Paul says they "*live as* enemies of the cross of Christ" (verse 18). No doubt they were antinomian Gnostics with whom Paul shared the belief that freedom from the tutelage of the elemental angels entitled one to ignore the laws promulgated by them (Gal. 4:8-10). But they inferred from this notion that physical depravity was now morally indifferent if indulged in by the illuminati who transcended conventional standards of "good and evil."

The brief reference in verse 20 to heaven as the true home of Christians (so that where their treasure is, their hearts ought to be also, Matt.6:19-21; Col. 3:1-4) very likely reflects the fact that Caesar Augustus had bestowed full Roman citizenship on all residents of Philippi, elevating them from a mere province to the status of a colony (like Hawaii, not like Puerto Rico). Unlike these profligate antinomians, who are doomed to destruction, all true, heavenly-minded Christians keep their eyes focused on heaven ("Keep watching the skies!"[219]), scanning for the first sign of Christ's appearing (cf., 1 Kings 18:44), which will signal the miraculous transformation of humble human bodies into "glorious" (i.e., shining, radiant, spirit-)

---

[218] Would this qualify them as Priapus cultists? (Look it up.)
[219] The famous last line of the 1951 flying saucer movie, *The Thing from Another World*.

bodies. Remember, Gnostics believed the resurrection had occurred fully in baptism, spiritually, and that there would be no (superfluous) resurrection of the body at the end of time. Well, Paul says in effect, they're right! *They won't* be attending "when the roll is called up yonder"! "They have received their reward in full" (Matt. 6:2, 5, 16). This line of thought, of elevated heavenly-mindedness, continues in 4:8-9, the original conclusion of this letter.

Allow me to double back for a moment to a brief passage (4:2-3) which interrupts the discussion of antinomianism versus the resurrection hope.

> I entreat Euodia and I entreat Syntyche to agree in the Lord. And I ask you also, true yokefellow, help these women, for they have labored side by side with me in the gospel together with Clement and the rest of my fellow workers, whose names are in the book of life.

The names "Euodia" or "Evodia" ("Lucky") and "Syntyche" ("Successful") are widely attested ancient Greek names, as "Clement" ("Peaceful") is a known Roman name. "True yokefellow" may also be intended as the name ("Syzygus") of some individual in the congregation, but that seems unlikely since no other occurrence of such a hypothetical name is known. Much ink has been spilled over whether we should treat all four as proper names, or as allegories,[220] or as somehow both. If we do have here a set of allegorical ciphers, what on earth do they stand for? For what would Paul be appealing? I don't get it. I'd sooner go with the theory that Euodia, Syntyche, and Clement are supposed to be actual individuals, and that Paul is winking at some colleague[221] (perhaps Epaphroditus, the bearer of the letter?), using the epithet "yokefellow" to apply his well-known skills as a mediator. But ultimately, who cares? Not me, that's for sure.

---

[220] Peter Carls, "Identifying Syzygos, Euodia, and Syntyche, Philippians 4:2f" *Journal of Higher Criticism* (8/2) Fall 2001), pp. 161-182.
[221] Carls, "Identifying Syzygos," pp. 163-164.

20

The Epistle to the Colossians
The Amazing Colossal Epistle

Epaphras' Epistle?

Colossae was one of a triad of cities in Asia Minor, along with Laodicea and Hierapolis. We hear that Laodicea received a letter from Paul (Col. 4:16) as well as a note from the Risen Christ (Rev. 3:14-22). Hierapolis may ring a bell, too: Papias was its bishop in the early second century, who collected (dubious) traditions about the apostles and gospel origins.[222]

You don't need to be a Tübingen radical to judge this epistle a pseudepigraph.[223] Most critical scholars deny Pauline authorship, and there are plenty of clues to that effect. You stumble over them at every turn, right out of the box. Although the vocabulary is pretty much standard for Paul's letters, the style is not. The long sentences, the lack of any coherent thread of argument, the piling on of genitives, and various other grammatical peculiarities just don't match Paul, and this sort of thing does not change from letter to letter by a single author.[224]

The epistle says the gospel has already penetrated the *whole world* (1:6), that it "has been preached to *every creature under heaven*" (1:23). What? Already in Paul's day? You mean the Great Commission (Matt. 28:19-20) is already completed? Well, that's nice to know.

The reference to Epaphras as ministering to the Colossians on his behalf, starting the church in an area Paul himself had not visited (1:7), may be a wink to the reader, signaling this man as the actual author using Paul's name. To speculate further, I cannot help thinking of the gospel stories of Jesus healing at a distance: the

---

[222] Ironically, though apologists delight in citing Papias as a witness to the supposed apostolic authorship, hence historical accuracy, of the gospels, what I think Papias, despite himself, actually attests is the gross unreliability of the much-vaunted oral tradition.

[223] Or, if you prefer, a pious fraud or a forgery. See Bart D. Ehrman, *Forgery and Counterforgery: The Use of Literary Deceit in Early Christian Polemics* (New York: Oxford University Press, 2013).

[224] The same issue arose in connection with Ephesians, as is only natural since that letter is clearly based on Colossians.

centurion's son/slave[225] (Matt. 8:5-13; Luke 7:1-10) and the Syro-Phoenician woman's daughter (Mark 7:24-30; Matt. 15:21-28). It's no coincidence that in both cases the one healed and the ones requesting the healings are *Gentiles*. Why? Though Jesus was supposed to have restricted his activities to Palestine, Christians pursuing the Gentile Mission (Acts 11:19-20) needed to appeal to him to legitimate their actions, since others disputed the propriety of preaching to Gentiles (Acts 11:1-3; Matt. 10:5-6). Naturally, there were diverse, independent attempts to authorize the mission. Peter, in a story derived from Ezekiel 1:1, 2:9; 4:14,[226] has Peter being convinced to preach to Gentiles (Cornelius' household) by a vision sent by the Holy Spirit (Acts 10:9-16; 11:5-10). Another approach was to just have Jesus, after his resurrection, command his disciples to undertake the Gentile Mission (Matt 28:19-20; Mark 16:15-16; Luke 24:46-49; John 20:21-23). But the healings at a distance stand about midway between those passages and Acts 10. The ones Jesus heals are at some distance, symbolizing the distance between Jesus' stomping ground and the subsequent mission fields of Europe and Asia Minor, where Paul, Barnabas, and Silas would one day venture. And those healed are the *next generation*, not the centurion but his son/slave, not the Syro-Phoenician but her daughter. Thus there is both a spatial (geographical) and a temporal (historical) distance between the Savior and the eventual Gentile converts. Get it?

Well, I wonder if the character of Epaphras is the same kind of distancing device, this time marking the historical distance from Paul, hinting that we are really reading a Paulinist but post-Pauline document. Our suspicions are only increased when we get to 2:5, "though I am absent in body, yet I am with you in spirit." Obviously, in the implied narrative this phrase simply means that Paul is far away as to the map but with them in his heart, but I can't help thinking it is a wink to the reader, hinting that Paul has departed this mortal coil and now speaks, as if mediumistically, through the pseudepigraphist.[227]

---

[225] Same word in Greek: *pais*.

[226] Randel Helms, *Gospel Fictions* (Buffalo: Prometheus Books, 1989), pp. 20-21.

[227] But doesn't Paul say the same thing in 1 Corinthians 5:3? Indeed "he" does. Don't ask the question if you don't want to hear the answer.

THE EPISTLE TO THE COLOSSIANS

Lyrical Theology

Like Philippians (2:6-11), Colossians quotes a hymn depicting Christ as a heavenly being (1:15ff), which seems anachronistic for Paul.[228] Was there "traditional" Christian hymnody already in Paul's day? Isn't it more likely that his Christians were just singing some of the Old Testament Psalms (Col. 3:16)? In any case, the hymn lyrics are quite fascinating. They speak of the unnamed Savior in terms reflecting Jewish Wisdom theology/mythology: "He is the image of the invisible God" (verse 15). Compare Wisdom of Solomon 7:25-26:

> For she is a breath of the power of God,
> and a pure emanation of the glory of the Almighty;
> therefore nothing defiled gains entrance into her.
> For she is a reflection of eternal light,
> a spotless mirror of the working of God,
> and an image of his goodness.

The same verse declares him to be "the first-born of all creation," again reflecting Divine Wisdom: "Wisdom was created before all things, and prudent understanding from eternity" (Sir. 1:4). "Yahweh created me at the beginning of his work, the first of his acts of old" (Prov. 8:22). It is downright amusing to behold the gymnastics theologians perform to evade the plain sense of the text. Arians (Jehovah's Witnesses) have no trouble with it, as they understand the pre-incarnate Christ, the Logos, as the first and highest creation, but Nicene orthodoxy forces its theological interpreters to offer the preposterous "explanation" that for Christ to be the "first-born of creation" just means he has the authority over the creation that a human first-born son inherits over his father's estate. Just a metaphor; nothing to see here. Move along.

Christadelphians, on the other hand, believe Christ had no personal existence before Bethlehem and thus was not around at the moment of creation. So, although for the opposite reason, they adopt the same desperate *ad hoc* hypothesis. "First-born of creation" *has* to be a metaphor. But it is ruled out by the parallelism with verse 18: "He

---

[228] But wouldn't the same question arise in the case of Philippians 2:6-11? I think so, and in both my *Pre-Nicene New Testament* and *The Amazing Colossal Apostle* I do in fact take the position of F.C. Baur and of the Dutch Radical critics that Philippians is pseudepigraphical. But here I am employing the more commonly held mainstream critical position. Even Bultmann held Philippians to be authentically Pauline.

is... the beginning, the first-born from the dead, that in everything he might be pre-eminent." In both cases, then, Christ has chronological priority *in each category*, the first created and the first resurrected, and therefore onto-theological priority.

All the Treasures of Sophia and Gnosis

"In him all the fullness of God was pleased to dwell" (verse 19) is already unpacked by verses 16-17: "for in him all things were created, in heaven and on earth, visible and invisible, whether thrones or dominions or principalities or authorities—all things were created through him and for him. He is before all things, and in him all things hold together." This is markedly Gnostic conceptuality: Christ has the whole Pleroma, the divine world full of spiritual entities, dwelling within himself (see also 2:19). It is a little bit different from classic Gnosticism, but it is only a variation in nuance. In classic, second-century Gnosticism, the Pleroma is the totality of the Godhead including all the (Neo-Platonist) emanations therefrom, called Aions. The Demiurge, the malevolent creator of the material world, produced a "lowerarchy"[229] parallel to the Aions of the Pleroma. These henchmen of the Demiurge, called Archons ("rulers"), were identified with the fallen Sons of God (Gen. 6:1-4), also known as the Principalities, Powers, and Authorities. The Colossians hymn seems to identify the Archons with the Aions, though still implying some sort of Fall of the Archons since Christ has to subsequently reconcile them to himself. Thus he contains the entire Pleroma.[230]

Colossians 1:20 has Christ reconciling to himself "all things" not only "on earth" but also "in heaven," which must refer to the rehabilitation of the Principalities and Powers. But let us not pass on too quickly. Does not the verse demand that all sinners have been reconciled by the cross, regardless of whether they repent? In short, the doctrine of Universalism. Would a writer put it this way if he believed that many souls would be forever lost, not placed back in the cosmic womb of Wisdom/Christ? That doesn't work out to "all things," does it? Even less so if the writer somehow believed sinners would suffer in hell! Forget it. Sure, other New Testament writers

---

[229] C.S. Lewis coined the term in *The Screwtape Letters*.

[230] Ernst Käsemann, *Essays on New Testament Themes*. Trans. W.J. Montague. Studies in Biblical Theology No. 41 (London: SCM Press, 1964), Chapter VII, "A Primitive Christian Baptismal Liturgy," pp. 149-168.

believed in hell, but not this guy.

Signed, Sealed, and Delivered

The writer refers to himself as "I, Paul"[231] (1:23) in the classic manner of a pseudonymous writer, making a *claim* to be Paul, something it would not occur to the real Paul to do since he would of course take his own identity for granted. Similarly, the reference to Paul's autograph as being on the letter (4:18) is a literary device: the writer only *says* he is signing because he knows the reader cannot see it, because he *hasn't* really signed it. He is writing something he hopes will be taken for a later copy of an original Pauline letter that *did* have a Pauline autograph. "Hey, look, folks! My signature!"[232] Even if you don't buy this, you'd at least have to admit that such "security alerts" ("No virus detected!") attest the fact that plenty of spurious "Pauline" letters were making the rounds when this epistle was written, which makes it a real possibility that the New Testament canon might contain some.

Whereas in 1 Corinthians 1:13 Paul scoffs at the absurdity that anyone might consider that he had been crucified, like Christ, for them, in Colossians 1:24 he is shown making the absolutely astonishing claim that his own sufferings make up what was lacking in the atoning sufferings of Christ! Paul is depicted here through the lens of later saint-worship. Note the parallelism:

> Now I rejoice in my sufferings
> for your sake,
> and in my flesh I complete what is lacking in Christ's afflictions
> for the sake of his body, that is, the church.

---

[231] The same "Look—it's me!" gimmick occurs in 1 Corinthians 16:21; Galatians 5:2; Ephesians 3:1; Colossians 4:18; 1 Thessalonians 2:18; 2 Thessalonians 3:17; Philemon 1:9, 19; 2 Corinthians 10:1 (but, as this last one is the beginning of the Severe Letter, chapters 10-13, "I, Paul" might be an edited version of an originally fuller salutation). The "I, So-and-so" mark of pseudonymity also appears in Revelation 1:9; 22:16; Daniel 7:15, 28; 8:1, 15, 27; 9:2; 10:2, 7; 12:5; Ezra 7:21.

[232] We find the same thing in 1 Corinthians 16:21; Galatians 6:11; 2 Thessalonians 3:17. Some might point to these instances and say, "You see? These other letters have this feature, but they're genuinely Pauline. So why not Colossians?" Uh, that sword cuts both ways. If it is a device to reinforce the convincing pseudonymity in the one case, why not in the rest?

Roman Catholics would later say pretty much the same thing about the tears of the Virgin Mary: they contributed to the atonement along with the crucifixion agonies of her Son. Let's face it: just because the Bible "can't" say such a thing doesn't mean it *doesn't*.

Angelolatry

The bulk of chapter 2 is devoted to a Gnostic-Christian polemic against Christian Torah-legalism. The Jewish Law of the Old Testament is considered the invention and imposition of the demonic Principalities and Powers to enslave and condemn humanity. Christ died on the cross to wrest this weapon out of their hot little hands (2:14-15). The Colossians do not understand that, in such misguided piety, they are really worshipping angels[233] (verse 18), namely the Principalities and Powers[234] who promulgated the Torah commandments: "Do not handle" any unclean thing; "Do not taste" pork or shellfish; "do not touch" a running wound, etc. (verse 21). They are, just as in Galatians 4:8-10, the "elemental spirits" (Col. 2:20) who seek to prolong their unsuspected reign over a gullible and immature humanity. As one of their own has said, "They do not understand either the source or the real character of the prohibitions they are breaking"[235] or keeping!

This is why our author emphasizes a spiritual "circumcision of Christ" which cuts off the whole "body of flesh" (verse 11) and not just a small bit of it, the foreskin. The standard, psychologizing reinterpretation of "the flesh" here, as if it meant some abstract "sinful nature," is merely an attempt to hide the Gnosticism of the text. The "uncircumcision of your flesh" (verse 13) means to equate the flesh

---

[233] Some scholars debate the evidence for any Jewish practice of worshipping angels, but I fear they are missing the point. Colossians 2:18 does not envision people *wittingly* worshipping them. Conventional Torah observance turns out to be Archon-worship.

[234] G.B. Caird, *Principalities and Powers: A Study in Pauline Theology.* Chancellor's Lectures for 1954 at Queen's University, Kingston Ontario (Oxford at the Clarendon Press, 1956); Clinton D. Morrison, *The Powers That Be: Earthly Rulers and Demonic Powers in Romans 13.1-7.* Studies in Biblical Theology No. 29 (Naperville, IL: Alec R. Allenson, 1960); Heinrich Schlier, *Principalities and Powers in the New Testament.* Quaestiones Disputatae 3 (New York: Herder and Herder, 1961); H. Berkhof, *Christ and the Powers.* Trans. John Howard Yoder (Scottdale, PA: Herald Press, 1970).

[235] C.S. Lewis, *The Screwtape Letters & Screwtape Proposes a Toast* (New York: Macmillan, 1970), Part 2, "Screwtape Proposes a Toast," p. 156.

itself with the uncircumcised (i.e., profane pagan) existence. It is no accident that smack dab in the middle of this discussion we find mention of the resurrection of believers (verse 12), because it is understood as a resurrection precisely *from* the body (cf., Romans 7:24, deliverance from "this body of death"[236]). This is the Gnostic doctrine of spiritual resurrection.

The baptized Christian has *already been resurrected* (3:1), a doctrine condemned as heresy in 1 Corinthians 15 and 2 Timothy 2:18. Christians form part of the giant cosmic light-body of the Savior (2:19). The "body of Christ" image elsewhere in Paul (save for Ephesians, the exception that proves the rule, since it is a rewrite of Colossians) refers to local congregations. The use of the term in Colossians and Ephesians gave rise to the Roman Catholic doctrine of the Mystical Body of Christ, but it comes from the Gnostic belief in the cosmic Christ-Aion. Some[237] argue that these terms do not mean in Paul the same things they do in the language of Paul's Gnostic opponents, but that he is repurposing their vocabulary, redefining it in order to "turn their own language against them," whatever that could mean. No, it is the apologist who is redefining them, not the author. And besides, a more confusing tactic cannot be imagined.[238]

The baptism theme continues in 3:9-10, "you have put off the old humanity [*anthropos*] with its practices and have put on the new, which is being renewed in knowledge after the image of its creator." The reference is to the resurrection symbolism of ancient baptism.[239] The individual would strip off his or her clothing, symbolizing the fleshly state, imposed upon the formerly purely spiritual Adam, after the Fall. The initiate would stand naked to denote the innocence of Adam before the Fall (Gen. 2:25). Then, back up out of the water, he or she would don a bright white robe symbolizing the pre-Fall light-body of the Adam Kadmon. The actual restoration of that spirit-body

---

[236] A Gnostic term. See Richard Reitzenstein, *The Hellenistic Mystery-Religions: Their Basic Ideas and Significance*. Trans. John E. Steely. Pittsburgh Theological Monograph Series 15 (Pittsburgh: Pickwick Press, 1978), p. 449.

[237] Ralph P. Martin, *Colossians: The Church's Lord and the Christian's Liberty: An Expository Commentary with a Present-Day Application* (Exeter: Paternoster Press, 1972), p. 29: "Paul seeks to disinfect these heretical watchwords by giving to them a specifically Christian content."

[238] It reminds me of an old pal of mine who was a schizophrenic. You could carry on a long, convoluted discussion with him, trying to refute some assertion of his, only to have him exclaim, "But that's just what I *mean*!" Hoo boy.

[239] Jonathan Z. Smith, *Map Is not Territory: Studies in the History of Religions* (Chicago: University of Chicago Press, 1993), Chapter I, "The Garments of Shame," pp. 11-17.

must await the death of the physical body, but it has, in principle, already taken place. Again, we see that resurrection, for the Gnostic Christian, was *from the flesh*.

The Adam mythology continues in 3:10-11: you "have put on the new [*anthropos*], which is being renewed in knowledge after the image of its creator. Here there cannot be Greek and Jew, circumcised and uncircumcised, barbarian, Scythian, slave, free man, but Christ is all, and in all." Here is the Primordial Adam, the *anthropos*, generic for "human being" just like the Hebrew *adam*.[240] He is the "image of God" (Gen. 1:27), and baptism returns one to that state. That is why all these distinctions between ethnicity, religion, and class are obliterated. In the Adam Kadmon all souls were contained; none were yet divided into warring factions. Baptism into *gnosis* returns us to that, at least in the sense of equality. The final escape from imprisonment in the body will unite all these fragments of the shattered Man of Light.

A passing note on Colossians 2:20-23: when the author lists vain commandments preoccupied with transient matters of the flesh, dictated by "human precepts and doctrines," he admits that "these have indeed an appearance of wisdom in promoting rigor of devotion and self-abasement and severity to the body," but in fact "they are of no value, serving only to indulge the flesh."[241] This is a striking and profound insight reminiscent of the Buddhist "Middle Way." Prince Siddhartha initially exerted himself in terrible austerities, hoping to silence the cravings of the flesh. But at length he realized he was only indulging the flesh in a different way, boasting in a kind of ascetical athletics (like Kafka's "Hunger Artist"). Henceforth he pursued a moderate course, being preoccupied with the flesh neither by wining and dining it nor by trying to starve it out.

No Uppity Slaves

Notoriously, Colossians 3:22-4:1 commands Christian slaves not only to obey their masters but even to do so enthusiastically, not just to avoid a beating. (This section is part of the *Haustafeln* code, as we saw in Ephesians.) Why does not Paul (or whoever) demand freedom for slaves? Well, he may not have felt he dared tell wealthy Christians

---

[240] By contrast, in Hebrew, *ish* refers to a male, just as, in Greek, *aner* means a male.
[241] RSV marginal reading.

what to do, since freeing their slaves would entail economic hardship. He certainly had no pull with non-Christian masters who would not be reading this anyway. Nor had he any business urging Christian slaves to run away to freedom, since they should be taking their lives into their hands if they did so. Once captured, they could be crucified, which wouldn't have done anybody any good. We receive the impression overall that, like the Hellenistic Mystery Cults, Christianity existed as a movement of personal piety within the prevailing social structures.

No, the real problem with Paul's failure to crusade for abolitionism lies elsewhere. I have just suggested that the lack of apostolic opposition to slavery is only what one should expect in the historical context, that to expect Christian abolitionism in this setting would be anachronistic. But the indignation aroused by Colossians 3:22-4:1 arises from the fact that Christian theological rhetoric crows about the "radical demands of discipleship," the discontinuous intervention, like a bolt out of the blue, of the Word of God, revealing "what no eye has seen, nor ear heard, nor the heart of man conceived" (1 Cor. 2:9a). "Has not God made foolish the wisdom of the world?" (1 Cor. 1:20b). In other words, shouldn't the moral imperatives of God ride roughshod over mundane socio-economic circumstances? Sure. And the obvious fact of the Bible's easy tolerance of slavery (among other things) gives the lie to the claim that the Bible is a pure revelation from beyond human ken. Nobody would be squawking about this if the theological over-praise of the Bible hadn't invited it.

21

The First Epistle to the Thessalonians
Can the Dead Fly?

Gospel Greetings

Some think this letter is the earliest of Paul's epistles, while others dismiss it as a pseudepigraph. I will operate here on the former assumption in order to see what sense can be made of the text that way, though I will note the anomalies that led F.C. Baur and others to deny Pauline authenticity. For instance, what are we to make of the lack of the typical Pauline salutation? Usually Paul packs in various anticipations of themes to be discussed in the body of the letter. On the one hand, the terse salutation (characteristic of ancient letters) might attest that 1 Thessalonians is an early product, written before Paul had hit upon the device of making the salutation into a miniature letter in and of itself. On the other, it may denote the clumsiness of a *pasticheur*, rushing to get down to business and simulating only those features of a Pauline epistle that had caught his attention. At any rate, the short salutation "Grace to you and peace" is a theological play on the standard Greek salutation, *chairē*, "rejoice," making it instead *charis*, "grace." "Peace" is the standard Jewish greeting, *shalom* (cf., John 20:19, 21, 26).

Defensive Posture

After praising the Thessalonians, recent converts, Paul goes on to offer a defense, apparently against accusations made against him by some who sought to budge the Thessalonians from their new faith. Had they been taken in by a charlatan? There was no shortage of them in the ancient world. To this, Paul offers a three-pronged apologia. First, he appeals to what Calvin called the "effectual call." Paul knows his readers are among the elect because his preached message "connected" with them when they heard it (1:4-5; 2:13; cf., 1 Cor. 1:22-24).

Second, there is Paul's blameless conduct (1:5b; 2:3-12). His defense is strikingly reminiscent of the words of Dio Chrysostom as he contrasts his own role as a philosopher with that of popular Cynic preachers whom he accuses of ulterior motives, flattery (or, alternatively, scathing abuse of their hearers)[242] and reluctance to engage with the real-life problems for which their hearers sought guidance.

> But to find a man who with purity and without guile speaks with a philosopher's boldness, not for the sake of glory, nor making false pretensions for the sake of gain, but who stands ready out of good will and concern for his fellowman, if need be, to submit to ridicule and the uproar of the mob – to find such a man is not easy, but rather the good fortune of a very lucky city, so great is the dearth of noble, independent souls, and such the abundance of flatterers, charlatans and sophists. In my own case I feel I have chosen that role, not of my own volition, but by the will of some deity.[243]

Third, he commends the Thessalonians for having endured the same sort of persecution from their idol-worshipping countrymen (1:6) that, first, Jesus, then Paul and his colleagues received from Jews back in Judea (2:14-16). As Baur noted, this seems quite odd, given that the only persecution Christians are ever said to have received in Judea was that following the stoning of Stephen, a persecution *spearheaded by Paul himself!*[244] Worse yet, verse 15 condemns Jews *en masse* in the terms of prevalent Greco-Roman anti-Semitism and without guile speaks with a philosopher, making Jews the enemies of the human race.[245] Can Paul, himself a Jew, have written this? Still worse, if possible, is the transparent reference to the fall of Jerusalem to the Romans in 70 C.E.[246] "God's wrath has come upon them at

---

[242] Ingmar Bergman, *The Seventh Seal*. In *Four Screenplays by Ingmar Berman*. Trans. Lars Malmstrom and David Kushner (New York: Simon and Schuster, 1960), p. 124, portrays the chief of a wandering band of Flagellant penitents during the Black Plague excoriating local sinners in such terms: "You there, who stands staring like a goat, will your mouth be twisted into the last unfinished gasp before nightfall? [...] You back there, with your swollen nose and stupid grin, do you have another year left to dirty the earth with your refuse?"

[243] Dio Chrysostom, *Discourses* 32:11-12, quoted in Abraham J. Malherbe, *Paul and the Popular Philosophers* (Minneapolis: Fortress Press, 1989), p. 45.

[244] Ferdinand Christian Baur, *Paul the Apostle of Jesus Christ: His Life and Works, his Epistles and Teachings. A Contribution to a Critical History of Primitive Christianity*, 2 vols. Trans. Eduard Zeller. Theological Translation Fund Library (London: Williams & Norgate, 1873-1875; rpt. Peabody: Hendrickson Publishers, 2003), vol. II, p. 87.

[245] Baur, *Paul the Apostle of Jesus Christ*, p. 87.

[246] Baur, *Paul the Apostle of Jesus Christ*, p. 88.

last!"[247] Let's see... wasn't Paul supposed to have been decapitated in 63?

But how does their endurance of persecution count as a defense of Paul and his mission? I think he is appealing to their *cognitive dissonance*. They would naturally be having second thoughts: "Is it really worth *this*? Maybe I'll switch back to Serapis. How about you, Biggus?" To clamp the lid on such stinkin' thinkin', Paul lionizes the Christians of Thessalonica. He hopes the esteem he showers upon them will compensate for the scorn they are receiving for having embraced this wacky new cult of Jesus.

Plus, Paul reminds them that they will get the last laugh when the Lord arrives to kick the heathen butts of those who torment them. This is the sort of "chop-licking attitude"[248] that made Nietzsche despise the phony forgiveness Christians claim to dispense so benevolently.[249] And it represents a sub-type of "future this- worldly theodicy." Peter Berger describes it this way: "When the proper time comes (typically, as a result of some divine intervention), the sufferers will be consoled and the unjust will be punished."[250] Why is God allowing these troubles? Who knows? But if it's going to stop soon, who cares?

Paul admits he had been a bit worried about their buckling under persecution even though he had tried to prepare them for it (2:17-3:13; cf., Mark 4:14-17). But Timothy visited them and returned to Paul with good news as to their steadfastness, and that's all Paul needed to hear. Old Scratch didn't get the better of them after all. Note Paul's depiction of Satan: he somehow thwarted Paul's plans to return to Thessalonica to strengthen the church (2:18) and was

---

[247] Many scholars would bracket these verses as a later interpolation. Winsome Munroe, *Authority in Paul and Peter: The Identification of a Pastoral Stratum in the Pauline Corpus and 1 Peter*. Society for New Testament Studies Monograph Series 45 (Cambridge at the University Press, 1983), p. 93, regards 2:15-16 as part of a wider "Pastoral Stratum" laid over the letter; see also William O. Walker, Jr., *Interpolations in the Pauline Letters*. Journal for the Study of the New Testament Supplement Series 213 (London: Sheffield Academic Press, 2001), pp. 210-220. But I am skeptical that such a surgical excision is sufficient to save the patient.

[248] John Beversluis, *C.S. Lewis and the Search for Rational Religion* (Grand Rapids: Eerdmans, 1985), p. 24.

[249] Max Scheler, *Resentiment*. Trans. Lewis B. Coser and William W. Holdheim (Milwaukee: Marquette University Press, 1994), Chapter III, "Christian Morality and Resentiment," pp. 74-75; Gerd Theissen, *Sociology of Early Palestinian Christianity*. Trans. John Bowden (Philadelphia: Fortress Press, 1978), pp. 100-101.

[250] Peter L. Berger, *The Sacred Canopy: Elements of a Sociological Theory of Religion* (Garden City: Doubleday Anchor Books, 1969), p. 68.

meanwhile working through persecution to tempt them to apostasy. Better luck next time, Satan!

You Better not Pout, You Better not Cry

Paul next deals with issues arising from the expectation (theirs and his) of the soon coming of Jesus. First, Thessalonian Christians must be prepared for the End Times denouement (cf., Matt. 3:2, 7-10). Only the holy[251] will be saved at the arrival of Christ (3:12-13; 4:3-6, "the Lord is an avenger," i.e., at the Second Coming; 5:2-9, 23-24). Holiness is what God requires, but he also makes it possible, so don't be *too* scared.

Paul warns against idleness (4:11-12; 5:14), a problem the Thessalonians need to deal with before the Parousia (Second Coming). No Christian slackers! Why was this a problem? It might have been a matter of individuals being so heavenly minded that they were no earthly good, blithely assuming that more industrious brethren would take up the slack while they took care of the praying. That is entirely plausible, but there are a couple of other possibilities.

First, and this would fit admirably into the discussion of the near Parousia, some might have figured there was simply no point in continuing their mundane jobs since there would be no earthly future to provide for. Albert Schweitzer[252] argued that Jesus' commands to give away possessions and wealth to the poor were by no means short-sighted and fanatical, because they were predicated on precisely this premise. It was an "interim ethic": on the very verge of the End, secular work must be dropped, as Peter, Andrew, James, and John did (Mark 1:16-20). Money must be used for the only thing it remains good for, feeding the starving poor in the scant weeks remaining. After that, the redeemed will sit down to the Messianic Banquet, with new wine, manna, and steaks carved from Behemoth and Leviathan. (Of course, it didn't quite work out that way!)

Nor is this entirely a speculative theory. At least we do know of modern apocalyptic movements who pursued exactly this logic. These are the Cargo Cults of Melanesia, including the Tuka Movement of Fiji, starting in 1882, whose prophet Navosavakandua

---

[251] Thomas Cook, *New Testament Holiness* (Fort Washington, PA: Christian Literature Crusade, n.d.).

[252] Albert Schweitzer, *The Mystery of the Kingdom of God: The Secret of Jesus' Messiahship and Passion.* Trans. Walter Lowrie (New York: Schocken Books, 1964), pp. 94-97.

exhorted the people to abandon all they owned to ready themselves for the imminent coming of the divine Twins Nathirikuamoli and Nakausambaria, who should usher in the millennium.[253] In 1893, one Tokeriu founded the Milne Bay Prophet Movement. He announced the coming of a massive tidal wave. Only his believers would survive to enjoy supernatural prosperity. But before the cataclysm, they must consume all their pigs and their garden produce.[254] Followers of the prophet Mambu in the Madang District of New Guinea, around 1938, were told to consume all their stores of food to prepare for the arrival of the millennium.[255] A Cargo Cult on the island of Buka in the Solomons, led by a prophet named Paki, prophesied a deadly tidal wave prefacing the arrival of the magical Cargo ship bearing goods and food for believers. To be ready, they had to abjure all work, shutting down the island's pottery trade.[256] This was in 1932. A couple of years later, another prophet, Sanop, warned that "those owning large gardens or many pigs should give their food away in feasts if they wished to qualify for a share in the Cargo."[257] In 1939, a movement in Biak heralded the coming of the mythical hero Mansren ("the Lord") to bring the goodies. "Gardens were harvested and pigs slaughtered; if this were not done, the *koreri* [the "regeneration," as in Matthew 19:28] would never come, manna would not fall, and the people would be condemned to a life of toil in the gardens."[258] I very much doubt Albert Schweitzer knew about any of this, but he had exactly pegged the logic of the interim ethic: unless you proved your faith in the good news of the coming kingdom by burning all your bridges behind you, you would not enter it. And this may well have been the thinking of the sanctified slackers of Thessalonica.

A second possibility is that the idlers in question were charismatic itinerants like the superapostles of 2 Corinthians who, like today's TV evangelists, cultivated the donations of their audiences.[259] We know this became something of a problem in the early church because the late-first, early-second-century church manual called the *Didache* ("The Teaching of the Twelve Apostles to the Nations") warns about these gospel vagabonds.

---

[253] Peter Worsley, *The Trumpet Shall Sound: A Study of "Cargo" Cults in Melanesia* (New York: Schocken Books, 1968), pp. 23.

[254] Worsley, *Trumpet*, pp. 52-53.

[255] Worsley, *Trumpet*, p. 107.

[256] Worsley, *Trumpet*, p. 115.

[257] Worsley, *Trumpet*, p. 117.

[258] Worsley, *Trumpet*, p. 139.

[259] Munro, *Authority in Paul and Peter*, pp. 82-83.

No prophet who orders a meal under the spirit's influence shall eat of it; if he does, he is a false prophet [...] But whoever says in the spirit, "Give me money," or something else, you shall not listen to him. [...] If the one who comes is a traveler, help him all you can. But he must not stay with you more than two or if necessary three days. If he wants to settle among you and has a trade, let him work for his living. But if he has no trade, see to it in your understanding that no one lives among you in idleness because he is a Christian. If he will not do this, he is trading on Christ. Beware of such men. (11:9-12:5)[260]

Episcopalian Resurrection

There was some worry among the Thessalonians about "the dead in Christ." It seems Paul had left them with the impression that the Parousia would arrive so quickly that he simply had assumed all would live to see it and didn't bother to mention the doctrine of the resurrection of the righteous dead. He also must have assumed that, as all their dead loved ones had been pagan idolaters, they would not be joining the party. So why tell them about the coming resurrection? The problem is that, in Paul's absence, some of the Thessalonian Christians had died, and their loved ones feared they were lost for good. (Perhaps this was the intention of Mark 13:13b, "He who endures to the end will be saved.") Paul now comforts them (4:13-18) with the assurance that, not only will the recently deceased Christians not find themselves at a disadvantage, but they will actually be *ahead* of the game; they will rise first!

The business about Jesus "coming with his saints" (3:13) refers to the resurrection of these very same saints. These "saints" are not an angel host as in Revelation 19:14, much less the return of a previously harvested group of saints caught up in a Secret Rapture (an innovation introduced by John Nelson Darby in the nineteenth century),[261] but rather the recently dead Christians who rise to meet the returning Christ at his arrival (cf., Matt. 25:6; Acts 28:15). Thus 1

---

[260] Edgar J. Goodspeed, trans., *The Apostolic Fathers: An American Translation* (New York: Harper& Brothers, 1950), pp. 16-17.
[261] Ernest R. Sandeen, *The Roots of Fundamentalism: British and American Millenarianism, 1800-1930.* Twin Brooks Series (Grand Rapids: Eerdmans, 1978), pp. 62-63.

Thessalonians 3:13 would seem to be interpreted by 4:14, then 16.

The details of the Parousia (4:16) are reminiscent of those in 1 Corinthians 15:51-52.[262] Remember that 1 Corinthians 15 speaks of a pneumatic ("spiritual") body without flesh and blood and does not seem to anticipate a resurrected life here on earth. Likewise, 1 Thessalonians 4:17 ("then we who are alive, who are left, shall be caught up together with them in the clouds to meet the Lord in the air; and so [i.e., in this manner] we shall always be with the Lord.") must mean that the risen dead and the raptured living will forever dwell with Christ "in the air," not on earth. This looks like the same notion found in John 14:3, as opposed to that in Revelation 20-22 and Matthew 19:28-29, which picture the resurrected dwelling on the earth.

In both 1 Corinthians 15:51 and 1 Thessalonians 4:15 Paul whispers to the readers that he is sharing a mystery with them. Here he says he is appealing to "the word of the Lord." Does he mean he is giving the gist of a saying of Jesus of Nazareth? Probably not. More likely he means the Old Testament. Compare 1 Thessalonians with the Isaiah Apocalypse (Isa. 26-27).

In that day this song will be sung in the land of Judah:
"We have a strong city;
   he sets up salvation
   as walls and bulwarks.
Open the gates,
   that the righteous nation which keeps faith
   may enter in.
Thou dost keep him in perfect peace,
   whose mind is stayed on thee,
   because he trusts in thee.
Trust in [Yahweh] for ever,
   for the Lord [Yahweh]
   is an everlasting rock.
For he has brought low
   the inhabitants of the height,
   the lofty city.
He lays it low, lays it low to the ground,

---

[262] Nor is this the only close parallel to the Corinthian letters; the parallels are so striking as to have led Baur to deem 1 Thessalonians as a whole a pseudepigraph based largely on the Corinthian letters. Baur, *Paul the Apostle of Jesus Christ*, vol. II, p. 86.

casts it to the dust.
The foot tramples it,
   the feet of the poor,
   the steps of the needy."
 The way of the righteous is level;
   thou dost make smooth the path of the righteous.
In the path of thy judgments,
   O [Yahweh], we wait for thee;
thy memorial name
   is the desire of our soul.
My soul yearns for thee in the night,
   my spirit within me earnestly seeks thee.
For when thy judgments are in the earth,
   the inhabitants of the world learn righteousness.
 If favor is shown to the wicked,
   he does not learn righteousness;
in the land of uprightness he deals perversely
   and does not see the majesty of [Yahweh].
O [Yahweh], thy hand is lifted up,
   but they see it not.
Let them see thy zeal for thy people, and be ashamed.
   Let the fire for thy adversaries consume them.
O [Yahweh], thou wilt ordain peace for us,
   thou hast wrought for us all our works.
O [Yahweh] our God,
   other lords besides thee have ruled over us,
   but thy name alone we acknowledge.
They are dead, they will not live;
   they are shades, they will not arise;
to that end thou hast visited them with destruction
   and wiped out all remembrance of them.
But thou hast increased the nation, O [Yahweh],
   thou hast increased the nation; thou art glorified;
   thou hast enlarged all the borders of the land.
O [Yahweh], in distress they sought thee,
   they poured out a prayer
   when thy chastening was upon them.
Like a woman with child,
   who writhes and cries out in her pangs,
   when she is near her time,
so were we because of thee, O [Yahweh];
   we were with child, we writhed,

we have as it were brought forth wind.
We have wrought no deliverance in the earth,
    and the inhabitants of the world have not fallen.
Thy dead shall live, their bodies shall rise.
    O dwellers in the dust, awake and sing for joy!
For thy dew is a dew of light,
    and on the land of the shades thou wilt let it fall.
Come, my people, enter your chambers,
    and shut your doors behind you;
hide yourselves for a little while
    until the wrath is past.
For behold, *the LORD is coming forth out of his place*
    to punish the inhabitants of the earth for their iniquity,
and the earth will disclose the blood shed upon her,
    and will no more cover her slain.
In that day [Yahweh] with his hard and great and strong
sword will punish Leviathan the fleeing serpent, Leviathan the
twisting serpent, and he will slay the dragon that is in the sea.

In that day:
"A pleasant vineyard, sing of it!
    I, [Yahweh], am its keeper;
    every moment I water it.
Lest any one harm it,
    I guard it night and day;
    I have no wrath.
Would that I had thorns and briers to battle!
    I would set out against them,
    I would burn them up together.
Or let them lay hold of my protection,
    let them make peace with me,
    let them make peace with me."
In days to come Jacob shall take root,
    Israel shall blossom and put forth shoots,
    and fill the whole world with fruit.
Has he smitten them as he smote those who smote them?
    Or have they been slain as their slayers were slain?
Measure by measure, by exile thou didst contend with them;
    he removed them with his fierce blast in the day of the east
wind.
Therefore by this the guilt of Jacob will be expiated,

and this will be the full fruit of the removal of his sin:
when he makes all the stones of the altars
   like chalkstones crushed to pieces,
   no Asherim or incense altars will remain standing.
For the fortified city is solitary,
   a habitation deserted and forsaken, like the wilderness;
there the calf grazes,
   there he lies down, and strips its branches.
When its boughs are dry, they are broken;
   women come and make a fire of them.
For this is a people without discernment;
   therefore he who made them will not have compassion on them,
   he that formed them will show them no favor.

In that day from the river Euphrates to the Brook of Egypt [Yahweh] will thresh out the grain, and *you will be gathered* one by one, O people of Israel. *And in that day a great trumpet will be blown*, and those who were lost in the land of Assyria and those who were driven out to the land of Egypt will come and worship [Yahweh] on the holy mountain at Jerusalem.[263]

Several such Old Testament passages reappear in the New, cited from the Greek Septuagint, where the Hebrew Yahweh has become the Greek *Kyrios*, "Lord." It was an easy transition from the Lord Jehovah to the Lord Jesus, and the old prophecies were reapplied.

One more thing: Paul does not seem to envision the possibility of a heavenly afterlife following immediately upon death while the righteous await resurrection. If he had, wouldn't he have comforted the mourning Thessalonians with *this* knowledge? Instead, he says, "Oh, don't worry! Uncle Mel isn't dead as a doornail. You'll be seeing him soon at the Parousia!" Remember, for the "dead in Christ" to return with the Lord refers to their resurrection, since Paul explicitly compares it with Jesus' own resurrection: "Since we believe that Jesus died and rose again, *even so*, through Jesus, God will bring with him those who have fallen asleep" (1 Thess. 4:14). And, after all, he does call the dead "those who have fallen asleep"—*not conscious*, if

---

[263] T. Francis Glasson, *The Second Advent: The Origin of the New Testament Doctrine* (London: Epworth Press, 1947), pp. 168-170.

the metaphor means anything at all.

Parting, Prayer, and Prophecy

In 1 Thessalonians 5:16-18 Paul says it is God's will that we pray, rejoice, and thank God constantly, i.e., that we do not lose sight of God in distressing circumstances (the lesson of the homiletic midrash in Matthew 14:28-31). Paul cannot mean by "pray without ceasing" what Russian "Jesus Prayer" piety takes it to mean, the uninterrupted, autonomic "background noise" of a kind of resonating mantra.[264]

Prophecy is the subject in 5:19-22: "Do not quench the Spirit, do not despise prophesying, but test everything; hold fast what is good, abstain from every form of evil." This forms one single sentence in Greek. To reject congregational prophesying *period* would be to put out the fire of the Spirit, so permit people to stand up and prophesy, but evaluate their utterances. Weigh them and take heed when they sound legitimate. If they don't, disregard them.

Churches sometimes teach their members to walk on eggshells, tiptoeing around and restricting their freedom in order to avoid doing anything that *somebody* *might* look askance at. That means having to adopt the hyper-scrupulosity of the neurotic "weaker brethren." First Corinthians 10:28-33 actually advises that, but 1 Thessalonians 5:22 does not. It means not "avoid all appearance of evil" (i.e., anything that anyone else would think untoward even if unreasonably), but "Don't take any wooden nickels." In fact, in one of the Agrapha (sayings ascribed to Jesus in various ancient Christian writings), Jesus says, "Be wise money-changers."[265] Ignore what seem to be false prophecies, but profit from the genuine.

How to judge prophetic utterances? In 1 Corinthians 12:3 (cf., 1 Cor. 12:10; 14:29 and 1 John 4:1-3), Christological doctrine is the litmus test: prophetic oracles affirming docetism or that Jesus was merely the channeler for the Christ spirit must be bogus. Here we see the beginning of an inevitable process whereby charismatic revelation

---

[264] *The Way of a Pilgrim, and, The Pilgrim Continues his Way.* Trans. R.M. French (New York: Seabury Press, 1970).

[265] Montague Rhodes James, ed. and trans., *The Apocryphal New Testament: Being the Apocryphal Gospels, Acts, Epistles, and Apocalypses* (Oxford at the Clarendon Press, 1953), p. 35; Joachim Jeremias, *Unknown Sayings of Jesus.* Trans. Reginald H. Fuller (New York: Macmillan, 1957), pp. 89-93.

gets suppressed in favor of institutional dogma.[266] If you heed prophecy indiscriminately, you get blown about by every wind of doctrine. Nobody wants that, and this passage implies that the Thessalonians had already had their fill of it. But 1 Thessalonians urges them not to throw the baby out with the baptismal water. (I hate to say it, but such a scenario implies a later date, a later stage of institutional evolution, than seems reasonable for the infant Thessalonian congregation.)

We find yet another reason to doubt Pauline authorship in 5:17: "I adjure you by the Lord that this letter be read to all the brethren." Why should Paul have added this? Isn't the letter explicitly addressed to the whole congregation (1:1)?

> But how could the apostle himself have found it necessary formally to adjure the Church to which his Epistles were addressed, not to leave them unread? That could be done only by an author who was not writing in the living pressure of the circumstances of which he treated, but transporting himself while writing into an imagined situation, and who wished to vindicate for his own pretended apostolic Epistles the consideration with which the original apostolic Epistles had become invested by the growth of custom.[267]

---

[266] Hans von Campenhausen, *Ecclesiastical Authority and Spiritual Freedom in the Church of the First Three Centuries*. Trans. J.A. Baker (Stanford: Stanford University Press, 1969), Chapter IV, "Spirit and Authority in the Pauline Congregation," pp. 55-75.
[267] Baur, *Paul the Apostle of Jesus Christ*, vol. II, p. 96.

22

The Second Epistle to the Thessalonians
The Son of Perdition

Deja Vue All Over Again

This letter reads largely like a rehash of 1 Thessalonians, with one crucial difference. Most critical scholars consider it pseudepigraphical, and with good reason. It sounds like a new and corrected version of 1 Thessalonians, aiming to replace the earlier letter. We start out the same way, 1:4 repeating the business about the Thessalonians' faith being reported throughout the churches, just as in 1 Thessalonians 1:7-8. The next verse repeats that suffering is proof that God has chosen them, recalling both the emphasis on persecution as the Christian's lot and the reassurance that God has chosen them, as we read in 1 Thessalonians chapter 3. Likewise, chapter 3, verses 6-15, deals again with the problem of Christian idlers, already discussed in 1 Thessalonians 5:14.

Again we hear that the Thessalonians, hard pressed by their enemies now, will have the last laugh at the Parousia. It is worth noting, however, that 1:5-12 absolutely precludes the notion, widespread today among fundamentalists, that Paul taught Christians will be secretly raptured before the End Time tribulation, biding their time as bodiless spirits in heaven, awaiting the Final Judgment seven years later. Why? Simply because "Paul" affirms that he and his readers will be delivered from the very persecution they are *now* enduring when Christ returns with his angels and the fires of judgment. This means Paul's own contemporaries were undergoing the Great Tribulation.

One other note: the mention of "eternal destruction" in verse 9 is the closest thing to a reference to Hell we find in any epistle ascribed to Paul, whether genuine or spurious, and it is not very close. The phrase would most naturally imply that the wicked will be "destroyed forever," not tormented forever.

Not So Fast!

The main point of the letter is to throw a wet blanket over

eschatological (End Times) fervor ("The day of the Lord is at hand!") ignited by some prophecy, some rumor, or some spurious epistle with Paul's name on it. Did the writer not know the exact origin of the fanatical enthusiasm? That is what we are supposed to think, but the real intent is to cover all theoretical possibilities and so to prevent future flare-ups. He is not really addressing the Thessalonian church of Paul's day. But he does mean to forestall further damage done by people in his own (later) day reading 1 Thessalonians with its incitements to Rapture fanaticism.

And he is concerned to get Paul out of a jam. Just as Luke[268] and Matthew[269] both found themselves chagrinned by Mark's sayings about the Parousia coming in the generation of Jesus' contemporaries and hoped to replace Mark's with their own versions,[270] so did the author of 2 Thessalonians seek to replace 1 Thessalonians, toning down the Millerite fanaticism and making it look like Paul had already tried to nip such lunacy in the bud. For now we read that Paul had "actually" given a more moderate version of eschatological teaching: Oh yes, Christ will return, but all in good time! It cannot happen before a checklist of important events transpire. (Even within our text of Mark the same thing had happened, with corrections and mitigations of earlier predictions such as Mark 9:1. Chapter 13 gives a similar list of items that prove that "the end is not yet.") Second Thessalonians 2:1-12 can scarcely have been written by the same man who wrote 1 Thessalonians 5:1-3.

> But as to the times and the seasons, brethren, you have no need to have anything written to you. For you yourselves know well that the day of the Lord will come like a thief in the night. When people will say, 'There is peace and security,' then sudden destruction will come upon them as travail comes upon a woman with child, and there will be no escape.

The great irony is that, though 2 Thessalonians wants us to write off 1 Thessalonians as a misleading forgery (which indeed it may well be!), 2

---

[268] Hans Conzelmann, *The Theology of St. Luke.* Trans. Geoffrey Buswell (New York: Harper & Row, 1961), pp. 95-97, etc.

[269] Joachim Jeremias, *The Parables of Jesus.* Trans. S.H. Hooke (New York: Scribners, 1972), pp. 51, 56. Jeremias argues that, as Jesus originally gave these parables, there was no hint of a "delay of the Parousia" motif, but that Christians reinterpreted them in order to cope with the delay.

[270] Compare Mark 9:1 with Luke 9:27, see also Luke 17:20-21; 19:11-27; Acts 1:6-7; Matt. 24:48; 25:5.

Thessalonians thus reveals *itself* as a polemical forgery! Second Thessalonians 2:5-6 says that Paul is only reminding the Thessalonians of things he had taught them earlier. I think the writer is really thinking of the materials he has reproduced from 1 Thessalonians, as I have already mentioned.

The Man of the Lie

Paul often speaks of the Parousia, but seldom of any accompanying details. But 2 Thessalonians 2:3-12 does. It gets interesting fast, once the author mentions the Antichrist, though he doesn't actually call him that, referring instead to "the man of sin" (or "of lawlessness," depending on which manuscripts you read) and "the son of perdition" (2:3). ("Man of sin" is also a proper name for this villain, "Belial,"[271] used in 2 Corinthians 6:15 and in the Dead Sea Scrolls). Baur dismisses all these trappings as incompatible with real Paulinism.

> It is therefore scarcely probable that an author who expresses his views of the last things with such caution and reserve as in 1 Cor. xv., should, in a writing of earlier date, have entered into the question so fully and given evidence of a belief entirely preoccupied with Rabbinical opinions.[272]

But whoever wrote this, it is pretty clear that these ideas stem from the Book of Daniel. Compare 2 Thessalonians 2:4, speaking of him "who opposes and exalts himself against every so-called god or object of worship, so that he takes his seat in the temple of God, proclaiming himself to be God," with Daniel 11:31b, 36-39.

---

[271] Wilhelm Bousset, *The Antichrist Legend: A Chapter in Christian and Jewish Folklore.* Trans. A.H. Keane (London: Hutchinson, 1896), pp. 152-156.

[272] Ferdinand Christian Baur, *Paul the Apostle of Jesus Christ: His Life and Works, his Epistles and Teachings. A Contribution to a Critical History of Primitive Christianity,* 2 vols. Trans. Eduard Zeller. Theological Translation Fund Library (London: Williams & Norgate, 1873-1875; rpt. Peabody: Hendrickson Publishers, 2003), vol. II, p. 91. Baur could not know of the Dead Sea Scrolls, unearthed in 1947, which attest such notions earlier than Baur supposed, but that does not affect his argument; one could simply substitute "Essene" or "Qumran" for "Rabbinical." But is not 2 Corinthians 6:14-7:1 redolent of Qumran? Yes, and this is one of the reasons many critical scholars regard the passage as a non-Pauline interpolation. See William O. Walker, Jr., *Interpolations in the Pauline Letters.* Journal for the Study of the New Testament Supplement Series 213 (London: Sheffield Academic Press, 2001), pp. 199-209.

> And they shall set up the abomination that makes desolate. [...] And the king shall do according to his will; he shall exalt himself and magnify himself above every god, and shall speak astonishing things against the God of gods. He shall prosper till the indignation is accomplished; for what is determined shall be done. He shall give no heed to the gods of his fathers, or to the one beloved by women;[273] he shall not give heed to any other god, for he shall magnify himself above all. He shall honor the god of fortresses instead of these; a god whom his fathers did not know he shall honor with gold and silver, with precious stones and costly gifts. He shall deal with the strongest fortresses by the help of a foreign god; those who acknowledge him he shall magnify with honor. He shall make them rulers over many and shall divide the land for a price.

What is "the rebellion" (2 Thess. 2:3)? "Apostasy" might be a better translation, or "falling away." This is a standard piece of apocalyptic mythology spelled out in Mark 13:12 ("And brother will deliver up brother to death, and the father his child, and children will rise against parents and have them put to death") and Matthew 24:10-12 ("And then many will fall away, and betray one another, and hate one another. And many false prophets will arise and lead many astray. And because wickedness is multiplied, most men's love will grow cold"). It is part of the Antichrist myth in many ancient sources[274] and fits into that framework here, too. Ditto for the "lying wonders" performed by the Antichrist (1 Thess. 2:9).[275] We find the same thing in Revelation 13:13-15.

How about "the Restrainer" (verse 6) who or which presently functions as a dam to prevent the apocalyptic deluge? Several theories exist. Many early Christian writers believed the reference was to the Roman Empire which, for all its faults, did preserve a measure of order.[276] Whereas Revelation equates Rome with the Antichrist,

---

[273] Probably Tammuz, as in Ezekiel 8:14. Paul Louis Couchoud, *The Book of Revelation: A Key to Christian Origins*. Trans. C. Bradlaugh Bonner (London: Watts, 1932), thought that the number of the Beast in Revelation 13:17-18 signified the similar dying-and-rising deity Attis (pp. 139-140).

[274] Bousset, *Antichrist Legend*, pp. 121-122.

[275] Bousset, *Antichrist Legend*, pp. 175-182.

[276] "Yes, they certainly know how to keep order... let's face it, they're the only ones who *could* in a place like this." Graham Chapman, John Cleese, Terry Gilliam, Eric Idle, Terry Jones, and Michael Palin, *Monty Python's The Life of Brian (of Nazareth)* (New York: Ace Books, 1979), p. 49.

Tertullian and others viewed it as the last bulwark against him. And, come to think of it, Revelation chapter 17 does have the resurrected Beast destroy Rome, so you can see where Tertullian, et. al., got the idea.

Some modern interpreters think the Restrainer to be the Holy Spirit, while Oscar Cullmann[277] agrees with various ancient writers who believed the Restrainer was Paul himself preaching the gospel to all nations before the End could come (cf., Mark 13:10; Rev. 14:6). Still others think the Restrainer is code (common in apocalyptic texts and the Dead Sea Scrolls) for some particular individual whose identity our author expected the readers to be able to figure out (cf., Mark 13:14; Rev. 13:18).

Trying Too Hard

But there is another clue to another puzzle here, perhaps a puzzle our author did not intend anyone to solve, and that is the question of authorship and authenticity. ""I, Paul, write this greeting with my own hand. This is the mark in every letter of mine; it is the way I write" (3:17). There are two marks of *inauthenticity* in this single verse. As I have noted in previous chapters, "I, Paul" seems to be a typical case of "protesting too much," found in pseudepigraphical works, defensively making a claim of Pauline authorship, something Paul himself would hardly think of doing. He knew he was Paul, and so did his readers. This, however, is a dead giveaway that the unknown author is trying to pass himself off as Paul. Likewise with the business about his distinctive signature. You would point this out only if the reader could *not* see it for himself. Such a statement is meant to convey what it conveys to readers still today: "Oh! The original must have borne an actual Pauline autograph!" And this is something the real Paul would not bother to say. An actual signature would speak for itself. This means 2 Thessalonians was *originally* written *as if* a subsequent copy of a Pauline epistle. But it is a "copy" without an original.

---

[277] Oscar Cullmann, *Christ and Time: The Primitive Christian Conception of Time and History.* Trans. Floyd V. Filson (Philadelphia: Westminster Press, 1960), pp. 164-166.

23

The Letter to Philemon
Make Yourself Useful!

Philemonade

For an ancient letter, even this is pretty long. Most of them could fit on a Post-it. Many commentators would have us believe that this letter's length is inversely proportional to its importance because it contains the first glimmer of Christian realization that perhaps slave-holding and the gospel are incompatible. But that may be no more than spin, as we will soon see.

Philemon presents itself as a personal letter from the Apostle Paul to one particular family, not a substantial treatise like the others. The back-story is not hard to reconstruct. Paul writes from prison, where he has been enjoying the company of a runaway slave named Onesimus. The young man knew Paul from the apostle's visits to the family Onesimus worked for, that of the Colossian businessman Philemon,[278] his wife (?) Apphia, and their son (?) Archippus ("Horse trainer"). They lived in a house large enough to accommodate weekly church meetings, and this fact raises a difficult question: was this the church at Colossae to which that epistle was addressed? Colossians 4:17 lists an Archippus as a member of the church there. But Colossians 2:1 is unequivocal that the Colossian congregation had never seen Paul in person. You have to wonder, in that case, if someone writing in Paul's name and somewhat familiar with Colossians intended to pass off Philemon as a postscript to the Epistle to the Colossians.[279] I will return to this possibility in due time.

Whether historical or fictional, the premise of this letter is that Onesimus had absconded with some of the household cash (verse 19). Once on the road, he began to ask himself, like the Prodigal Son (Luke 15:17), what course might be open to him. If he should be

---

[278] It is not absolutely certain that Paul had spent time with this family, since he speaks of having *heard of* Philemon's good works *from others* verses 5, 7 (cf., Col. 1:4). But verse 19 seems to imply Paul's personal acquaintance at least with Philemon, since he seems to be claiming credit for Philemon's conversion to Christianity. Also, his request (even if an idle word of optimism) that Philemon get a guest room ready for him seems to imply this would be *another* visit with close friends.

[279] He must not have read Colossians very closely, since Colossians 4:9 already knows an Onesimus as an integral member of the Colossian congregation, which would have to make Colossians later than Philemon.

nabbed by the authorities, Onesimus could find himself warming up a wooden cross. The only friendly face he figured he could count on was Paul, and he knew where to find him. Paul was happy to see him, especially as the youth was eager to see to Paul's needs, get him supplies, and run to the post office for him. But Paul was already in enough trouble, and he didn't want to be charged with harboring a runaway slave. Somewhere along the line he persuaded Onesimus (verse 10) to accept the gospel (he had for whatever reason not found it very attractive back home among the pious household of Philemon). And then he convinced Onesimus to return to Philemon and face the music. After all, the kid had not only run away, he had robbed his master to boot. He was potentially taking his life into his hands by retracing his hasty steps. No Frederick Douglass, he swallowed hard and went back to Ol' Massa, tail between legs, carrying this letter from Paul and hoping it would work. If the bishop of Ephesus, a man named Onesimus (commended in the Ignatian Epistle to the Ephesians), was the same as the Onesimus on whose behalf the Letter to Philemon was written, it must have been a resounding success.

The most impressive thing about the Letter to Philemon is, in my opinion, the clever undertone of humorous innuendo. Paul didn't just seek Philemon's forgiveness for Onesimus; he wanted him to free the slave and send him back to Paul so he could continue to serve as the apostle's personal attendant (verse 13). And he is pretty coy about it, employing a string of puns on the name "Onesimus" (which means "useful" or "beneficial"). "Formerly he was *useless* to you, but now he is indeed *useful* to you and to me" (verse 11). "Yes, brother, I want some [*ahem*] *benefit* from you in the Lord" (verse 20). "Nudge, nudge, wink, wink, say no more!" And talk about manipulation! Paul knows Onesimus is in no position to compensate Philemon for the amount he stole (and has since used up for travel, shelter, and food), much less for his own market value as a slave, so Paul volunteers to cover it. "Put it on my tab!" Of course, Paul and Philemon know perfectly well that Philemon is just going to have to swallow the loss. And how can he turn the old apostle down? Paul "gently" reminds him of the debt *he* owes *Paul*: his very soul! Heck, let's call it even.

Now what about that nasty little matter of pseudonymity? Well, there's the tell-tale self-reference: "I, Paul, write this with my own hand" (verse 19), usually a clue that a pseudonymous writer is protesting too much. But there is another reason to suspect Paul did not write the Letter to Philemon, noted long ago by Rudolf Steck and the Dutch Radical critic W.C. van Manen.[280] Philemon bears a striking resemblance to Pliny the Younger's letter to Sabianus (easily available, since Pliny himself collected and published his correspondence):

> The freedman of yours with whom you said you were angry has been to me, flung himself at my feet, and clung to me as if I were you. He begged my help with many tears, though he left a good deal unsaid; in short, he convinced me of his genuine penitence. I believe he has reformed, because he realizes he did wrong. You are angry, I know, and I know too that your anger was deserved, but mercy wins most praise when there was just cause for anger. You loved the man once, and I hope you will love him again, but it is sufficient for the moment if you allow yourself to be appeased. You can always be angry again if he deserves it, and will have more excuse if you were once placated. Make some concession to his youth, his tears, and your own kind heart, and do not torment him or yourself any longer - anger can only be a torment to your gentle self.
>
> I'm afraid you will think I am using pressure, not persuasion, if I add my prayers to his - but this is what I shall do, and all the more freely and fully because I have given the man a very severe scolding and warned him firmly that I will never make such a request again. This was because he deserved a fright, and is not intended for your ears; for maybe I *shall* make another request and obtain it, as long as it is nothing unsuitable for me to ask and you to grant.

But someone will say, "Wait a second, Price! This letter is decades later than Paul!" Right-o, my friend, but I'm not saying *Paul* copied Pliny's letter. Someone *else* did, long after Paul's time, and tried to pass it off as Paul's. But why would anyone want to? Stephan Hermann Huller[281] explained it pretty well. He turned the theory of Edgar J. Goodspeed[282] on its head. Goodspeed had suggested that

---

[280] Willem Christiaan van Manen, *A Wave of Hypercriticism: The English Writings of W.C. van Manen* (Valley, WA: Tellectual Press, 2014), pp. 145, 149.
[281] Stephan Hermann Huller, "Against Polycarp," unpublished manuscript.
[282] Edgar J. Goodspeed, *The Key to Ephesians: A Provocative Solution to a Problem in the Pauline Literature* (Chicago: University of Chicago Press, 1956), pp. xiv-xv.

Onesimus in later years, so grateful to his old mentor Paul, preserved the letter that won him his freedom and included it in the collection of Pauline Epistles he made. Huller counters that the Letter to Philemon was fabricated by or on behalf of Bishop Onesimus to provide him the credentials of a kind of apostolic succession.

Whoever wrote Philemon, what does it have to say about slavery? There is no condemnation of the institution itself, nor of Christians participating in it. We must not read too much into "you might have him back for ever, no longer as a slave, but as more than a slave, as a beloved brother" (verses 15-16). Nothing is said here to hint that "if he is a brother, he can no longer be a slave," and even if that *were* the point it would still be morally insufficient from the modern standpoint from which we judge the ancients: is it only wrong to have *fellow Christians* as slaves? But in any case, all it says is that, once Philemon frees Onesimus, if he does, Onesimus will no longer be a slave to Philemon, but he *will* be a Christian brother since Paul has converted him.

24
The Pastoral Epistles
Paul in the Rear-View Mirror

Post-Paul by Post

If no other writings carrying Paul's name are pseudonymous, 1 and 2 Timothy and Titus certainly are. Virtually every verse of the Pastoral Epistles, as the three of them are called, gives evidence of non-Pauline authorship. The vocabulary is indisputably different from that in the others and instead has much in common with both Luke and Acts (to say nothing of the Apostolic Fathers),[283] to the degree that some scholars are convinced that all are by the same author.[284] That author may be Polycarp, second-century author of one or two epistles[285] and likely the compiler of our twenty-seven book edition of the New Testament.[286]

The Pastorals also feature creedal materials uncharacteristic of the other ostensibly Pauline letters. Besides, the very existence of creedal and catechetical materials bespeaks a more advanced state of institutionalism. There are five "faithful sayings."

> The saying is sure and worthy of full acceptance, that Christ Jesus came into the world to save sinners. (1 Tim. 1:15)

> The saying is sure: If any one aspires to the office of bishop, he desires a noble task. (1 Tim. 3:1)

> The saying is sure and worthy of full acceptance... We have our hope set on the living God, who is the Savior of all men,

---

[283] P.N. Harrison, *The Problem of the Pastoral Epistles* (New York: Oxford University Press, 1921), pp. 18-86.

[284] Stephen G. Wilson, *Luke and the Pastoral Epistles* (London: SPCK, 1979); Jerome D. Quinn, "The Last Volume of Luke: The Relation of Luke-Acts to the Pastoral Epistles." In Charles H. Talbert, ed., *Perspectives on Luke-Acts*. Perspectives on Religious Studies, Special Studies Series No. 5 (Edinburgh: T&T Clark, 1978), pp. 62-75.

[285] P.N. Harrison, *Polycarp's Two Epistles to the Philippians* (Cambridge at the University Press, 1936).

[286] David Trobisch, *The First Edition of the New Testament* (New York: Oxford University Press, 2000); Trobisch, "Who Published the New Testament?" *Free Inquiry* 28/1 (December 2007-January 2008), pp. 30-33.

especially of those who believe. (1 Tim. 4:9-10)[287]

The saying is sure:

If we have died with him, we shall also live with him;
if we endure, we shall also reign with him;
if we deny him, he also will deny us;
if we are faithless, he remains faithful—
For he cannot deny himself. (2 Tim. 2:11-13)

When the goodness and loving kindness of God our Savior appeared, he saved us, not because of deeds done by us in righteousness, but in virtue of his own mercy, by the washing of regeneration and renewal in the Holy Spirit, which he poured out upon us richly through Jesus Christ our Savior, so that we might be justified by his grace and become heirs in hope of eternal life. The saying is sure. (Titus 3:4-8a)

To these might be added a sixth, a confessional statement with some marks of a Christological hymn like those in Philippians 2:6-11 and Colossians 1:15-20.[288] The introductory formula is not the same as in the other five, but it is pretty analogous.

Great indeed, we confess, is the mystery of our religion:

He was manifested in the flesh,
vindicated in the Spirit,
    seen by angels,
preached among the nations,
believed on in the world,
    taken up in glory.

The institutional organization of the churches, bristling with

---

[287] I'm sorry, but I just cannot accept the majority opinion that the faithful saying constitutes verse 8 (George W. Knight III, *The Faithful Sayings in the Pastoral Letters*. Baker Biblical Monographs [Grand Rapids: Baker Book House, 1979], Chapter IV, "1 Timothy 4:9 and its Saying," pp. 62-79), which seems to me just part of the discourse into which the traditional maxim has been inserted. And I think 10a is also part of the context.

[288] Jack T. Sanders, *The New Testament Christological Hymns: Their Historical Religious Background*. Society for New Testament Studies Monograph Series 15 (Cambridge at the University Press, 1971), pp. 15-17.

bishops, deacons, deaconesses, and consecrated widows and virgins, seems way too late for the time of Paul. The situation envisioned for Paul does not fit with any attested in either the Book of Acts or the Pauline Epistles. These last represent the original stance and character of Christianity as a *sect*, self-contained and living in tension with the surrounding society from which the sectarians have distanced themselves. The Pastorals, by contrast, imply a *church*, a second-generation version of the original sect which has moved back toward the ethos of the wider society, reassimilating to many of the conventional values it had repudiated.[289] Not surprisingly, the concept of "faith" seems to have shrunk in one sense and inflated in another, no longer denoting an existential life-stance but rather the assent to a checklist of orthodox doctrines.[290] The notion of apostolic succession appears here (2 Tim. 2:2), something which by its very nature implies and demands a definite, later stage of ecclesiastical validation.[291] Finally, the occasion of writing is clearly artificial: "Paul" says he will shortly be rejoining his colleagues Timothy and Titus, yet in these letters he outlines a whole church manual. Why bother? Why make the trip? What else could he add once he arrived?

The Anti-Sex League[292]

Basically, as Dennis Ronald MacDonald[293] demonstrates, the Pastoral letters are attempting to invoke the "real" Paul, the Catholic Paul, to combat a rival version of Paul, the Paul Tertullian later characterized

---

[289] Max Scheler, *Problems of a Sociology of Knowledge*. Trans. Manfred S. Frings. International Library of Sociology (London: Routledge & Keegan Paul, 1980), pp. 84-85.

[290] Rudolf Bultmann, *Theology of the New Testament*. Complete in One Volume. Trans Kendrick Grobel. Scribner Studies in Contemporary *Theology* (New York: Scribners, 1955), vol. I, pp. 314-330; vol. II, p. 135; Paul Tillich, *Dynamics of Faith*. Harper Torchbooks/Cloister Library (New York: Harper & Row, 1958), pp. 1-4, 30-38.

[291] The sporadic, temporary, charismatic leadership of the earlier generations of Christians, attested in 1 Corinthians, might be compared to the sequence of dynasties in Israel, while a succession of legitimated apostles and bishops, as in the Pastorals, recalls the long and exclusive continuance of the single Davidic dynasty in Judah. In Israel, the anointing of God could pass unpredictably from one king and his heirs to another, while in Judah, a king must have the legitimacy of the licensed dynastic line of descent.

[292] Of course, I'm stealing this from George Orwell's novel *1984*.

[293] Dennis Ronald MacDonald, *The Legend and the Apostle: The Battle for Paul in Story and Canon* (Philadelphia: Westminster Press, 1983).

as "the apostle of Marcion" and "the apostle of the heretics." Many early varieties of Christianity[294] eventually stigmatized as "heresies" claimed Paul as their fountainhead. One movement, centered in Asia Minor, that overlapped several of these is now referred to as Encratism (from the Greek *encrateo*, "self-control," implying celibacy). Originally this was the name of a specific ascetical sect founded by Tatian, the disciple of Justin Martyr, but gradually the use of the term in scholarly discussion has been widened to include the various sects that practiced asceticism, especially celibacy. There were Marcionites, Montanists, Jewish Christians, and Gnostics who fit the description. Relevant to our topic is the fact that encratites "remembered" Paul as teaching this doctrine. The chief evidence for this is a very long, second-century text called the Acts of Paul in which the apostle preaches that only those renouncing sex, even within marriage, can be saved. This book ascribes Paul's martyrdom to the ire of husbands whom Paul's preaching had alienated from their wives.[295] Some of these men were highly placed and persuaded local officials to slap the cuffs on Paul and dump him in the dungeon.

Encratites were also apocalyptic enthusiasts,[296] expecting this fallen age to end very quickly. In the meantime, they lived as if the kingdom of God had already arrived. They regarded sex as the original sin[297] and sought to return to Edenic innocence through baptism and celibacy.[298] Without the need for family structure, women could be on a par with men, both of them teaching, preaching, baptizing.[299] (The Pastoral writer doesn't like this; in fact, he is especially concerned to restrict the membership of the stipended Order of Widows and Virgins.) Encratites considered themselves citizens of heaven (Phil. 3:20), subjects of a kingdom not of this world (John 18:36), and thus they embraced communal anarchism and pacifism.[300] Having returned

---

[294] Walter Bauer, *Orthodoxy and Heresy in Earliest Christianity*. Trans. Philadelphia Seminar on Christian Origins (Philadelphia: Fortress Press, 1971); Bart D. Ehrman, *Lost Christianities: The Battles for Scripture and the Faiths We Never Knew* (New York: Oxford University Press, 2003).

[295] Stevan L. Davies, *The Revolt of the Widows: The Social World of the Apocryphal Acts* (Carbondale: Southern Illinois University Press, 1980).

[296] Peter Brown, *The Body and Society: Men, Women, and Sexual Renunciation in Early Christianity*. Lectures on the History of Religions, new series no. 13 (New York: Columbia University Press, 1988), pp. 31-32, 99.

[297] Brown, *Body and Society*, p. 86.

[298] Brown, *Body and Society*, p. 101.

[299] Brown, *Body and Society*, pp. 89-90.

[300] Jacques Ellul, *Anarchy and Christianity*. Trans. Geoffrey W. Bromiley (Grand Rapids: Eerdmans, 1991).

to Eden, they refused to eat meat (Gen. 1:29) or to drink wine (Gen. 9:20-21).[301]

MacDonald shows how the Pastorals would make the most sense if "Paul" were writing against all these points, as we will shortly see. Encratites embraced a radical Paul, and Polycarp(?) countered with a conventional, domesticated Paul.[302] Winsome Munroe[303] has carried the argument further, explaining the occasional "early catholic"[304] Paulinism met with in the non-Pastoral epistles as a sanitizing overlay by the same hand that wrote the Pastorals. (Such a procedure is hardly unknown: Rufinus did the same thing to the dicey text of Origen's *On First Principles*, toning it down for a more orthodox audience.)[305]

First Timothy

We are at least a little bit surprised to read in 1 Timothy 2:1-2 of "Paul's" priority that Christians are to pray for the Roman authorities, who will provide security for Christians to live tranquil, peaceable lives as good subjects of the Empire. Here the church seems to have morphed into the Rotary Club. We cannot miss the decidedly different sense we get from reading Romans, 1 and 2 Corinthians, Galatians, the so-called *Hauptbriefe* (Principle Epistles). What happened to the sectarian self-conception of being strangers in a strange land, a beachhead for the coming kingdom of God? That has all been ceded to the radicals, the encratites.

First Timothy 2:11-12 forbids women to teach, implying that they *were* teaching and that this writer wants it to stop. He is not trying to *prevent* it happening; he is trying to shut it down. In fact, women teachers and prophets were important in various encratite

---

[301] Brown, *Body and Society*, p. 97. A good modern example of an encratite sect would be the now sadly defunct Shakers.

[302] Winsome Munro, *Authority in Paul and Peter: The Identification of a Pastoral Stratum in the Pauline Corpus and I Peter*. Society for New Testament Studies Monograph Series 45 (New York: Cambridge University Press, 1983), pp. 131-140.

[303] Munro, *Authority in Paul and Peter*, passim; MacDonald, *Legend and the Apostle*, pp. 86-89.

[304] Ernst Käsemann, *New Testament Questions of Today* (London: SCM Press, 1969), Chapter XII, "Paul and Early Catholicism." Trans. Wilfred F. Bunge, pp. 236-251.

[305] *Origen On First Principles*. Trans. G.W. Butterworth. Harper Torchbooks/Cathedral Library (New York: Harper & Row, 1966), "Introduction," pp. xli-xlii, xlvii.

groups. The writer knows that women promote encratism in their teaching, something quite natural since it provided the only opportunity for them to exercise their gifts.

Encratites preached that salvation required the absolute renunciation of sex and, obviously, child-rearing and family (cf., Luke 14:26[306]). Accordingly, 1 Timothy 2:15 says just the opposite: "a woman will be saved through bearing children, if she continues in faith and love and holiness, with modesty." (More on this verse later on.)

The list of qualifications for bishops and deacons in 3:1-13 describes an institutional-hierarchical authority structure, centered in offices and credentials, totally unlike the free-wheeling charismatic-prophetic leadership of the encratites. And both bishops and deacons must be married, *not celibate,*[307] and married only once, not remarried once widowed, reflecting the Roman ideal of the *univirae* ("one-husbanded"), women who refused remarriage, considering it infidelity to their dear, departed husbands. And notice how, in utter contradiction to encratism's revolutionary rejection of "family values," 1Timothy 3:4-5 recommends domestic life as an ideal training ground for ministry.

First Timothy 4:3-5 vilifies both continence and vegetarianism in no uncertain terms as heresies whispered into someone's ear by Uncle Screwtape. Both, of course, were prominent mores of encratism, and their condemnation here is a far cry from Paul's advice in 1 Corinthians 7:38-40; 8:13; Romans 14:6, 14-21, to say nothing of Matthew 19:10-12.

Verse 7 warns readers ("Timothy") to "have nothing to do with old women's [or wives', same Greek word] tales."[308] Does the phrase simply refer to unreliable old rumors and superstitions, as we

---

[306] Thaddeé Matura, *Gospel Radicalism: The Hard Sayings of Jesus.* Trans. Maggi Despot and Paul Lachance (Maryknoll: Orbis Books, 1984), p. 59.

[307] Then where the heck did the Catholic Church get celibate priesthood? Eventually there was a rapprochement between the Church and some encratites (non-Gnostic ones). Just as the Catholic Church made a place for asceticism and voluntary poverty within itself, restricting it to monasteries, so did they reach an accommodation on celibacy: they admitted the logic of it, a la 1 Corinthians 7:32-37, but did not require it of all Christians as the encratites had. They admitted sex was sinful but a necessary evil to keep the human race going, something the encratites had not cared about, as they had expected the world to end very soon. So voluntary poverty and celibacy alike became "counsels of perfection" for the spiritual elite (monks, nuns, and priests).

[308] It is difficult to find a translation which does not paraphrase, masking any reference to "wives'" or "women's," though the New International Version tells it like it is. See MacDonald, *Legend and the Apostle,* p. 14.

use the term today? No, because, as far as we know, the phrase "old wives' tales" is first used right here in this text. So it is not yet a general term or a cliché but instead pegs the origin of the "heretical" encratite doctrine against which the Pastoral author strives so mightily. It was propagated by the Order of Widows. The tales in question, as MacDonald demonstrates,[309] must be those of Paul's adventures, yarns now available in the Acts of Paul.

What is the "bodily training" damned with faint praise in verse 8? Not athletic exercises or weight-lifting, but rather asceticism (fasting, isolation, sleep deprivation, continence, fasting, etc.). Our author does not and cannot very well condemn asceticism outright, but (in the spirit of Colossians 2:20-23), he minimizes its effectiveness, preferring conventional piety.

Pseudo-Paul wants to restrict church aid to "real widows" (5:3), apparently meaning literal widows whose husbands had died, because "widow" was commonly a designation for any woman of any age who pledged herself to Christ as her only husband.[310] (The Ignatian Epistle to Smyrna 13:1 refers to "the virgins who are called widows.") The Pastor (as he is called) wants to purge the rolls of women who have joined the order because they want to leave husband and family and live with their sisters in celibacy. If a woman still has living relatives, she belongs with them instead of mooching off the church (5:4). The Revised Standard Version adds words to 5:16 because the translators didn't understand what was going on. "If any believing woman has *relatives who are* widows, let her assist them; let the church not be burdened, so that it may assist those who are real widows." The point is not the same as in 5:4, which would otherwise make 5:16 redundant. Rather, the reference is to wealthier women who maintained a household (a kind of proto-convent) of consecrated women, apparently with assistance from the church.[311] The Pastor says, "Take care of 'em yourself!" The practice continued successfully for some centuries with patronesses like Melania the Elder and Melania the Younger. Acts 9:29-31 seems to depict such a situation.[312] This writer wants to change the Order of Widows from a precursor of convents and nuns to a simple geriatric relief fund (5:9) as depicted in Acts 6:1. Verses 5-6 malign the motives of any woman who leaves

---

[309] MacDonald, *Legend and the Apostle*, Chapter I, "The Oral Legends Behind the Acts of Paul," pp. 17-33.

[310] MacDonald, *Legend and the Apostle*, p. 76.

[311] MacDonald, *Legend and the Apostle* , p. 75.

[312] MacDonald, *Legend and the Apostle*, p. 50.

family and home to take refuge with the church, desiring to live a spiritual, non-domestic life, as Mary of Bethany does in Luke 10:38-42 (cf., 1 Cor. 7:34, "the unmarried woman or virgin is anxious about the affairs of the Lord, how to be holy in body and spirit; but the married woman is anxious about worldly affairs, how to please her husband."). First Corinthians 7:10 was content to leave it at saying, "the wife should not leave her husband." But 1 Timothy 5:5-6 assumes such a woman is merely shirking her household duties to watch soap operas and eat Malomars. Likewise, the visitation ministry of the consecrated women is caricatured as house-to-house gossip-mongering (5:13). Those who abandon their responsibility to care for their family are worse than unbelievers (5:8).

Verse 10, stipulating qualifications for eligible candidates for the ecclesiastical dole, nevertheless makes it clear that such women would have previously been engaged in acts of ministry, though not teaching, baptizing, or prophecy. Presumably they may now earn their keep only by continuing the "secular" voluntarism described here. The author bans "younger widows" from the order, which is still quasi-clerical since it requires a pledge not to marry. He doesn't think the "virgins called widows" have what it takes to stick to it. Whereas 1 Corinthians 7:36 okays consecrated women who are anxious about passing childbearing age (depending on your translation) dropping their celibacy oath, going ahead and having sex with their husbands, 1 Timothy 5:11-12 says younger women must not undertake the initial vow of continence ("the first pledge") in the first place lest they be subsequently tempted to marry after all and break their betrothal to Christ, still apparently considered inviolable, more so even than in Paul's day.

Why on earth would Paul advise Timothy to swig a little wine to settle his upset stomach? Well, of course, he didn't. It wasn't Paul, and he wasn't addressing an individual named Timothy. The prescription is there to needle the encratites who were absolute teetotalers.[313]

I mentioned earlier that there were various brands of encratites, including Gnostics and Marcionites. Both of them receive parting jabs at the end of 1 Timothy: "Avoid the godless chatter and contradictions of what is falsely called knowledge, for by professing it some have missed the mark as regards the faith" (6:20-21). You see, "contradictions" is the Greek word *antitheses*, which just happened to

---

[313]MacDonald, *Legend and the Apostle* , p. 58.

be the title of a Marcionite work in which various Old and New Testament passages were juxtaposed in order to show how different the Hebrew God was from the Father of Jesus. And "knowledge falsely so-called"? Of course, that's a poke at the Gnostics' trademark claim to possess secret knowledge, or *gnosis*.

2 Timothy

This epistle warns three times against false teachers who are likely to be identified with the encratite (Marcionite, Gnostic, etc.) teachers infiltrating Christian communities in Asia Minor. Second Timothy 2:16-18 envisions Gnostics teaching a completely realized eschatology. Chapter 3, verses 5-9 and 13, refer to gigolos and charlatans who cultivate groupies, which is of course a hostile caricature of sectarian apostles with whom the Pastor disagrees. Irenaeus describes the Gnostic miracle-worker Marcus, successor to Gnostic apostle Simon Magus, in pretty much the same terms:

> He devotes himself especially to women, and those such as are well-bred, and elegantly attired, and of great wealth, whom he frequently seeks to draw after him, by addressing them in such seductive words as these: "I am eager to make you a partaker of my Charis, since the Father of all does continually behold your angel before His face. Now the place of your angel is among us: it behooves us to become one. Receive first from me and by me [the gift of] Charis. Adorn yourself as a bride who is expecting her bridegroom, that you may be what I am, and I what you are. Establish the germ of light in your nuptial chamber. Receive from me a spouse, and become receptive of him, while you are received by him. Behold Charis has descended upon you; open your mouth and prophesy." On the woman replying, "I have never at any time prophesied, nor do I know how to prophesy;" then engaging, for the second time, in certain invocations, so as to astound his deluded victim, he says to her, "Open your mouth, speak whatsoever occurs to you, and you shall prophesy." She then, vainly puffed up and elated by these words, and greatly excited in soul by the expectation that it is herself who is to prophesy, her heart beating violently [from emotion], reaches the requisite pitch of audacity, and idly as well as impudently

utters some nonsense as it happens to occur to her, such as might be expected from one heated by an empty spirit. (Referring to this, one superior to me has observed, that the soul is both audacious and impudent when heated with empty air.) Henceforth she reckons herself a prophetess, and expresses her thanks to Marcus for having imparted to her of his own Charis. She then makes the effort to reward him, not only by the gift of her possessions (in which way he has collected a very large fortune), but also by yielding up to him her person, desiring in every way to be united to him, that she may become altogether one with him. (*Against Heresies* 1.13.3)[314]

Verse 8 refers to Jannes and Jambres, Hellenistic names for Pharaoh's sorcerer-priests who competed with Moses, counterfeiting his miracles. Here again are the miracle-working apostles who provided the prototypes for the Apocryphal Acts' adventures of Paul, Peter, Philip, Andrew, Thomas, and John.[315] Chapter 4, verses 3-4, regrets the widespread turning to teachers of false doctrines (and by now we can guess which ones) out of unwholesome curiosity, preoccupied with what the Buddha called "questions that tend not unto edification." All this is phrased as a prediction ("The time is coming when...") because of the fictional device of Pauline authorship. Since the actual intended audience lives in a generation subsequent to Paul, "Paul's" warning must have been prophetic, the classic pose of apocalyptic writers.

The famous affirmation of the inspiration and authority of scripture (3:16-17) would be superfluous, wholly pointless, unless scriptural authority were in dispute. And it was, by the Marcionites, who rejected the Jewish scriptures, replacing them with the pre-Pastoral Pauline Epistles. Similarly, back in 1 Timothy 2:5 we find a blow struck at Marcionism: "there is one God, and there is one mediator between God and men, the man Christ Jesus." This seems not to be a denial of polytheism or of the reality of other religions' deities (as is the somewhat similar sounding 1 Corinthians 8:4-6); rather, the object of criticism in 1 Timothy 2:5 looks like the

[314] Alexander Roberts, James Donaldson, and A. Cleveland Coxe, eds., *Ante-Nicene Fathers*, Vol. 1. Trans. Alexander Roberts and William Rambaut (Buffalo, New York: Christian Literature Publishing Co., 1885.)
[315] MacDonald, *Legend and the Apostle*, p. 47; Davies, *Revolt of the Widows*, Chapter III, "The Apostles," pp. 29-49.

Marcionite doctrine that the Hebrew Jehovah, Creator and Torah-giver, and the loving Father of Jesus both exist but are not partners in a binitarian pantheon. No, says the Pastor, these "two" Gods are *one* and the same, and Jesus was sent by that single deity.

Titus

Titus is essentially a "church order" manual of the same genre as the *Didache*, the later Apostolic Constitutions and the *Didascalia*, the Qumran Manual of Discipline and even the Gospel of Matthew as a whole, but most obviously in chapters 18 and 19. The letter frame is clearly fictional, as "Paul" says he is about to visit Titus in Crete, so why is he jumping the gun and giving him all this instruction *now*? And the pseudonymous author (Polycarp, as I think) knows good and well that such a document is anachronistic for the period he pretends to address; he reveals this by the simple fact of cloaking this ecclesiastical handbook in the guise of a different genre: a letter. They had epistles in Paul's day, but not church manuals.

The Pastoral agenda is again prominent. Titus 1:14-15 condemns encratite vegetarianism. Chapter 2, verses 3-5, take aim at the widows, restricting their teaching to instructing young wives to embrace Stepford-wife domesticity and to stick with their husbands, i.e., not to walk out on them to join a household of charismatic celibate women (something we see them doing frequently in the Apocryphal Acts). Titus 3:1 reiterates the need for Christians to be good conformists and loyal Roman citizens/subjects, not exactly the posture of the radical, anarchist, apocalyptic encratites who the Pastor fears are giving Christians in general a bad reputation. The situation might be compared to the chagrin felt by mainstream, moderate Muslims today when outsiders lump them together with Jihadist killers.

A Closer Look at 1 Timothy 2:11-15

What exactly is going on in one of the most infamous passages in the Pastorals?

> Let a woman learn in silence with all submissiveness. I permit
> no woman to teach or to have authority over men; she is to

keep silent. For Adam was formed first, then Eve; and Adam was not deceived, but the woman was deceived and became a transgressor. Yet woman will be saved through bearing children,[316] if she continues in faith and love and holiness, with modesty.

This passage, like all strange-sounding biblical texts, has been pelted with the stones of many and varied attempts to interpret it. It will doubtless be edifying to review some of them here. First, there is some debate over whether we should translate *gunē* and *andros* as "woman" and "man," or as "wife" and "husband." Either is lexically legitimate, but in context the difference becomes moot since the Pastoral writer allows (celibate) women only to wash the feet (1 Tim. 5:10) of visiting dignitaries (admittedly a noble, Christlike service, Luke 7:38; John 13:3-15). "Older women" are to teach "younger women" (Titus 2:3-4), and "women" are not "to teach... men" (2:12).

Is "I do not permit" a command, or merely a personal preference? Of course, the intention behind the latter suggestion is to make what follows no more than friendly advice, as when a TV cooking host says, "I always put just a pinch of arsenic in the recipe, but you may want to use more." Because if it's only advice, the "biblical feminist" can feel free to disregard it without flipping off "biblical authority." Well, it has to be taken as a command, because Titus is a church manual, not friendly chit-chat.

"For" introduces the Adam and Eve business. Does this imply the Eden allusion is an *illustration*, or a *scriptural warrant*? Again, it is easy to see what is at stake in this debate. A mere illustration need not be normative for "Bible-believing" readers. But I think it is supposed to be an argument from scripture, given that *gar*, "for," usually introduces reasons, rarely illustrations, even here in the Pastorals. The effect is to say that women must not be allowed to teach because, by their very nature (as seen in the prototype of women, Eve), they are easily deceived and thus easy marks for heretical teachers. Want proof? They are teaching that wacky encratite doctrine!

At this point I must discuss the fascinating theory of Catherine Clark Kroeger,[317] who proposes a new interpretation of the

---

[316] I recall how, in 1976, as I sat on a park bench piously reading my pocket New Testament, I came to this text, looked up from the page and said to myself, "This is [*Bullgeschichte*]!" (I am substituting Norman Perrin's apt euphemism if you don't mind). This was the turning point in my thinking about "biblical authority."

[317] Catherine Clark Kroeger, "1 Timothy 2:12 - A Classicist's View," in Alvera

controversial passage, which capitalizes on the Gnostic connection. What does the word *authentein* mean? Traditionally, the word is taken to mean "to domineer," and this sense of the root survives in our English word "authoritarian." Accordingly, the King James Version reads, "I do not permit a woman to teach or to *usurp* authority over men." Nothing wrong with that translation, but *authentein* can just as easily denote "to claim authorship/origination of" something. Of course, the two meanings are linked, as when we say the *author* of a book is the *authority* as to what his book means.[318] Anyway, Kroeger draws attention to one of the Nag Hammadi texts, The Origin of the World, one of several related variant versions of the Eden story. In The Origin of the World we read that Eve is the origin of Adam! She is a spiritual Aion, one of the entities emanated from the Godhead. She puts on flesh to become the androgyne from whom Rabbinical lore said Adam and Eve were created. In this version it is the male Adam who is split off from the androgyne's "side," not Eve. At first Adam lies inert at her feet, a soulless homunculus (as in Genesis 2:7), until Eve imparts life to him: "Adam, live! Rise up upon the earth!" Awaking, he exclaims, "You will be called 'the mother of the living' because you are the one who gave me life." Thus when the newly conscious Adam calls Eve "the Mother of All Living" (Gen. 3:20), he *includes himself.* Similarly, the heresiologist Epiphanius, bishop of Salamis, relates that certain encratite Montanist prophetesses claimed legitimation from Eve as the instructor and enlightener of Adam. Kroeger notes just how well this would fit 1Timothy 2:11-15 if we took *authentein* in the second sense: "I do not permit a woman to teach or to claim to be the origin of men."

Recall that 1 Corinthians 11:8-10 cites Eve's origin from Adam as a reason for a male hierarchy with wives subordinated to husbands. Could the Corinthian women prophets, too, have been claiming that Eve originated and instructed Adam, as a basis for claiming greater authority? Might Paul have already been trying to rebut such a claim? That seems to be exactly the logic of 1 Timothy 2:13-14: "for Adam was formed first, *then* Eve," i.e., contrary to the

---

Mickelsen (ed.), *Women, Authority & the Bible* (Downers Grove: InterVarsity Press, 1986), pp. 225-244.

[318] Deconstructive critics, like the New Critics before them, deny that any author lords it over the meaning of his text, which must instead speak for itself to every reader. I recall once hearing Stephen King describe the meaning of his novel *Carrie* and suddenly realizing he was *wrong!* It obviously means the same thing King said William Peter Blatty's book *The Exorcist* means: the parent-frightening transition from girlhood to full womanhood.

teaching that *woman* is the origin of *man*.

And it gets better: verse 14 says, "And Adam was not deceived, but the woman was deceived and became a transgressor." This sounds like a rebuttal to yet another feature of the myth in The Origin of the World, that the Archons (angelic henchmen of the Demiurge) *deceived* Adam, telling him that Eve had been created from him, when in fact it was the reverse. Against this, the author of the Pastorals affirms the traditional Jewish interpretation.

"Yet woman will be saved through *teknogonia* if they continue in faith and love and holiness with modesty" (1 Tim. 2:15). Can our writer possibly mean to say, "saved via bearing children"? Or, less ludicrous, "kept safe through delivery"? What is *teknogonia*? Since encratism is the issue throughout the Pastorals, the word would mean "domestic life," "family life." Our author thus seeks to combat the doctrine of salvation through rejecting sex and child-bearing. We might read the word *sōthēsetai* as "kept safe" rather than "saved," and it would then allude to the sentence passed on Eve in Genesis 3:16, "I will greatly multiply your pain in childbirth; yet your desire shall be for your husband, and he shall rule over you." The Pastor's point would be to reaffirm this arrangement against the female freedom made possible by encratite egalitarianism. At least he figures that God will keep obedient women safe through the birth-pangs to which he long ago sentenced them.

Was this prohibition of women teaching given as a general rule for all Christian congregations? Or was it meant to deal only with the specific situation in Ephesus (1 Tim. 1:3), where for some reason a group of women were teaching heresy? Given that the epistle is pseudepigraphical, the ostensible addressees are just as fictional as the supposed author, and this means the prohibition is intended for "whom it may concern" in any of the churches. And yet it was certainly a local problem (in Asia Minor, including Ephesus) that led to the prohibition. If encratism, Montanism, Gnosticism, etc., had not existed, the writer would not have responded this way. (And if chauvinist pigs could fly...) You might say the encratites of Asia Minor ruined things for Christian women everywhere. Again, this observation creates anxiety only for those who want women to teach and yet want to (think they) obey the Bible. The Pastoral writer said what he said, whether or not we like it. I don't.

25

The Epistle to the Hebrews
Finding Paul Appalling but Apollos Appealing

Who Shall Remain Nameless

We don't know *who* wrote Hebrews. We'll *never* know. Hebrews hits the ground running, not pausing to identify the writer or his addressees. As Origen said, "God only knows who wrote the Epistle to the Hebrews!" But the ancients thought they knew. The Alexandrian church (and the East in general) thought Paul wrote it, while the West, if Tertullian and Novatian in the third century are any examples, believed the epistle was the work of Paul's companion Barnabas.[319] That's just a shot in the dark, probably based on the hint in 13:23 that the author belonged to the circle of Paul's associates. Martin Luther picked a different suspect out of the Pauline line-up, namely Apollos from Alexandria (Acts 18:24-28), probably because Hebrews appears to reflect the kind of scripture-allegorizing Judaism characteristic of Philo of Alexandria.[320]

In modern times the mighty Adolf Harnack[321] conjectured that the book was written by Priscilla, a Pauline colleague mentioned in Romans 16:3; 1 Corinthians 16:19; 2 Timothy 4:19; and Acts 18:2, 18, 26. As subsequent discussions of Harnack's fascinating argument are usually oversimplified to the point of straw man caricature, it seems worthwhile to outline it here in some detail.

---

[319] There *is* a so-called Epistle of Barnabas, one of the Apostolic Fathers, but he probably didn't write that one, either.

[320] Despite the demurrals of some (e.g., William Robinson, *The Eschatology of the Epistle to the Hebrews: A Study of the Christian Doctrine of Hope.* Joseph Smith Memorial Lecture 4, October 14, 1950 [Selly Oak, Birmingham: Overdale College, 1950], pp. 6-7), I find it hard to discount Sidney G. Sowers's demonstration of conceptual and lexical parallels between Hebrews and Philo that demand a common (Alexandrian) religious-intellectual milieu. In fact, it looks to me that the author of Hebrews actually used Philo's work. See Sidney G. Sowers, *The Hermeneutics of Philo and Hebrews: A Comparison of the Interpretation of the Old Testament in Philo Judaeus and the Epistle to the Hebrews.* Basel Studies of Theology No. 1 (Zürich: EVZ-Verlag/Richmond: John Knox Press, 1965), Chapter V, "The Alexandrian Jewish Background to the Epistle to the Hebrews," pp. 64-74.

[321] Adolf Harnack, "Probability about the Address and Author of the Epistle to the Hebrews." Trans. Emma Runge Peter. Appendix A to Lee Anna Starr, *The Bible Status of Women* (New York: Fleming H. Revell, 1926), pp. 392-415.

First, there are clues suggesting that Hebrews was written to a congregation in Rome. First Clement, written from Rome (whether by Clement or not, since this text, too, is actually anonymous!) knows it and quotes it about 96 C.E. And near the end of Hebrews (13:24) we have a shout-out: "Those greet you who are from Italy." Harnack took this to mean that expatriate Italians with the author as he or she wrote wanted to give the recipients their regards, implying the readers, too, were Italians.[322] (It wouldn't have to imply this, though; it might mean that the author is writing *from* Italy, and those with him are sending their greetings to the saints in Antarctica or wherever else the epistle is headed.) Leaders of the church are called "hegemons" (Heb. 13:7), a term also used in 1 Clement and the Shepherd of Hermas, also penned in Rome. The recipient church is said (6:10) to be renowned for its hospitality, something elsewhere attested for Rome (as in the letter from Dionysus of Corinth to Bishop Soter of Rome). The readers have suffered persecution, and this might be that unleashed by Nero. Hebrews 13:7 implies the martyrdom of past leaders: Peter and Paul? The epistle seems to be aimed at one of the particular house churches in the city, as implied by the uniformity and homogeneity of the audience (unlike Romans and Corinthians, which seek to mediate disputes between factions). And according to Romans 16:5, 14, 15, various Roman Christians hosted small congregations in their homes.

The author was, as already mentioned, a member of the Pauline circle (cf., "Timothy our brother has been released, with whom I shall see you if he comes soon," 13:23). And yet the letter is anonymous. How are we to explain the omission of so famous an apostolic name as, say, Apollos, Barnabas, Silas, Clement, or Luke? You have to wonder if the text originally had a name on it which was suppressed. Who might that have been?

The frequent use of "we" and "you" implies the writer had lived among this group at some time in the past and is writing to personal acquaintances (13:19). Priscilla and Aquila had once lived in Rome but had to relocate to Ephesus (Acts 18:2). Hmmm...

The author(s) was/were not among the actual witnesses of Jesus and his preaching (2:3), but belonged to the second generation. This would fit Apollos or Barnabas, but tradition associated neither with Rome.[323]

The alternation between "we" and "I" implies that a single

---

[322] Harnack, "Probability," p. 395; Adolf Jülicher, *An Introduction to the New Testament.* Trans. Janet Penrose Ward (London: Smith, Elder, and Co., 1904), p. 163.
[323] Though the Pseudo-Clementines do place Barnabas there.

author is writing on behalf of a group or a team (as in 1 Corinthians, Philippians, 1 Thessalonians, etc., where Paul is clearly the one and only writer but includes the names of Timothy, Sosthenes, etc., along with his own.

What about Priscilla and Aquila? They were Pauline colleagues *and* a ministerial team in their own right *and* they hosted their own church, to whom they must have written while abroad. Looks like we're getting somewhere, doesn't it?[324]

Can we narrow it down even further? Was it Priscilla who wrote Hebrews, or Aquila? Well, Acts places her name first in two of the three references to the couple. Paul, too, lists her first in Romans 16:3, though admittedly not in 1 Corinthians 16:9. Second Timothy 4:19, despite its dim view of women teachers, lists Priscilla first. Priscilla herself was a teacher, not just the wife of one, since Acts 18:24-28 says *both* Priscilla and Aquila instructed Apollos. In Romans 16, both are called "helpers in Christ." The priority of her name implies she was the main teacher. John Chrysostom, in his summary reference to the passage, simply makes *her* the teacher of Apollos, neglecting any mention of Aquila. This implies her greater prominence was generally taken for granted. Chrysostom was no fan of women teachers and would more likely have skipped *her* name if he thought he could have.

If Hebrews had originally borne the name Aquila, why would anyone have chopped it? But a woman's name? That, unfortunately, is a different story. In fact, there is a demonstrable tendency in the early church to downplay Priscilla's name. Comparing manuscripts of Acts, Harnack noticed that Acts 18:2, in the earlier text, the Alexandrian,[325] has "he found... Aquila *and* his wife Priscilla... and he stayed with *them*." But the Western text of Acts has "he found... Aquila *with* his wife Priscilla... and he stayed with *him*." Call it a redactional change or a Freudian slip, it's probably no accident. Likewise, the Western text puts Aquila's name first in the story of the couple catechizing Apollos. The Alexandrian text of Acts 18 never mentions Aquila without Priscilla, but the Western text three times adds "Aquila," and *only* "Aquila" (verses 3, 7, 22).

According to Acts 18:27, "the brethren" at Ephesus wrote a

---

[324] Naturally, it might be someone we never heard of: the Apostle Bif, Chad the Evangelist, or Mahalalel the Motivational Speaker. But if we're looking for the most "probable" candidate, we're perforce reduced to "the usual suspects," names preserved in the text.

[325] Attested in, e.g., the fourth-century Codex Sinaiticus and Codex Vaticanus.

letter of recommendation for Apollos, newly brought up to speed, to the Corinthian church. The "brethren" must, given the rest of the chapter, be just Priscilla and Aquila, especially since the Ephesian congregation is founded only subsequently, by Paul, in chapter 19. Yet the Western text clumsily changes the wording so that the *Corinthians* write the letter! In other words, the later editor has omitted Priscilla and Aquila as authors of an epistle! Is there an echo in here?

Tertullian lists Paul's great helpers: Onesiphorus, Aquila, Stephanas—but no Priscilla. Thus we have a consistent pattern of suppression of Priscilla. Might we not ascribe the omission of any authorial name from Hebrews the same way? As the egalitarianism of the early days of Christian sectarianism faded, women teaching was frowned on, and copyists snipped Priscilla's name from Hebrews, along with the surrounding tissue of the whole opening salutation.

Tucked away in a footnote, Harnack comments, "Without laying great stress upon it, I should like to mention the observation that in the large catalogue of heroic believers (Ch. 11), women were mentioned three times (vs. 11, 31, 35), and that in two of these places (vs. 11 and 35) they are rather far-fetched." Harnack scarcely thought it worth mentioning, yet latter-day scholars dismiss the whole argument as if the content of this footnote constituted the whole of it. It's almost a continuation of the old pattern of suppressing Priscillian authorship...

To the Hebrews?

There is no particular reason to accept the traditional guess as to the identity of the recipients. Did they really have to be Jews for the epistle's preoccupation with scripture and atonement ritual to make sense? Seeing as how many of the early Christian converts must have been Gentile "God fearers," I don't think so. These were Gentiles who had dumped paganism to attend synagogue but did not want to become full proselytes, unwilling to embrace the ritual and dietary laws that, while altogether natural for Jews, were imposingly alien to Gentiles. They would already have been pretty familiar with scripture in the Greek Septuagint translation, so the focus in Hebrews on scripture and Jewish ritual would make sense even for such a Gentile readership.[326] Hebrews 9:14 says the readers had turned to the living

---

[326] Robinson, *Eschatology of Hebrews*, p. 5.

God, apparently referring to their discarding their original pagan polytheism (cf., 1 Thess. 1:9). They had already made this change when they became God-fearers, so our author need not have been describing their Christian conversion.

It is obvious that the Writer to the "Hebrews" is trying mightily to convince his readers not to abandon their Christian faith in order to escape persecution. All the talk about how passé the Old Testament religion has become certainly means that the readers are thinking of returning to the synagogue, Judaism being a legally tolerated religion in the Roman Empire, unlike Christianity. That might assure the apostates, weary from persecution and discrimination, of a smoother ride, but, our writer is telling them, that is a dead end. And this would fit Gentile God-fearers as well as Jews. The warning not to be sucked in by "diverse and strange [or "foreign"] teachings" (13:9) sounds odd if the reference is to Judaism.[327] But there is no reason to think it is. Some of the wavering (Roman?) Christians had no doubt come to Christ from various Gentile Mystery Religions like Mithraism, the Attis cult, or Isis worship, and they're contemplating going back to *them*. The similarity between these cults and Christianity, both being redemption religions centering on dying-and-rising savior gods, had no doubt facilitated their members' transition to Christianity in the first place and would make it just as easy to retrace one's steps. These potential apostates, of course, would not be impressed by all the epistle's discussion of Melchizedek, Moses, Aaron, and atonement. But they were probably in the minority.

The dire warnings the author makes lest anyone abandon his Christian identity have rightly caused considerable angst among modern fundamentalists who cherish the doctrine of "eternal security,"[328] the belief that, once a person accepts Jesus as Lord and Savior, he cannot forfeit salvation no matter what he might do subsequently: child molestation, bestiality, necrophilia, genocide, card-playing, you name it. That ticket to heaven is irrevocable. This teaching is not aimed at providing a blank check for libertinism. Rather, the point is to affirm that, since good behavior cannot earn salvation, bad behavior cannot cancel it. Otherwise, salvation should depend upon the believer, not on the grace of Christ. And there is no way to read Hebrews 6:4-8 and 10:26-31 as compatible with that

---

[327] Sowers, *Hermeneutics*, p. 74, n. 31.

[328] Harry A. Ironside, *The Eternal Security of the Believer* (Neptune, NJ: Loizeaux Brothers, 1946), pp. 33-40; M.R. De Haan, *Eternal Security: Five Radio Sermons* (Grand Rapids: Radio Bible Class, 1973), p. 31.

notion. Rather, that way lieth damnation.

Even worse, as I read it, the Hebrews 10 passage enters into the ancient debate over post-baptismal sin, *any* sin. Early Christians believed that baptism washed away all one's sins, but that subsequently one had better keep one's nose clean. This would not have seemed all that odd given that they expected Christ to return very soon, and it ought to be possible with God's help to avoid sinning. But as the years went by, it got tougher and tougher to stay on the wagon. This led many believers to delay baptism till they were on their deathbed, hoping they'd have the opportunity. The Shepherd of Hermas, written in the late first century in Rome (though added to later), proclaims a second opportunity for effective repentance, after which you're on your own. By contrast, Hebrews 10 takes a rigorous stance: one sin after baptism, and, pal, you're toast, *burnt* toast. Hebrews 12:16-17 invokes the example of foolish "Esau, who sold his birthright *for a single meal.*" Ouch! Imagine what would happen to a guy who, say, denied his Lord three times.[329]

Date Book

It is common to hear Hebrews dated in the early 60s because the elaborate description of the Temple rituals is given in the present tense, implying they are still going on, and the Temple was destroyed in 70 C.E. But, as Loisy[330] pointed out, there is a big problem with this. Hebrews *never mentions the Jerusalem Temple.* Instead, it discusses the furnishings and protocols of the desert Tabernacle. It does this because the argument largely depends upon the Exodus 25:9 story of Moses being commanded to make an earthly replica of the heavenly Tabernacle, which he saw in a vision atop Mount Sinai. The present tense, then, merely denotes a kind of virtual reality tour with no historical reference.

There is also the near-ubiquitous New Testament problem of the delay of the Parousia. Why does chapter 11 hold up for emulation the example of Abraham and others who died *without seeing the*

---

[329] But I am persuaded by Alfred Loisy, *The Birth of the Christian Religion.* Trans. L.P. Jacks (London: George Allen & Unwin, 1948), p. 82, that the story of Peter's denial must be a smear circulated by partisans of Paul. See also Robert H. Gundry, *Peter: False Disciple and Apostate according to Saint Matthew* (Grand Rapids: Eerdmans, 2015).
[330] Jülicher, *Introduction,* p. 160-161.

fulfillment of God's promises?[331] Clearly, our author knows not only that the generation contemporary with Jesus has passed away (Mark 13:30; Heb. 2:3), but also that it is quite probable the same disappointment awaits his readers. He is trying to prepare his readers for the big let-down. All this seems to require a pretty late date. The upper limit for the date of composition for Hebrews is the use of it in 1 Clement, generally estimated to have been written in 96 C.E. So Hebrews can't be later than that (unless, of course, we have been dating 1 Clement too early. The ascription to Clement is only a matter of tradition, since the epistle, like Hebrews, does not tell us who wrote it.)

Who Is Hebrews Talking About?

In view of the striking conceptual and lexical parallels between Hebrews and the Dead Sea Scrolls, Israeli archaeologist Yigael Yadin[332] suggested that Hebrews was addressed to Jewish Christians who had formerly been members of the Qumran (Essene?) sect of the Dead Sea Scrolls. Hans Kosmala[333] went further, arguing the case that the recipients of Hebrews were not yet Christians and were still members of a Diaspora group of Essenes. (This debate may be moot in light of the theories of Jacob L. Teicher and Robert Eisenman that the Dead Sea Scrolls sect is to be identified with the Jerusalem Church.[334]) John C. O'Neill[335] went so far as to argue that the Epistle to the Hebrews was not originally discussing Jesus at all, as every single instance of the names "Jesus" and "Christ" are textually or contextually insecure. Textual variants or grammatical anomalies imply a long series of insertions in order to Christianize an originally Essene/Qumran document (with the addition of chapter 13, which many scholars have long suspected was not original to the text anyway,

---

[331] Robinson, *Eschatology of Hebrews*, p. 6.

[332] Yigael Yadin, "The Dead Sea Scrolls and the Epistle to the Hebrews," *Scripta Hierosolymitana* 4 (Jerusalem, 1957).

[333] Hans Kosmala, *Hebräer-Essener-Christen: Studien zur Vorgeschichte der früchristlichen Verkündigung* (Leiden, 1959). The works cited in this note and the previous one are unavailable to me, and I am citing them from Sowers, *Hermeneutics*, p. 65.

[334]Jacob L. Teicher, *The Dead Sea Scrolls: Documents of the Jewish-Christian Sect of Ebionites* (1951); Robert Eisenman, *James the Brother of Jesus: The Key to Unlocking the Secrets of Early Christianity and the Dead Sea Scrolls* (New York: Viking Press, 1997).

[335] J.C. O'Neill, "Jesus in Hebrews" *Journal of Higher Criticism* 6/1 (Spring 1999), pp. 64-82.

trying to give Hebrews, actually a sermon text or a treatise, the superficial appearance of a letter). The original Son of God for the writer was the Dead Sea Scrolls Teacher of Righteousness. We would come full circle if Teicher was correct in identifying the Teacher of Righteousness (a code name in any case) as Jesus!

But I promised I would behave and follow the trail of mainstream biblical scholarship, so let's get back to that.

Christology: Adopted Son?

On first reading, the Christology of the Epistle to the Hebrews would seem to be a clear instance of incarnationism.

> In many and various ways God spoke of old to our fathers by the prophets; but in these last days he has spoken to us by a Son, whom he appointed the heir of all things, through whom also he created the world. He reflects the glory of God and bears the very stamp of his nature, upholding the universe by his word of power. (Heb. 1:1-3a; cf., Wisdom of Solomon 7:24-26)

The Word or Wisdom of God took on human flesh to redeem a sinful humanity. We would still have to deal with the Arian question as to whether that entity were of the same nature as God or rather the first of the creations of God (to which we shall return). But John A.T. Robinson[336] complicated the matter further when he pointed out how, but for a couple of verses, we should take our author for an adoptionist, one who believed that a righteous mortal man had been rewarded with an honorific status as God's Son and installed in heavenly glory. "Nowhere, in fact, in the New Testament more than in Hebrews do we find such a wealth of expressions that would support what looks like an adoptionist Christology – a Jesus who becomes the Christ."[337] Here are some verses that do sound pretty adoptionistic.

> having become as much superior to angels as the name he has obtained is more excellent than theirs. (1:4)

---

[336] John A.T. Robinson, *The Human Face of God* (Philadelphia: Westminster Press, 1973).
[337] Robinson, *Human Face,* p. 156.

> Thou hast loved righteousness and hated lawlessness;
> therefore God, thy God, has anointed thee
> with the oil of gladness beyond thy comrades. (1:9)

> So also Christ did not exalt himself to be made a high priest,
> but was appointed by him who said to him, "Thou art my
> Son, today I have begotten thee." (5:5)

> He was faithful to him who appointed him, just as Moses also
> was faithful in God's house. (3:2)

I have to say I find that some of the verses Robinson cites (Heb. 1:13; 2:9-10, 16, 12; 5:1-6, 8; 7:28) do not seem to make his point.

What is Robinson's solution? How does he make sense of these groups of verses that seem to point in opposite directions? He opts for adoptionism. He takes the seemingly incarnationist language of Hebrews 1:1-3 as *metaphorical*[338] (a red light should be flashing), applying Wisdom language to Jesus as the second Adam, the ideal Man. I confess, this sounds to me like a desperate harmonization, very much like what James D.G. Dunn[339] tries to do with Philippians 2:6-11, where he interprets the apparent pre-existence language as a contrast between Adam (created in the "form of God"), who over-reached, coveting the knowledge that would make him equal to God, and Jesus, an earthly human who spurned such temptations.[340] I don't think either reinterpretation works. Robinson's "metaphorical" approach is almost explicitly tantamount to allegorizing the text. How can Robinson explain away Hebrews 3:2?

> But we see Jesus, who for a little while was made lower than
> the angels, crowned with glory and honor because of the
> suffering of death, so that by the grace of God he might taste
> death for every one.

Robinson notes that the crucial Greek phrase, *brachy ti* ("for a bit, for a little while") could also be translated "a bit lower," which would reflect the meaning of the Psalm 8 text being quoted in Hebrews 3:2.

---

[338] Robinson, *Human Face*, p. 156.

[339] James D.G. Dunn, *Christology in the Making: An Inquiry into the Origins of the Doctrine of the Incarnation* (London: SCM Press, 2nd ed., 1989), pp. 114-121.

[340] I'm not sure what that temptation could have meant for a mortal man, unless we're talking about Doctor Faustus.

He wants it to mean the same thing in both verses, so that Hebrews 3:2 is only saying that Jesus was no more than a man, though he went on to be awarded heavenly glory. But this only makes sense if we are looking for a reading of the words to comport with Process Theology, as Robinson is obviously doing in *The Human Face of God*. Why note that Jesus was (and always had been) "a bit lower than the angels" unless the point was to challenge a belief in Jesus' pre-existent divinity? But that was no concern of the Writer to the Hebrews; it fits instead with Robinson's. I don't buy it.

I am always suspicious of scholars synthesizing sophisticated theological models that are never set out in any particular text, then using that construct (of their own devising) as a lens through which to interpret specific texts as if they were allusions to the construct. Then they read the whole thing into various verses and call the result "biblical theology." The famous "Suffering Servant/Son of Man" hybrid is a notorious example.[341] I feel safer choosing an exegetical paradigm that is at least ancient even if not explicitly set out in the Bible itself. And it seems to me the best framework for making sense of both the adoptionist and the incarnationist texts in Hebrews is that of Arius, Asterius, and Eusebius of Nicomedia (not the church historian) in the fourth century.

These theologians believed that Jesus was the incarnation of the divine Logos, but that this entity was a creature of God. Therefore he was changeable. During the incarnation he was perfected through obedience and suffering. He was then rewarded with divine honors and could henceforth be *called* "God," "the Son of God," "the Christ," etc. And he was the trailblazer, "the pioneer and perfecter of our faith" (Heb. 12:2; cf., 2:10) by virtue of having trod the path we all must tread in order to gain salvation. This was the Christology and the soteriology opposed by Athanasius, who held that the Logos was of the very same nature as God, hence perfect and immutable. In flesh he suffered all that humans suffer, but he saves believers by transferring to them his divine immortality, which he did not have to win but had always possessed. It seems to me that the Arian doctrine

---

[341] Rudolf Otto, *The Kingdom of God and the Son of Man: A Study in the History of Religion*. Trans. Floyd V. Filson and Bertram Lee-Woolf (Boston: Starr King Press, 1957), Book Two, Chapter 11, "The Son of Man as the Suffering Servant of God," pp. 249-255; Oscar Cullmann, *The Christology of the New Testament*. Trans. Shirley C. Guthrie and Charles A.M. Hall (Philadelphia: Westminster Press, 1969), pp. 160-161; Hugh J. Schonfield, *The Passover Plot: New Light on the History of Jesus* (New York: Bantam Books, 1967), Part Two, Chapter 3, "The Suffering Just One and the Son of Man," pp. 207-219.

is a pretty good representation of the Christology of Hebrews. Christ (the Logos) both pre-existed his earthly sojourn *and* was rewarded for his endurance by being adopted into divine stature once he was perfected.

Orbiting Altar

The Writer to the Hebrews tries to persuade his(?) readers not to go back to the synagogue: why retreat to an obsolete, earlier model? The logic is the same as that in the Gospel of John, which says Jesus Christ is the real thing of which the various Jewish feasts and rites were merely anticipations. Again, we are reminded of Colossians 2:16-17, which relegates the rituals of Judaism to a kind of charade pointing to Christ, having no real substance in their own right. Or think of Mark 2:18-19: since fasting was preparatory to the coming of God's kingdom, why waste your time continuing to fast when the kingdom has already dawned? But the approach taken by Hebrews is fantastically more complicated. Jesus does not just die as a sacrifice for sins; he has to offer his blood as a Yom Kippur sacrifice in the heavenly tabernacle which Moses beheld and tried to copy in crude matter here below. But that creates a problem, since Jesus as the Davidic Messiah belonged to the tribe of Judah, and all Israelite priests had to belong to Levi's tribe. So how could he qualify?

Our author reaches all the way back to Psalm 110 and Genesis 14:18-20 to enlist the enigmatic figure of Melchizedek, the priest king who offered Abraham bread and wine and whose pre-Jewish priesthood the Judean kings carried on. Whoever this Melchizedek was, he was superior in dignity even to Father Abraham, who offered to him in tribute a share of the plunder from the victory over the Elamite kings. When you consider that Levi and all his descendants were at that moment genetically latent within Abraham, this means that the Levitical priesthood was paying a tithe to Melchizedek, which only underscores his superiority over the traditional Israelite priesthood. Okay, Jesus *wasn't* a Levitical priest, but what if he were ordained to a higher, greater priesthood? Well, as the now-enthroned Son of David, Psalm 110 would apply to him, making him a priest in Melchizedek's sacerdotal order. *Voila!* Jesus is a superior priest, not one of those two-bit Levites.[342] The whole thing

---

[342] Mythicist scholar Earl Doherty, *The Jesus Puzzle: Did Christianity Begin with a Mythical Christ?* (Ottawa: Canadian Humanist Press, 1999), p. 122, 310-311, points to

sounds sort of weird, granted, but it does make a certain kind of sense.

But so what? In practical terms, what difference does it make? There is a parallel between the Levitical priests and the atoning sacrifices they offered incessantly. As to the priests, they kept dying. As mortal men, they wore out their allotted lifespan and could not continue in office, so naturally you needed to have a lot of them. But why? It seems atonement was equally transient. It didn't stick. If the sacrifices had been effective, then it would have been "one and done," right? But the Israelites, flawed humans like the rest of us, kept committing sins and kept needing sacrificial atonement, year after year. It's like treating a disease but not being able to cure it. Wouldn't it be great if there were a superior High Priest who could finally get the job done? That would require him to offer a superior sacrifice: not merely animal blood, but rather his own. And that's just what the crucified Jesus was doing. In his death he was the sacrificial victim, and, once he ascended through the veil (i.e., sloughed off his mortal flesh) separating this world from the heavenly World of God, he assumed his High Priestly role as mediator before God. Having entered that heavenly tabernacle, the one Moses glimpsed, he offered his own blood as the effective sacrifice to cleanse his people from sin.

Apparently, the writer intends that Jesus' priestly sacrifice would purify Christians so they should sin no more. Otherwise, they'd be right back in the same old leaky Levitical boat, wouldn't they? Accordingly, Hebrews says that if anyone dares sin after baptism, it would require Christ to die again to deal with it, and that he has no plans to do. "There is no more sacrifice for sins" (Heb. 10:26). Yikes! But this sobering picture is mitigated somewhat, somehow, because the ascended Christ is always on duty asking God to give sinners a break. God has not known what it is to be tempted and to succumb to it, but Jesus Christ has shared our miserable lot; "he knoweth our frame, he remembereth that we are dust" (Psalm 103:14 KJV).

Hebrews 8:4 ("Now *if he were on earth*, he would not be a priest at all") as indicating that the writer assumed Jesus was a purely celestial entity who had never set foot on earth. But I think the point is rather that Jesus lived and died in a physical body on the solid earth, but that he functions as a priest in the heavenly Tabernacle, there offering his own shed blood as a sacrifice, presumably in a state of eternal timelessness. Doherty contends that any priestly sacrifice of Christ's own blood must be identified with his death on the cross, and that if Jesus were not a priest on earth, the crucifixion sacrifice must have been a celestial event, not a historical one, and rather like, I would suggest, the cosmic self-sacrifice of Purusha in the Rig Veda. But I don't think Hebrews is referring to the shedding of his blood (on earth) as the priestly ministry, but only the offering of the already shed blood on the heavenly altar.

"Nobody knows the troubles I've seen. Nobody knows but Jesus." He can empathize (or at least sympathize) with us. He never sinned, true, but he's seen sin up close. Hebrews, I think, portrays Jesus in just the same way Roman Catholics picture the Virgin Mary, always asking her son (cf., John 2:3) to go easy on the poor hapless sinners.[343]

Jesus' likeness to Melchizedek is predicated upon the fact that both are undying immortals (Heb. 7:16).[344] They both possess "the power of an indestructible life." Of Melchizedek, the writer says he is "without father or mother or genealogy, and has neither beginning of days nor end of life, but resembling the Son of God he continues a priest forever" (7:3). Who *is* this guy? Much was made of him by various ancient religious thinkers. Philo and Josephus both understood him to be the very first priest of God Most High, even though he was a Canaanite. The Dead Sea Scroll "11Q13 Melchizedek" depicts him as an angelic redeemer appointed to judge the wicked at the End of Days. The text even calls him "Elohim," God. The mind-numbing pages of the Gnostic texts Pistis Sophia and the Books of Jeu make him an angelic being who pours out baptismal water, like Aquarius, on believers and who regathers sparks of the Pleromatic Light trapped within the malevolent Archons. The fourth-century Melchizedekian sect believed their namesake to be the heavenly intercessor for angels, while Jesus performed the same function for mortals. The Nag Hammadi apocalypse *Melchizedek* is a Sethian Gnostic scripture which seems to regard Melchizedek as an avatar of both Seth (himself anciently considered a messianic figure) and Jesus Christ. Indeed, in my judgment, Hebrews understands Melchizedek as a divine theophany who appeared to the victorious Abraham.

Most scholars think Melchizedek's divine stature was a large-scale embellishment of the simple fact that, when Melchizedek pops up in Genesis 14, nothing is said of his parents or earlier genealogical descent. It was evidently on this basis that Philo and Josephus inferred that he had been the very first priest. They were no doubt thinking of the priestly genealogies in 1 Chronicles which served as credentials for the current priestly orders. If Melchizedek served as God's priest without such credentials, it must have been because he was the very first domino in the series.

---

[343] As Jesus was moved up in the hierarchy, pretty much taking the place of his Father, Mary moved into Jesus' slot as intercessor on behalf of humanity.
[344] Even though Jesus did die for a few hours, death was a mere respite before he took up his life again, as in John 10:17.

But a great deal more might be, and was, inferred from the brief mention in Genesis. If no parents or other ancestors were ascribed to Melchizedek, it must mean he *had* none but simply descended from heaven to earth. Also, remember that Psalm 110:4 declares the king a priest in Melchizedek's order just after (in verse 3) recounting his birth from the womb of the dawn goddess Shahar. This is already evidence that Melchizedek was supposed to be a god (as were the ancient Judean kings).

Fred L. Horton, Jr.,[345] tries to reduce what Hebrews says of Melchizedek to the ancient priest's lack of hereditary credentials. That is, he thinks this is all the author of Hebrews meant by "without father or mother or genealogy, and... neither beginning of days nor end of life, but resembling the Son of God he continues a priest forever." Horton says Hebrews assumes the mere mortality of this priest-without-a-resume because it would provide a scriptural precedent for Jesus, a High Priest without the proper Levitical *bona fides*. Certainly that is part of it, but it seems to me Horton is really attempting to insulate and to isolate the Melchizedek character in Hebrews from the theological freakiness of almost the entire Melchizedek tradition which he so ably chronicles, and which has rubbed off on Hebrews. This is the same sort of maneuver we saw John A.T. Robinson attempting on Jesus himself in this epistle and James D.G. Dunn[346] performing on the savior in Philippians 2:5-11:

---

[345] Fred L. Horton, Jr., *The Melchizedek Tradition: A Critical Examination of the Sources to the Fifth Century A.D. and in the Epistle to the Hebrews.* Society for New Testament Studies Monograph Series 30 (New York: Cambridge University Press, 1976), pp. 162-163.

[346] By the way, some thirty-five years ago I had the great treat of talking briefly with James Dunn at a conference in Toronto. I gave him a sketch I had made of Melchizedek and, impudent whippersnapper that I was, I took the opportunity of questioning a statement he had made to the effect that the Qumran sectarians were not referring to the biblical Melchizedek when they wrote of the good "Melchizedek" as opposed to the evil "Melchiresa." Maybe, he suggested, the Qumran Melchizedek was just cooked up as a foil to Melchiresa (which strikes me as if someone first created the comic book villain the Reverse Flash, then dreamed up the Flash as his opposite number). I asked him if it was really likely that scripture-junkies like the Qumran sect could have seen no connection with a biblical character named Melchizedek. He backed down. As Alvie Singer once said, "Boy, if life were only like this!" (Woody Allen, "Annie Hall," in *Four Screenplays of Woody Allen: Annie Hall, Interiors, Manhattan, Stardust Memories* [New York: Random House, 1982], p. 16). Sometimes it *is*!

no heavenly pre-existence here, folks, so move along.[347]

Don't Give Up!

The famous "faith chapter," Hebrews 11, says a number of important things about the exercise of faith and presents a long catalogue of Israelite men and women who pleased God because of their willingness to believe in his promises against all odds and with no supporting empirical evidence. But the underlying theme seems to be dogged endurance of present troubles, something rendered all the more difficult by the fact that the promised deliverance at the Parousia has been forever delayed. The Olivet Discourse was written late enough to have had to deal with the same problem: "he who endures to the end will be saved" (Mark 13:13). The key passages are these:

> These all died in faith, not having received what was promised, but having seen it and greeted it from afar, and having acknowledged that they were strangers and exiles on the earth. (11:13)

> And all these, though well attested by their faith, did not receive what was promised, since God had foreseen something better for us, that apart from us they should not be made perfect. (11:39-40)

It is obvious that Hebrews means to encourage its readers not to knuckle under to persecution, but, to some, the connection with eschatological disappointment is not so obvious. The exhortation is parallel to that in Revelation 6:9-11.

> When he opened the fifth seal, I saw under the altar the souls of those who had been slain for the word of God and for the witness they had borne; they cried out with a loud voice, "O

---

[347] I consider it to be of a piece with the strange neo-rationalism of fundamentalists who insist that the fire-breathing dragon Leviathan in Job chapter 41 is really just a crocodile, or that Pharaoh's magicians did not really transform their staffs into snakes but only cast them on the floor where all could see the wands were stiffened, stuffed snake carcasses. They want to believe in the supernatural, just not too *much* of it! Only the stuff that made it into the approved theological worldview.

Sovereign Lord, holy and true, how long before thou wilt judge and avenge our blood on those who dwell upon the earth?" Then they were each given a white robe and told to rest a little longer, until the number of their fellow servants and their brethren should be complete, who were to be killed as they themselves had been.

Why do most readers not see this? It simply does not occur to them that the first-century Christians were already suffering the serial embarrassment undergone in more recent times by Jehovah's Witnesses (who predicted the Second Coming in 1914, 1925, and 1975), the Millerites/Adventists (who had it scheduled for some time in1843, then on March 21, 1844, April 10, 1844, October 22, 1844), and Harold Camping (September 6, 1994, then May 21, 2011, then October 21, 2011). Non-members do not hesitate to laugh these Chicken Littles to scorn. They do not relish the prospect that their own religion began with the same delusional fanaticism.

There is another interesting sidelight here. We read in 11:39-40 that the great heroes of the faith, their course complete, nonetheless linger at the Pearly Gates, unwilling to enter into the joy of their Lord until the readers finish their difficult journeys here below. They are being characterized in terms strongly reminiscent of the Bodhisattvas of Mahayana Buddhism, who defer their well-deserved entry into Nirvana in order to help bring home lesser mortals.

Despicable Shame (12:1-3)

The Christian pilgrimage is here likened to a race in a stadium, the bleachers packed with ghostly spectators, the saints of the past. They are waving their pennants and munching ectoplasmic hotdogs as they cheer for their favorites! Is Abraham rooting for the Presbyterian runner? Is Moses waving on the Seventh-Day Adventist? Is David yelling encouragement at the Anglicans? Or are the holy ghosts Politically Correct, hoping that all the runners cross the finish line simultaneously, so that everybody/nobody wins? Just as a robot rabbit rocketing along a rail spurs racing dogs to pursue it, the Writer to the Hebrews depicts the crucified Christ as the moving target at which the readers are to aim. "Let us run with the perseverance the race that is set before us, looking to Jesus the pioneer and perfecter of our faith, who for the joy that was set before him endured the cross, despising the shame" (12:1-2). Are we to understand Jesus overcoming his revulsion at being displayed in such an ignominious manner among the jackal-like mortals? I don't think so. Instead, it seems to me the point is that Jesus was *undaunted* at the prospect of flogging, jeering, nakedness, and crucifixion. He laughed in the face of the torment that necessarily stood in his path. He disdained the suffering for the prospect of the great good he was determined to achieve. Fourth Maccabees says exactly the same thing of the martyrs who submitted to the tortures of Antiochus Epiphanes rather than renounce the faith of Judaism. "All of these, by despising sufferings that bring death, demonstrated that reason controls the emotions."

26

The Catholic Epistles
General Delivery

Other Epistles by Other Apostles

The seven epistles we will be discussing in this chapter are a rag-tag batch. What William Wrede[348] said of the New Testament canon as a whole seems to be true especially of these General Epistles.

> Consider the following: suppose that we are living two thousand years from now and are interested in the social democratic movement in our nineteenth century. Most of the literature of social democracy is lost, but we do still have a reasonable number of sources – two popular biographies of Lassalle, an academic treatise of Marx, a few letters of Lassalle, Engels and one or two unknown workers active as agitators; then a few pamphlets two or three pages long and finally a socialist inflammatory writing describing the socialist picture of heaven upon earth – i.e., a collection of literature something like the New Testament.

Wrede cautions against assuming that the near-random selection of materials that chanced to come down to us tells us all we need to know about the religion that produced them, or that we can extract from them a systematic outline of the religion's beliefs. This is, I say, especially important to remember as we survey the seven so-called General Epistles and why they were collected for inclusion in the New Testament canon.

Though each contains distinctive and memorable gems, the letters pale in comparison to the much more substantial Pauline Epistles. Would they have seemed sufficiently important in their own right to have been included in the canon? I suspect not. To see why they were, we need to ask what motives underlay the selection of writings for the New Testament canon. The official party line, a product of orthodox-catholic theology, holds that the twenty-seven

---

[348] William Wrede, "The Task and Methods of 'New Testament Theology.'" Trans. Robert Morgan. In Robert Morgan, ed., *The Nature of New Testament Theology*. Studies in Biblical Theology, Second Series 25 (Naperville: Alec R. Allenson, 1973), p. 82.

books stood out from the larger crowd because they were *apostolic* in origin (written by Jesus' disciples, Paul, or apostolic sidekicks like Luke and Mark), *orthodox* in theology (conforming to the creeds emerging in the second century), and *catholic* in their use (not restricted to any one region or sect).[349] But a writing bearing an apostolic name would be declared a forgery if its teaching were deemed "heretical,"[350] and largely unknown writings like 2 and 3 John or Jude could be accepted on the coattails of a better-known work with which it was associated (1 John in the one case, James in the other). Scholars seem to be in agreement that the formation of the twenty-seven book New Testament was prompted by the Marcionites, the first to promulgate a uniquely Christian set of scriptures.[351] Marcion denied that the Old Testament Yahweh and the Father of Jesus were the same deity. Jesus had come to reveal his Father and to proclaim his Father's offer to adopt the creatures of Yahweh as his own children. Thus Marcion denied any Christian relevance of the Old Testament and left it to Judaism. He (and/or his followers) substituted for it a new Christian scripture, the Gospel and the Apostle. The Gospel was a shorter, earlier version of what we now call Luke. The Apostle was a collection of all ten known epistles ascribed to Paul, also in a shorter, more pristine form. Marcion believed the twelve disciples of Jesus were unable to grasp the revolutionary message of Jesus and wound up confusing Christianity with Judaism, equating the Father with Yahweh and Jesus with the Jewish Messiah. This was why Jesus had to draft Paul into his service, to preach the true gospel.

The earliest Paulinists we know of (not counting the ostensible, possibly fictive, addressees mentioned in the letters) were Marcionites and Gnostics. The Catholic (and later Montanist) theologian Tertullian called Paul "the apostle of Marcion" and "the apostle of the heretics" (*Against Marcion* III, 5, 4). There is a deafening silence among Catholic Christians in the second century regarding Paul's epistles—until Irenaeus and Tertullian begin to quote them to try to refute Marcion from his own sources. They had to take

---

[349] M.A. Smith, *From Christ to Constantine* (London: Inter-Varsity Press, 1971), pp. 64-67; Henry Chadwick, *The Early Church*. Pelican History of the Church 1 (Baltimore: Penguin Books, 1967), p. 44; John R.W. Stott, *Understanding the Bible*. Special Crusade Edition (Minneapolis: World Wide Publications, 1972), pp. 199-200.

[350] Chadwick, *Early Church*, p. 44.

[351] Hans von Campenhausen, *The Formation of the Christian Bible*. Trans. J.A. Baker (Philadelphia: Fortress Press, 1977), pp. 163, 203; Chadwick, *Early Church*, p. 81; John Knox, *Marcion and the New Testament: An Essay in the Early History of the Canon* (Chicago: University of Chicago Press, 1942).

Marcionism seriously because it was spreading like wildfire throughout the Mediterranean basin. Once they saw the Marcionite Sputnik arc its way into orbit, Catholics like Polycarp and Irenaeus had to scramble to catch up, compiling their own Christian canon to co-opt and to compete with Marcion's.

They decided it would be most expedient to embrace the "heretical" Pauline writings once they had sanitized them by the addition of a "Pastoral Stratum"[352] to the texts. And they composed three new "Pauline" epistles, 1 and 2 Timothy and Titus, to conventionalize and Catholicize Paul, to make him into "Saint Paul." Likewise, the same hand (probably Polycarp[353]) padded out the Marcionite gospel, larding it with Old Testament pastiche, to produce our Luke. But that was not enough; they added sanitized versions of three other current gospels. Mark may have originally been a "Secret Gospel" teaching Gnosticism.[354] Matthew in its extant form has Jesus commence his teaching by warning readers to ignore the Marcionite rejection of the Law and the Prophets (Matt. 5:17-19). John was at first a Gnostic gospel written, some said, by Cerinthus. Bultmann demonstrated that John was Catholicized by an "ecclesiastical redactor,"[355] whom I should, again, identify as Polycarp of Smyrna.[356] Acts was composed as a sequel to Luke, with the goal of reconciling (co-opting) Paulinists (i.e., Marcionites[357]) and Catholic Christians, whose figurehead was Peter, by having both apostles work the same miracles, give parallel speeches, etc.[358] (see my chapter on Acts). We also read in Acts of the Twelve (notably Peter, James, and John) and the brothers of Jesus (especially James the Just), because the author

---

[352] Winsome Munro, *Authority in Paul and Peter: The Identification of a Pastoral Stratum in the Pauline Corpus and 1 Peter.* Society for New Testament Studies Monograph Series 45 (New York: Cambridge University Press, 1983).

[353] Von Campenhausen, *Formation*, p. 181.

[354] Morton Smith, *The Secret Gospel: The Discovery and Interpretation of the Secret Gospel* (New York: Harper & Row, 1973); Smith, *Clement of Alexandria and a Secret Gospel of Mark* (Cambridge: Harvard University Press, 1973).

[355] Rudolf Bultmann, *The Gospel of John: A Commentary.* Trans. G.R. Beasley-Murray, R.W.N. Hoare, and J.K. Riches (Philadelphia: Westminster Press, 1971), pp. 219-220.

[356] Cf., John 15:5: "He who abides in me, and I in him, he it is who bears *much fruit*" (*karpon polun* in Greek).

[357] Joseph B. Tyson, *Marcion and Luke-Acts: A Defining Struggle* (Columbia: University of South Carolina Press, 2006).

[358] Ferdinand Christian Baur, *Paul the Apostle of Jesus Christ: His Life and Works, His Epistles and Teachings: A Contribution to a Critical History of Early Christianity.* Trans. Eduard Zeller. Theological Translation Fund Library. (London: Williams & Norgate, Two Volumes, 1873-1875; rpt. Two Volumes in One, Peabody: Hendrickson Publishers, 2003), vol. I, p. 6.

wanted to emphasize the importance of non-Pauline apostles, to dilute the Marcionite concentration on Paul.[359]

And here is the reason the General (or "Catholic") Epistles are included at all. They were intended as a counterweight to Marcion's favorite, Paul,[360] the theological elephant in the room. In general, these brief epistles correspond to the non-Pauline apostles we meet in Acts: Peter, John, James the Just, and, implicitly, Jude, another of the brothers of Jesus (Acts 1:14). Note that the so-called Johannine Epistles are actually anonymous. No doubt their traditional ascription to John, son of Zebedee, reflects the compiler's agenda. The attempt to counter-balance Paul is finally pretty lame due to the slim pickings available. (Why did the compiler not include the Epistle of Barnabas, since he, too, is prominent in Acts? No great mystery there: Barnabas' antipathy toward the Old Testament must have seemed dangerously close to Marcionism.)

James

This beloved digest of practical piety speaks for itself, but its background questions require discussion. Who wrote it (or *didn't*)? What are its major influences? How Christian is it?

A lot of men in the ancient world were named "James" (Iacobos in Greek, Yakub in Hebrew). Which one of them (if any!) wrote this document? I think the best guess is that "James" by itself, no epithet, no qualifier, no patronymic, is designed to make the reader think at once of James the Just, "brother of the Lord" (Gal. 1:19), and the *primus inter pares* of the Jerusalem Pillars (Gal. 2:9). All the *other* guys had to add on "the son of Zebedee," "of Alphaeus," "the Less," etc. But James the Just might be a pseudonym. Jerome thought so. By no means denigrating the epistle, Jerome suggested that some admirer of the historical James had written it in his honor. One big reason for thinking so is the good Greek in which the letter is written. The Holy Land had been thoroughly Hellenized, true, but given the description of James in early sources as a strict, Torah-observant Jew (Gal. 2:12), it seems rather unlikely he could have been as fluent in Greek as this letter would imply. Here is the description of James from the second-century Jewish-Christian historian Hegesippus:

---

[359] Knox, *Marcion*, p. 160.
[360] Knox, *Marcion*, p. 161; David Trobisch, *The First Edition of the New Testament* (New York: Oxford University Press, 2000), pp. 59-60.

> He drank no wine or intoxicating liquor and ate no animal
> food; no razor came near his head; he did not smear himself
> with oil, and took no baths. He alone was permitted to enter
> the Holy Place, for his garments were not of wool, but of
> linen. He used to enter the Sanctuary alone, and was often
> found on his knees, beseeching forgiveness for the people, so
> that his knees grew hard like as a camel's from his continually
> bending them in worship of God and beseeching forgiveness
> for the people. (quoted in Eusebius, *Ecclesiastical History*
> 2.23.5-6)[361]

I can't resist reproducing the unflattering portrait of James from Nikos
Kazantzakis's *The Last Temptation of Christ*.[362] Somehow it seems
consistent with the early tradition.

> Jacob the Pharisee appeared, his arms loaded with amulets.
> He was publishing the special grace of each: these cured
> smallpox, colic and erysipelas; these expelled demons; the
> most powerful and expensive killed your enemies.... He
> noticed the ragamuffins and cripples, recognized them. His
> envenomed mouth cackled maliciously: "Go to the devil!" and
> he spat three times into the air to be rid of them.

When asked his opinion of his brother Jesus, he replies, "He's no
brother of mine; I want no part of him!"[363] (cf., John 7:3-7).

A related issue is that of the apparent Stoic coloring of the
epistle. Right out of the gate, we hear instruction reminiscent of the
basic principle of Stoicism.

> Count it all joy, my brethren, when you meet various trials,
> for you know that the testing of your faith produces
> steadfastness. And let steadfastness have its full effect, that
> you may be perfect and complete, lacking in nothing. [...]
> Every good endowment and every perfect gift is from above,
> coming down from the Father of lights with whom there is no

---

[361] Eusebius, The *History of the Church*. Trans. G.A. Williamson. Penguin Classics
(Baltimore: Penguin Books, 1965), p. 100.
[362] Nikos Kazantzakis, *The Last Temptation of Christ*. Trans. P.A. Bien. Bantam Modern
Classics (New York: Bantam Books, 1961), p. 361.
[363] Kazantzakis, *Last Temptation*, p. 363.

variation or shadow due to change. (1:2-4, 17)

The popular philosophy of Stoicism, virtually a religion unto itself, taught that the only thing of value is *virtue* and that all else is indifferent. They believed that the mythical Zeus stood for the divine Logos permeating and directing all events. This meant that every event that befalls a person, pleasant or unpleasant, is ordained by God to increase the individual's virtue, to build his character. The only right response to the day's events, even if you have to swallow hard, is to greet them, appreciate them. Your chariot was crushed by a meteorite on the way to work? So what? You should be glad for the opportunity afforded you to grow in patience and to cultivate inner detachment from material possessions (cf., 1 Cor. 7:29-31). Eventually, you'll really start feeling it. Virtue, as Aristotle knew, is a skill, and this is how you hone it.

Stoicism had an "all or nothing" view of virtue: you either had it or you didn't. Virtue had to be perfect or it wasn't virtue. Again, James sounds pretty Stoic:

> For whoever keeps the whole law but fails in one point has become guilty of all of it. For he who said, "Do not commit adultery," said also, "Do not kill." If you do not commit adultery but do kill, you have become a transgressor of the law. (Jas. 2:10-11)

It would not be surprising to find elements of Stoic philosophy in a Jewish setting. Josephus saw a close analogy between Pharisaism and Stoicism, describing the first in terms of the second.

> Now, for the Pharisees, they live meanly, and despise delicacies in diet; and they follow the conduct of reason; and what that prescribes to them as good for them they do; and they think they ought earnestly to strive to observe reason's dictates for practice. [...] and when they determine that all things are done by fate, they do not take away the freedom from men of acting as they think fit; since their notion is, that it hath pleased God to make a temperament, whereby what he wills is done, but so that the will of man can act virtuously or viciously. (*Antiquities* XVIII, I. 3)[364]

---

[364] *The Works of Flavius Josephus.* Trans. William Whiston (London: Ward, Lock & Co., n.d.), p. 471.

Stoics held that living by reason is the way to live according the divine Reason (the Logos). They also believed that all circumstances are predestined since all is arranged in accordance with the Logos' providence but that human choice is free, since it is up to the individual whether he will react wisely to circumstances and so grow in virtue. Fourth Maccabees is even more overtly Stoic in its exhortations:

> The subject that I am about to discuss is most philosophical, that is, whether devout reason is sovereign over the emotions. So it is right for me to advise you to pay earnest attention to philosophy. For the subject is essential to everyone who is seeking knowledge, and in addition it includes the praise of the highest virtue ~ I mean, of course, rational judgment. If, then, it is evident that reason rules over those emotions that hinder self-control, namely, gluttony and lust, it is also clear that it masters the emotions that hinder one from justice, such as malice, and those that stand in the way of courage, namely anger, fear, and pain. Some might perhaps ask, "If reason rules the emotions, why is it not sovereign over forgetfulness and ignorance?" Their attempt at argument is ridiculous! For reason does not rule its own emotions, but those that are opposed to justice, courage, and self-control; and it is not for the purpose of destroying them, but so that one may not give way to them. I could prove to you from many and various examples that reason is dominant over the emotions, but I can demonstrate it best from the noble bravery of those who died for the sake of virtue, Eleazar and the seven brothers and their mother. All of these, by despising sufferings that bring death, demonstrated that reason controls the emotions. (4 Macc. 1:1-9)

This means that "James" could be simultaneously Jewish and Stoic, but would James the Just have dipped into Greek philosophy? The letter is explicitly addressed "to the twelve tribes in the Diaspora," and it was most probably written by a Diaspora Jew.

Just how Christian is this epistle? There is no real discussion of Jesus, only a pair of mentions (1:1 and 2:1). The references to "the Lord" could just as well be to Yahweh. This almost makes one suspect that the letter was originally a product of Hellenistic Judaism and that Polycarp (or whoever) superficially Christianized it so he could use it as an epistle of James the Just to beef up his "other apostles" section.

Ironically, the thing that most strongly implies the letter *is* a Christian document is its critical stance toward Paul! Our author plainly has Romans open in front of him. James 2:14-26 is a point-for-point rejoinder to Romans 3:27-4:6.

> *Paul*: Then what becomes of our boasting? It is excluded. On what principle? On the principle of works? No, but on the principle of faith. For we hold that a man is justified by faith apart from works of law. (Rom. 3:27-28)

> *James*: What does it profit, my brethren, if a man says he has faith but has not works? Can his faith save him? [...] So faith by itself, if it has no works, is dead. (2:14, 17)

> *Paul*: Or is God the God of Jews only? Is he not the God of Gentiles also? Yes, of Gentiles also, since God is one. (Rom. 3:29-30a)

> *James*: You believe that God is one; you do well. Even the demons believe—and shudder. (Jas. 2:19)

> *Paul*: What then shall we say about Abraham, our forefather according to the flesh? For if Abraham was justified by works, he has something to boast about, but not before God. For what does the scripture say? "Abraham believed God, and it was reckoned to him as righteousness." (Rom. 4:1-3)

> *James*: Do you want to be shown, you shallow man, that faith apart from works is barren? Was not Abraham our father justified by works, when he offered his son Isaac upon the altar? You see that faith was active along with his works, and faith was completed by works, and the scripture was fulfilled which says, "Abraham believed God, and it was reckoned to him as righteousness." (2:20-23)

It is a very longstanding problem that James contradicts Paul on this crucial issue of justification by faith. You can see why Martin Luther denigrated James as "an epistle of straw," relegating it to an appendix to the New Testament. But it is worse than that. It would be bad enough if James got Paul right, but in fact he misunderstood him. The author of the Epistle of James was not a contemporary of Paul. For one thing, he knows Paul only from a published Pauline epistle, not personally (contra Gal. 1:19; 2:9). For another, "James" has lost sight of the real issue for Paul. Paul was talking about "works of the law," works required by the Torah, the ritual and dietary regulations whose purpose was to safeguard Jewish ethnicity over against Gentile assimilation. But our author thinks Paul means moral good deeds. Ironically, the two writers might not have clashed if the two of them had sat down to discuss the issue (though Galatians 2:9 implies they *did* disagree on the question). But James doesn't even *understand* Paul. Good luck squaring *that* with a doctrine of scriptural inspiration and authority.

First Peter

Right off the bat, we have the same problem we had with James: the Greek seems way too good for a bumpkin like Simon Peter (Acts 4:13). It's hard to get around that. Some hit upon the desperate expedient of making Silvanus the real author, writing the letter for Peter's signature.[365] How do we know this Silvanus was any better versed in Greek than Peter? And besides, "By Silvanus, a faithful brother as I regard him, I have written briefly to you" (5:12) would ordinarily mean no more than that Silvanus carried the letter for Peter (cf., Eph. 6:21-22; Phil. 2:25; Col. 4:7-9), and that the "faithful brother" business denotes a letter of recommendation for Silvanus to minister among them (as in Romans 16:1-2). At most, it might imply he was the apostle's stenographer (cf., Rom. 16:22). The futility of this contrivance is illustrated in this statement of J.N.D. Kelly: "Of course, if he [Peter] is the author of I Peter, he can hardly have composed it himself." Huh? Then he *isn't* the author of 1 Peter.

Plus, 1 Peter 4:12-19; 5:8-9 refer to widespread persecutions, but no such thing occurred in the lifetime of Simon Peter. As far as our ancient sources tell us, there was no systematic persecution of Christians till the reign of Trajan, who died in 117.

But the real killer for Petrine authorship, I would say, is the way the author describes the Passion of Jesus Christ.

---

[365] J.N.D. Kelly, *The Epistles of Peter and Jude.* Harper's New Testament Commentaries (New York: Harper & Row, 1969), p. 31. Granted, Kelly didn't insist on Silvanus, but it must have been some friend of Peter with better Greek than the Galilean fisherman could muster (p. 32).

For to this you have been called, because Christ also suffered for you, leaving you an example, that you should follow in his steps. He committed no sin; no guile was found on his lips. When he was reviled, he did not revile in return; when he suffered, he did not threaten; but he trusted to him who judges justly. He himself bore our sins in his body on the tree, that we might die to sin and live to righteousness. By his wounds you have been healed. For you were straying like sheep, but have now returned to the Shepherd and Guardian of your souls. (1 Pet. 2:21-25)

This might sound familiar. It is obviously derived from Isaiah 53:4-9.

> Surely he has borne our griefs
>   *and carried our sorrows;*
> yet we esteemed him stricken,
>   smitten by God, and afflicted.
> But he was wounded for our transgressions,
>   he was bruised for our iniquities;
> upon him was the chastisement that made us whole,
>   and *with his stripes we are healed.*
> *All we like sheep have gone astray;*
>   we have turned every one to his own way;
> and [Yahweh] has laid on him
>   the iniquity of us all.
> He was oppressed, and he was afflicted,
>   yet he opened not his mouth;
> like a lamb that is led to the slaughter,
>   *and like a sheep that before its shearers is dumb,*
>   *so he opened not his mouth.*
> By oppression and judgment he was taken away;
>   and as for his generation, who considered
> that he was cut off out of the land of the living,
>   stricken for the transgression of my people?
> And they made his grave with the wicked
>   and with a rich man in his death,
> *although he had done no violence,*
>   *and there was no deceit in his mouth.*
> Yet it was the will of [Yahweh] to bruise him;
>   he has put him to grief;
> when he makes himself an offering for sin,

> he shall see his offspring, he shall prolong his days;
> *the will of* [*Yahweh*] *shall* prosper in his hand;
>   he shall see the fruit of the travail of his soul and be
> satisfied;
> by his knowledge *shall the righteous one, my servant,*
>   *make many to be accounted righteous;*
>   *and he shall bear their iniquities.*

The striking thing here is that the writer knows only the *scripture passage* that early Christians thought predicted Jesus' sufferings. If the author were really the historical Simon Peter, wouldn't we expect him to share his own tearful memories of Jesus' vicious whipping and cruel crucifixion? But our author does not. He only "knows" about all this from having read scripture, and *Old* Testament scripture at that![366]

Frank L. Cross[367] made a form-critical breakthrough in the study of this epistle when he showed how much sense the letter would make (most of it, anyway) if it had originated as an Easter baptismal liturgy/homily. Up until 4:12 (as subsequent scholars pointed out; see below), 1 Peter speaks repeatedly, almost incessantly, about *suffering*, both the sufferings of the Redeemer and of his believers. Yet the word "death" is not used of Jesus. Why? Not because the author was some kind of docetist, but rather because of the punning relationship between the early Christian name for Easter, namely, the Pascha (transliterating the Hebrew for Passover), and two Greek words for "suffering," i.e., *paschō* and *pathēma* (from which we get "pathos"). Thus the Pascha was (re)defined as the feast of the Suffering of Christ. This early, they had not divided Good Friday from Easter but commemorated both together: Easter vigil *and* sunrise celebration.[368] The references to Christian suffering (until 4:12) do not in fact have Roman persecution in view but rather the baptismal notion of uniting with the Passion of Christ in the waters of baptism (cf., Rom. 6:2-4).[369] If the author were already thinking of Christians suffering at the hands of Rome, could he possibly have written 2:13-17; 3:13,[370] which

---

[366] G.A. Wells, *The Jesus of the Early Christians: A Study in Christian Origins* (London: Pemberton Books, 1971), pp. 153-154, asks if this odd fact does not even raise the question of whether there was any historical memory of the event at all, and consequently, *was* there any original event for anybody to remember? Maybe the whole thing began as fiction based on passages like Isaiah 53 and Psalm 22.

[367] F.L. Cross, *I. Peter: A Paschal Liturgy* (London: A.R. Mowbray, 1954).

[368] Cross, *Paschal Liturgy*, p. 18.

[369] Cross, *Paschal Liturgy*, Chapter III. "Suffering in Christ," pp. 18-22.

[370] Cross, *Paschal Liturgy*, p. 13.

speak of the Emperor as a guardian of civil order who punishes the wicked and protects the righteous?[371] This isn't exactly the Beast from the Abyss (Rev. 13:5-8)!

Another widely attested theme of Easter preaching was the deliverance of the Israelites from Egypt in the Exodus, obviously because of the very name Pascha (Passover).[372] Note that 1 Peter 1:18-19 (like 1 Corinthians 5:7), speaks of Christ as the Passover lamb whose blood provides redemption, as the lamb's blood smeared on the lintels and doorframes of the Goshen ghetto did. Likewise, 1 Peter 1:13 urges its audience to "gird up your minds," now recognizable as a reference back to Exodus 12:11, where the Israelites, ready to leave Egypt at any moment, ate "with your loins girded." First Peter 1:16 quotes Leviticus 11:44-45, "You shall be holy, for I am holy," and this, too, is a reference to the Exodus: "For I am Yahweh who brought you up out of the land of Egypt." Again, 1 Peter 2:9-10 reproduces most of Exodus 19:4-6.

> You have seen what I did to the Egyptians, and how I bore you on eagles' wings and brought you to myself. Now therefore, if you will obey my voice and keep my covenant, you shall be my own possession among all peoples; for all the earth is mine, and you shall be to me a kingdom of priests and a holy nation. (Exod. 19:4-6)

> But you are a chosen race, a royal priesthood, a holy nation, God's own people, that you may declare the wonderful deeds of him who called you out of darkness into his marvelous light. Once you were no people but now you are God's people; once you had not received mercy but now you have received mercy. (1 Pet. 9-10)

So much for the Easter character of 1 Peter; what has it got to do with *baptism?* It was apparently R. Perdelwitz in 1911 who first recognized 1 Peter as a baptismal homily, though W. Bornemann came up with the same idea on his own in 1919. Very many scholars have endorsed it since then. First Peter 3:20-21 explicitly mentions water baptism, and

---

[371] G.A. Wells, *Did Jesus Exist?* (London: Elek/Pemberton Books, 1975), p. 45: "The author of this latter statement surely knew of no tradition which made Pilate responsible for Jesus' death!"

[372] That the Exodus was connected with Christian baptism is evident from 1 Corinthians 10:2.

in a manner suggesting the occasion is a baptism ceremony: "Baptism *now* saves you." Admittedly, the "now" could just as easily be a contrast with the immediately preceding analogy with Noah saving his family during the Flood, another comparison common in ancient baptismal imagery. Ark then, baptism now. But there are several more "nows" (1:6, 12; 2:2, 10, 25; 3:21), which *do* tip the balance toward the listeners dripping, or getting ready to drip.

Cross regards 3:19-20a, the descent of Christ into Hell, as another baptismal reference, as Holy Saturday was part of the Easter complex, and the mythic trip to the Netherworld was an element of baptismal imagery. But his reasoning is based on an ancient copyist error. Remember, the ancient manuscripts left no spaces between words, and what a scribe took as "*en ō kai,*" or "in which also," must originally have been the name "Enoch." It was Enoch who, in 1 Enoch 6-8; 12:3-13:10; 18:12-21:10, journeyed to the prison of the fallen Watchers who had corrupted humanity, leading to the Flood (Gen. 6:1-4). They prevailed on him to plead with God for mercy, but he returned with the divine reply, "Tough luck." Thus it was Enoch, not Jesus, who went to proclaim to the spirits imprisoned since the days of Noah.[373]

First Peter also addresses its audience as those who have been *reborn* (1:3, 23), which was believed to happen, not when one signed the card in the back of an evangelistic booklet or walked forward at a Billy Graham Crusade, but when one was baptized. The tell-tale reference at 2:2 to drinking milk is an obvious rebirth image. Ancient Christians, in their First Communion, were actually given three cups to drink: water, *milk*, and wine.

We find in 2:3-3:7 one of the *Haustafeln* (household codes) defining proper duties for, in this case, husbands, wives, and household servants. Cross thinks this was a reiteration of the moral catechism imparted to the baptismal candidates beforehand. Winsome Munro makes this part of the Pastoral Stratum subsequently inserted into the epistle, as in Colossians and Ephesians,[374] but I have to think of Luke 3:10-14, where *prior to baptism*, John gives moral instructions to various groups (including soldiers and toll collectors) on their proper duties. This is especially interesting in light of the strong possibility that the Ecclesiastical Redactor of Luke was the same as the author of the Pastoral Epistles and the Pastoral Stratum.

---

[373] J. Rendel Harris as discussed in Kelly, *Peter and Jude*, p. 152. Kelly rejects the suggestion, though, ironically, he does think the scenario of the disobedient spirits comes right out of 1 Enoch. Uh, *what* do two plus two equal?

[374] Munro, *Authority in Paul and Peter*, p. 37.

Conzelmann already pointed out the bourgeois character of the Baptizer's instructions, unique to Luke among the gospels, as one of several indications of Luke toning down earlier apocalyptic enthusiasm in order to reacclimate Christians to a long stay in the mundane world.[375]

Finally, Cross notes a surprising new possible reading of 1 Peter 3:3, where women are told not to braid their hair and not to bedeck themselves with gold jewelry and fancy gowns. We have always taken this to mean that pious women must shun such adornment as a matter of course, and Mennonite and Amish women have obeyed. But it turns out that Hippolytus of Rome, speaking of baptismal decorum in the second century, wrote, "the women... shall have loosed their hair, and laid aside their gold ornaments. Let no one go down to the water having any alien object with them."[376] And, of course, male and female alike had to disrobe and get baptized naked ("Naked I came from my mother's womb, and naked I shall return" Job 1:21), then don a white robe (cf. Col. 3:9-10; Eph. 4:22-24).[377] Presumably, once the ceremony was over, the women could get dolled up again.[378]

C. Leslie Mitton demonstrated that the author of 1 Peter made significant use not only of Exodus and Isaiah but also of Ephesians. Consider the parallels.

> *Ephesians 1:3:* Blessed be the God and Father of our Lord Jesus Christ, who has blessed us in Christ with every spiritual blessing in the heavenly places.

> *1 Peter 1:3:* Blessed be the God and Father of our Lord Jesus Christ! By his great mercy we have been born anew to a living hope through the resurrection of Jesus Christ from the dead.

> *Ephesians 1:18-20:* having the eyes of your hearts enlightened, that you may know what is the hope to which he has called

---

[375] Hans Conzelmann, *The Theology of Saint Luke.* Trans. Geoffrey Buswell (New York: Harper & Row, 1961), p. 102.

[376] Cross, *Paschal Liturgy*, p. 34. Once, when I was about to get put under for surgery, the doctors told me they might have to cut my wedding ring off my chubby finger. I see a real analogy here. (Turns out they didn't have to, though.)

[377] Jonathan Z. Smith, "The Garments of Shame." In Smith, *Map Is not Territory: Studies in the History of Religions* (Chicago: University of Chicago Press, 1993), pp. 4-8.

[378] This reminds me of the joke in which a Catholic monk is scrutinizing early New Testament manuscripts and suddenly slaps his forehead, exclaiming, "Oh my God! It said 'celebrate!'"

you, what are the riches of his glorious inheritance in the saints, and what is the immeasurable greatness of his power in us who believe, according to the working of his great might which he accomplished in Christ when he raised him from the dead and made him sit at his right hand in the heavenly places.

1 Peter 1:3-5: Blessed be the God and Father of our Lord Jesus Christ! By his great mercy we have been born anew to a living hope through the resurrection of Jesus Christ from the dead, and to an inheritance which is imperishable, undefiled, and unfading, kept in heaven for you, who by God's power are guarded through faith for a salvation ready to be revealed in the last time.

Ephesians 2:18-22: for through him we both have access in one Spirit to the Father. So then you are no longer strangers and sojourners, but you are fellow citizens with the saints and members of the household of God, built upon the foundation of the apostles and prophets, Christ Jesus himself being the cornerstone, in whom the whole structure is joined together and grows into a holy temple in the Lord; in whom you also are built into it for a dwelling place of God in the Spirit.

1 Peter 2:4-6, 11: Come to him, to that living stone, rejected by men but in God's sight chosen and precious; and like living stones be yourselves built into a spiritual house, to be a holy priesthood, to offer spiritual sacrifices acceptable to God through Jesus Christ. For it stands in scripture: "Behold, I am laying in Zion a stone, a cornerstone chosen and precious, and he who believes in him will not be put to shame." [...] Beloved, I beseech you as aliens and exiles to abstain from the passions of the flesh that wage war against your soul.

Ephesians 1:20-22: which he accomplished in Christ when he raised him from the dead and made him sit at his right hand in the heavenly places, far above all rule and authority and power and dominion, and above every name that is named, not only in this age but also in that which is to come; and he has put all things under his feet and has made him the head over all things for the church.

1 Peter 3:22: who has gone into heaven and is at the right hand of God, with angels, authorities, and powers subject to him.

Ephesians 3:9: and to make all men see what is the plan of the mystery hidden for ages in God who created all things.

1 Peter 1:20: He was destined before the foundation of the world but was made manifest at the end of the times for your sake.

Ephesians 3:20: Now to him who by the power at work within us is able to do far more abundantly than all that we ask or think.

1 Peter 1:12: It was revealed to them that they were serving not themselves but you, in the things which have now been announced to you by those who preached the good news to you through the Holy Spirit sent from heaven, things into which angels long to look.

Ephesians 4:17-19: you must no longer live as the Gentiles do, in the futility of their minds; they are darkened in their understanding, alienated from the life of God because of the ignorance that is in them, due to their hardness of heart; they have become callous and have given themselves up to licentiousness, greedy to practice every kind of uncleanness.

1 Peter 1:14: As obedient children, do not be conformed to the passions of your former ignorance.

As Willi Marxsen notes,[379] the original homily text ended with 4:11. The author of it made use of Ephesians with no particular hidden agenda; he simply liked Ephesians and used it. But once the material from 4:12 on was added and the name "Peter" was affixed, we have what F.C. Baur called a "Catholicizing" document, one which, like 2 Peter and Acts, either presupposes or tries to facilitate a reconciliation between Paulinist and Petrinist Christian factions. The ascription to

---

[379] Willi Marxsen, *Introduction to the New Testament: An Approach to Its Problems* (Philadelphia: Fortress Press, 1974), p. 234.

Peter combined with the Paulinist content puts a new spin on the text. It gives us a "Peter" who sounds just like Paul. I should think it was the Ecclesiastical Redactor, Polycarp, who made these alterations to advance his agenda of co-opting Paul.

Second Peter

Everything about this letter fairly *screams* "pseudepigraph!" Its pseudonymity is very nearly the subject of the letter.[380] The form of the name, "Symeon Peter," appears to be an archaizing device, like "Simeon" in Acts 15:14. Even the gospels do not refer to him in this way. The author claims (3:1) to be writing a sequel to his first letter, 1 Peter, but that cannot be, for the Greek of this letter is markedly different from that of 1 Peter. Equally fluent, it is however almost Byzantine in its complexity. And the author seems momentarily to forget himself, that he is supposed to be "Symeon Peter," when he writes, "you should remember the predictions of the holy prophets and the commandment of the Lord and Savior through your apostles. First of all you must understand this, that scoffers will come in the last days with scoffing,[381] following their own passions" (3:2-3). *Wait* a second! Isn't this guy supposed to *be* one of those apostles from the misty past who *predicted* the events of the reader's day?

Here's what accounts for this embarrassing slip of the mask. The writer copied most of the Epistle of Jude into his own chapter 3, and at this point he is reproducing Jude verses 17-18: "But you must remember, beloved, the predictions of the apostles of our Lord Jesus Christ; they said to you, 'In the last time there will be scoffers, following their own ungodly passions.'" Jude wasn't claiming to be an apostle, so he didn't trip over an anachronism. The author of 2 Peter somehow failed to notice the problem he was creating when he just copied the passage from Jude.

But back to 2 Peter. He changes the content of the ancient apostolic prediction.

"Where is the promise of his coming? For ever since

---

[380] Michael Green does a heroic job of defending the Petrine authorship (E.M.B. Green, *2 Peter Reconsidered*. Tyndale New Testament Lecture, 1960 [London: Tyndale Press, 1961]), but we must remember that, as F.C. Baur always said, while anything is *possible*, the historian asks what is *probable*.

[381] That's probably why we call them scoffers.

the fathers fell asleep, all things have continued as they were from the beginning of creation." They deliberately ignore this fact, that by the word of God heavens existed long ago, and an earth formed out of water and by means of water, through which the world that then existed was deluged with water and perished. But by the same word the heavens and earth that now exist have been stored up for fire, being kept until the day of judgment and destruction of ungodly men. But do not ignore this one fact, beloved, that with the Lord one day is as a thousand years, and a thousand years as one day. The Lord is not slow about his promise as some count slowness, but is forbearing toward you, not wishing that any should perish, but that all should reach repentance. (3:3-4)

Uh-oh! Looks like the Parousia has been delayed! Christians had been scurrying around like Jehovah's Witnesses, preaching, "Millions now living will never die!" And now maybe they're wishing they hadn't, because, like Harold Camping's dupes, now they're taking it from all sides (and one might say, deservedly so!). They no doubt felt like the disappointed Emmaus disciples, dreading the ridicule they were sure to receive when they got back home. "For ever since the fathers fell asleep, all things have continued as they were from the beginning of creation." Bultmann said the same thing: "History did not come to an end, and, as every schoolboy knows, it will continue to run its course."[382]

Who are "the fathers" who "fell asleep" long ago ("ever since...")? They are those apostles who predicted today's scoffers. One of those apostles, of course, was Simon Peter, now apparently writing from the Great Beyond. Mark 13:30 promises that "this generation will not pass away before all these things [apocalyptic omens] take place." But most of these contemporaries *did* die. So in Mark 9:1, Jesus promises that "*some* standing here will not taste death before they see the kingdom of God come with power." But more and more died, until only one was left: "The saying spread abroad among the brethren that this disciple was not to die" (John 21:23), but he *did*, and the author of the Johannine Appendix (John chapter 21) decided he'd better reinterpret "the saying" just as the Adventists found it expedient to reinterpret William Miller's prediction. Second Peter

---

[382] Rudolf Bultmann, "New Testament and Mythology." In Hans Werner Bartsch, ed., *Kerygma and Myth: A Theological Debate.* Trans. Reginald H. Fuller. Harper Torchbooks/Cloister Library (New York: Harper & Row, 1961), P. 5.

takes another approach, admitting there *has* in fact been a considerable delay, just as the scoffers allege, but that they (and we) ought to understand (reinterpret) that delay as a gracious reprieve: God is giving sinners an extension, more time to repent. If he could *shorten* the days for the sake of humanity (Mark 13:20), why shouldn't he *lengthen* them for the same reason?[383] At any rate, we are talking about someone who is writing long after the passing of that whole "apostolic" generation. Not Pete.

The author of the so-called Gospel according to Matthew could not have been the disciple Matthew because he did not share his own memories but instead just embellished a previous work, Mark's gospel. And 2 Peter cannot have been the work of Simon Peter the disciple for the same reason. Can we really imagine this Prince of Apostles thinly veiling the obscure Epistle of Jude as a chapter of his own work? The apologetic dodge is that, well, er, maybe Peter and Jude independently utilized the same irresistibly terrific text. (What would William of Occam have to say about such multiplication of hypotheses?) And is Jude all *that* great? As we will shortly see, Jude itself is a derivative echo of 1 Enoch. Just picture Simon Peter reading Jude: "Oh *wow!* I gotta get me one of *these!*") And even if Jude *were* irresistible as epistolary filler, can Peter the Great have had so little to say of his own?

Another blatant tip-off to the pseudepigraphical character of 2 Peter is its brief discussion of Paul. The writer is very obviously a man of the second century. For one thing, he forbids any individual interpretation of scripture, in favor of the ecclesiastical party line, which, like the College of Cardinals' "incense smoke filled room" selection of a new pope, is simply identified with the truth of God (2 Pet. 1:20-21). And those scriptures include the collected epistles of Paul ("all his letters," 3:15-16)! What? Collected already in Peter's lifetime? And considered "scripture"? Come on! Here we find the Catholicizing epistle *par excellence*. Note the gingerly "kid gloves" treatment of "our beloved brother Paul" and the attempt to control (in a Catholic direction) the interpretation of the Pauline Epistles. Anyone else's readings of them are the perverse spewings of deranged

---

[383] Most readers seem, inadvertently, to make the author a text-twisting idiot when they take 2 Peter 3:8, "with the Lord a day is as a thousand years, and a thousand years as one day" (quoting Psalm 90:4), to mean that Jesus did mean the Parousia would happen "soon," but (heh-heh) he was talking in terms of God's time scale, not *ours*. Of course, all our author meant was "Don't worry: God's got all the time in the world. He's in no hurry."

minds. So, the writer warns his readers, "Go ahead and read those letters, brethren; just remember, they don't mean, they *can't* mean, what those nasty Marcionites, encratites, and Gnostics *say* they mean."[384] That would, of course, be "private interpretation" (1:20 KJV).

All the preceding allows us to award the title of "pious fraud" when we come to 2 Peter 1:16-18:

> For we did not follow cleverly devised myths when we made known to you the power and coming of our Lord Jesus Christ, but we were eyewitnesses of his majesty. For when he received honor and glory from God the Father and the voice was borne to him by the Majestic Glory, "This is my beloved Son, with whom I am well pleased," we heard this voice borne from heaven, for we were with him on the holy mountain.

Sure you did. *Sure* you were. And I was there when Lincoln gave the Gettysburg Address. Note the pompous ecclesiastical lingo: "the holy mountain," "the Majestic Glory." Not following cleverly devised myths? Hell, this is *one* of them![385]

Jude

Who is this "Jude," anyway? Not an uncommon Jewish name, right? Actually, our word "Jew" comes from this name, "Judah." Our author is, or at least wants us to *think* he is, a *particular* Jude, namely the brother of someone named "James" (Jacob). Well, *that* narrows it down, right? Isn't that kind of like saying you're "Bill, the brother of Frank"? There are a lot of Jameses, too. But I think scholars are right to point out that, if the writer deems "James" as so obvious or famous as not to need further specification, it has to be a James Christian readers would automatically identify as James the Just, pope of the Jerusalem church. Hence Jude is supposed to be another of the brothers of Jesus listed in Mark 6:3. But is it really he? Well, it's always possible, but it seems unlikely to me since the brief letter is largely

---

[384] It reminds me of the historically recent "opening up" of the Bible to the Roman Catholic laity: "Go ahead and read it for yourself, but we'll tell you what it means."

[385] Opponents of the Christ Myth Theory like to gloat over the "fact" that not even the ancient critics of Christianity ever claimed that Jesus was cut from whole cloth. But don't these verses imply that at least some of them *did*?

cribbed from 1 Enoch, a book some early Christians (like Tertullian) thought ought to be included in the Old Testament. Jude, whoever he actually was, thought so, too.

Everybody knows by now that this brief epistle quotes 1 Enoch verbatim:

> It was of these also that Enoch in the seventh generation from Adam prophesied, saying, "Behold, the Lord came with his holy myriads, to execute judgment on all, and to convict all the ungodly of all their deeds of ungodliness which they have committed in such an ungodly way, and of all the harsh things which ungodly sinners have spoken against him." (Jude 14-15, quoting 1 Enoch 3:9)

But that's not the end of it. Jude's use of Enoch is more extensive than is usually recognized. David Persuitte[386] has shown that Jude is full of clear allusions to and paraphrases of 1 Enoch. For instance, Jude verse 6 ("And the angels that did not keep their own position but left their proper dwelling have been kept by him in eternal chains in the nether gloom until the judgment of the great day.") is derived from 1 Enoch 10:12b, "Bind them tight for seventy generations in the caverns of the earth, till the day of their judgment... till the judgment that lasts for ever and ever is consummated." Jude 12b ("waterless clouds, carried along by winds; fruitless trees in late autumn, twice dead, uprooted") comes from 1 Enoch 2:3, "Behold the summer and the winter, how all the earth is filled with water, and clouds and dew and rain rest upon it," and from 1 Enoch 3:1, "Observe and behold how all the trees appear as though they had withered and shed all their leaves." Jude 13 ("wild waves of the sea, casting up the foam of their own shame; wandering stars for whom the nether gloom of darkness has been reserved for ever.") is taken from 1 Enoch 2:1, "Observe everything taking place in the heavens, how they do not alter their orbits, and the lights which are in the heaven, how they all rise and set, in order each in its season, and transgress not against their assigned order," as well as from 1 Enoch 10:4-6, "And again the Lord said to Raphael, 'Bind Azazel hand and foot and pitch him into the darkness... and cover him with darkness, and let him remain there forever, and blindfold him to prevent his seeing light.'"[387]

---

[386] Personal correspondence.

[387] Witness the sad predicament of fundamentalists who don't want to admit Jude is quoting the Book of Enoch as scripture because they figure that would make it

Jude 9 alludes to a tale of Satan and the Archangel Michael disputing over the corpse of Moses. Huh? Where does he get *this?* Simple: Origen tells us that Jude is lifting the story from a no-longer-extant writing (which Origen and his teacher, Clement of Alexandria, lucky stiffs, *did* have access to): The Assumption of Moses.[388] The implied back-story runs as follows: Moses died and at once Satan and Michael both appeared on the scene, each with a body bag. Of course, the Archangel argued that Moses belonged in Heaven with his old friend Jehovah, while Satan replied that the same peccadillo that got Moses banned from the Promised Land (smacking the rock in the wilderness instead of just ordering it to produce water, Num. 20:10-12), ought to disqualify him from entering Heaven, too. (Or maybe it was his murdering the Egyptian in Exodus 2:12.)[389] Obviously, Michael won the argument, or the title of the book would be "Moses Goes to Hell in the Devil's Hand Basket."[390]

So Jude strings together various bad examples from the Old Testament: the Jihadist massacre of Israelites, following the orgy of Baal-worship, who "fraternized" with Moabite hussies (Num. 25); the fall of the sons of God (Gen. 6:1-4); the nuking of Sodom and Gomorrah and their suburbs (Gen. 19). What do these episodes have in common? All involve forbidden sex, violating the order of nature and/or the sacred. In Numbers 25, Israelites worship a false deity in a sacred orgy. The damning sin of Sodom was "unnatural lust," not homosexuality but the desire of the men of Sodom to gang rape Lot's visitors who were angels. This directly reflects (they "*likewise* acted immorally") the blasphemous intercourse between the sons of God (by

---

canonical, as Tertullian avowed. They say they love the Bible but don't want more of it. So they are reduced to saying (somehow with a straight face) that the "historical Enoch" *did* say this, that it somehow got preserved in the Book of Enoch though the rest of the book is spurious, and that Jude just happened to have heard the same oral tradition of Enoch's words elsewhere. Either that, or the Holy Ghost just whispered the information into Jude's attentive ear. You hear someone spouting this kind of stuff and you start slowly backing your way toward the door.

[388] See Montague Rhodes James, *The Lost Apocrypha of the Old Testament: Their Titles and Fragments*. Translations of Early Documents, Series I. Palestinian Jewish Texts (Pre-Rabbinic). (London: SPCK, 1920, 1936), pp. 43-47. This fascinating volume is almost as rare as The Assumption of Moses itself! I finally found a copy, but it was like searching for Von Junzt's *Unaussprechlichen Kulten.*

[389] James, *Lost Apocrypha*, p. 48.

[390] Isn't it strange that fundamentalists who scoff at the Roman Catholic belief in the bodily assumption of the Virgin Mary nonetheless believe the very same thing about Moses because, thanks to the accidents of history, Jude managed to make it into the canon, and they are *stuck* with it!

now understood as angels) and mortal women.

The second sequence of damning sins and damned sinners includes Satan vying with Michael over Moses' remains; Cain (believed to be the offspring of Eve and Satan, thus implicitly continuing the motif of boundary-violating intercourse); the prophet Balaam, implicated in the Moabite apostasy; and the upstart Korah (Num. 16) who dared to usurp the prerogatives of Moses and Aaron.

Against whom is all this aimed? Jude is warning against libertine Gnostics who he fears have infiltrated Christian congregations (verses 4 and 12). The "acts of the apostates" just reviewed reveal Jude's chief gripes against such Gnostic antinomians: they conduct orgiastic celebrations (verses 12-13) of their freedom from the Old Testament laws, and they (dangerously) mock the Archons/fallen angels (verse 8 and 10) who imposed those laws upon a superstitious and gullible humanity. This linkage explains why Jude seems to jump from one topic (immorality) to another (blaspheming "the glorious ones"). In fact, he is not changing the subject at all.

Were there actually such wild and crazy Gnostics? The Nag Hammadi Gnostic texts give a very different impression, depicting the strict mores of various groups of celibate ascetics. But there do seem to have been libertine Gnostics. Irenaeus, Epiphanius, and others describe their astonishing excesses. Some scholars dismiss all that as mud-slinging pure and simple. But the Nag Hammadi texts corroborated Irenaeus' descriptions of the extravagant myth systems of the various Gnostics. Irenaeus ridiculed them, but he did not misrepresent them. I should think the same is true of his descriptions of some Gnostics' sexual outrages. Nor are such groups unknown in later centuries. But even if all such charges were mere libel, that doesn't change the fact that this is what Jude was referring to. There's no reason to think he did not believe the worst of Gnostics.

No doubt the lasting contribution of the Epistle of Jude is the concluding benediction: "Now to him who is able to keep you from falling and to present you without blemish before the presence of his glory with rejoicing, to the only God, our Savior through Jesus Christ our Lord, be glory, majesty, dominion, and authority, before all time and now and for ever. Amen."

The Epistles of John

There is no particular reason (outside of the inertia of hide-bound tradition) to ascribe these three letters to John, son of Zebedee, or to *anyone* named John for that matter, for all three are anonymous. The writer presents himself only as "the Elder." His intended recipients would have known his name which indeed might have been John, Tarzan, or Poindexter for all we know. As I suggested above, the name "John" was probably bestowed by the canonical compiler (or Ecclesiastical Redactor), whom, following David Trobisch,[391] I identify with Polycarp of Smyrna. He wanted to counterbalance the one-sided Marcionite emphasis on Paul with other "apostolic" epistles, and these three brief letters came in quite handy.

I believe the canonical order in which the three "Johannine" Epistles occur is just the reverse of the order in which they were written. Here is the scenario I envision for their writing. Let us imagine a group of several local congregations (cf., Rev. 1:11) who looked to the Elder for guidance, which he provided by means of his stable of circuit-riders, referred to in these letters as "the brothers." These were itinerant prophets and teachers who traveled from church to church in teams of two (cf., Mark 6:7). Some of the Elder's delegates began to embrace Gnostic and docetic doctrines but decided to keep these new beliefs to themselves, that is, until they next hit the road. When their turn to make the rounds came up, they took the opportunity to disseminate this new variant. They must have met with disparate and confused reactions in the churches they visited, so they agreed not to report this to the Elder or their colleagues when they got home. Maybe they did the same thing on their next few outings.

Meanwhile, alarmed reports started circulating among the congregations to the effect that the Elder's representatives, hence the Elder himself, could no longer be trusted to teach sound doctrine. Of these developments the Elder remained blissfully ignorant, that is, until one day when he welcomed home a pair of his missioners who reported they had been refused hospitality by Diotrephes, the patron of one of the local congregations. He would not allow anyone to shelter them and forbade them to address the church. The rebuffed brethren had no idea why. Nor could the sole church member, a man named Gaius, who did welcome them on the sly, enlighten them, perhaps because he had been away when the trouble began and did not know why everyone else slammed the door in these men's startled faces.

---

[391] David Trobisch, "Who Published the New Testament?" *Free Inquiry* 28/1 (December 2007-January 2008), pp. 30-33.

The baffled itinerants could tell the Elder only of Diotrephes' new policy. The Elder, outraged, assumed Diotrephes was full of himself, repudiating the Elder's supervision and seizing total control of the congregation for himself. So the Elder fired off a letter rebuking Diotrephes, but no reply was forthcoming, perhaps because Diotrephes refused even to meet with the Elder's messenger. Next the Elder dispatched a new pair of representatives, telling them to go directly to the house of Gaius. One of them, Demetrius, carried the letter we call 3 John, a private missive to him, not to the congregation. The Elder knew his missioners would need their usual lodging at this stop on their journey. As for Diotrephes, the Elder planned to show up in person to set things right (cf., 2 Cor. 10:1-2, 11; 12:17, 20; 13:2-3, 10).

When that day came and he demanded to speak with Diotrephes, the latter told him his side of the story, whereupon the Elder finally realized what had been going on behind his back. He lost no time in excommunicating the subversives who had been peddling their poison with his name on the bottle. He even adopted Diotrephes' own "zero tolerance" policy and started writing letters to all his congregations telling them to slam the door if any of these former colleagues, now heretics, should show up, as we see in the so-called 2 John 10-11.[392]

But, as he disliked putting pen to papyrus (2 John 12), he soon tired of writing notes to the several congregations and decided instead to send out a circular letter to the whole bunch of them, and that is our 1 John. As we would expect, the issue of docetism emerges as the most prominent issue in the epistle, though it entails other matters which stand on their own even if one neither knows nor cares about the now-arcane topic of phantom-Christology. The Elder offers a trusty litmus test for visiting prophets and teachers from his brotherhood who may be heretics but have not revealed themselves to him (2:19). Do they affirm the incarnation of Jesus Christ, that he "came in the flesh" (4:1-3a)? And do they draw a line between the Christ-Spirit and the human Jesus as his temporary channeler (2:22), as the Corinthian Gnostics did (1 Cor. 12:3)? Twice he stigmatizes these docetist itinerants as ventriloquist dummies speaking the oracles of the fabled Antichrist (2:22; 4:4:3), or as simply being a legion of

---

[392] An old friend of mine, a Philosophy professor and faithful Russian Orthodox Christian, once told me how, whenever Mormons or Jehovah's Witnesses would come a-knocking, he would yell, "Get the f– out of here!" and slam the door in their faces. The Elder would have been proud of him!

Antichrists (2:18; cf. Mark 13:22).

Our author starts right out polemicizing against docetism: "That which was from the beginning, which we have heard, which we have seen with our eyes, which we have looked upon and touched with our hands, concerning the word of life— the life was made manifest, and we saw it, and testify to it, and proclaim to you the eternal life which was with the Father and was made manifest to us— that which we have seen and heard we proclaim also to you" (1:1-3a). Does the anonymous Elder mean to say that he himself (along with the other disciples, "we") personally saw and touched the incarnate Jesus, satisfying himself that he was no phantom? That inference, though quite natural, seems less likely to me than that the "we" denotes the whole Christian community[393] (as in John 1:14; 3:11; 21:24 and as implied in 3:11). Justin Martyr, writing in the latter half of the second century, can still say, "We do not trust mere statements, but by necessity believe those who predicted these things before they happened, for we are actual eyewitnesses of events that have happened and are happening in the very manner in which they were foretold" (*First Apology*, 30). He can't mean that he himself had witnessed the miracles of Jesus. He must mean that Christians *as a community* saw them, and that he is a member of it. That sounds like 1 John to me.

The epistle gives readers mixed signals on the related topic of *perfectionism*. On the one hand, we read that anyone who thinks he has never sinned is kidding himself and ought to confess his sins to God (1:8-10), confident that the heavenly Christ will put in a good word for him with the Almighty (2:1b-2a). We even hear of "mortal," "fatal," or "deadly sin," which is so severe that it would be a sheer waste of time to pray for mercy for anyone who has committed it (5:16-17). Too bad he doesn't say what it was![394] On the other hand (and in this case, the left hand sure does not know what the right hand is doing!), we read that genuinely regenerated Christians *do not*, because they *cannot*, sin. It's flat-out impossible because such a one is born of God and shelters divine nature within him (3:9). What gives? The only way to make sense of this mess is to suppose that our 1 John has been composed from two very different versions of the letter. The

---

[393] Rudolf Bultmann, *The Johannine Epistles: A Commentary on the Johannine Epistles.* Trans. R. Philip O'Hara, Lane C. McGaughy, and Robert W. Funk. Hermeneia - A Critical and Historical Commentary on the Bible (Philadelphia: Fortress Press, 1973), pp. 10-11.

[394] Protestant fundamentalists like to pretend this "mortal sin" refers to anyone's unwillingness to receive Christ as his personal savior, but that is patent text-twisting intended to ward off the Catholic notion of mortal sin.

Elder must have penned the original, warning against his former colleagues, now Gnostics, together with their boast of sinless perfection. But these very people got hold of a copy and redacted it so that it now *taught* Gnostic perfectionism instead of denouncing it. The tip-off is the attribution of sinlessness to their possession of a divine spark inside, a signal Gnostic doctrine. Eventually, some scribe found himself with two very different versions of 1 John. Scribes were notoriously (and understandably) reluctant to leave any textual material out. Who knew which reading was original? So who dared to risk skipping or omitting what might be the Word of God? So it all went in.[395] So our canonical 1 John juxtaposes the antipodal versions of the letter.

And, speaking of scribal screw-ups, how about the famous "Trinity" reference squeezed in between chapter 5, verses 8 and 9? "There are three that bear witness in heaven, the Father, the Word, and the Holy Spirit, and these three are one." This one no longer even merits a footnote in modern Bibles. It appears only in a couple of very late Greek manuscripts[396] and was obviously shoe-horned into the text by someone who figured the Bible wasn't "scriptural" enough in its teaching.[397] So much for the constantly repeated reassurance that textual criticism threatens no point of Christian doctrine![398]

Even the classic statements about Christian love seem to serve the anti-Gnostic purpose of the letter. It assumes that the schismatics had a nasty attitude of aloof arrogance toward those they considered unenlightened (2:9-11; 4:20). But did they? We cannot know, but we do know from their writings that Valentinians viewed their role quite analogously to that of the compassionate Bodhisattvas of Mahayana Buddhism, concerned to aid in the salvation of the unenlightened, not to scorn them like the stuffed-shirt elitists depicted in John 7:49. The Elder may simply have inferred such a dismissive superiority complex on their part. In any case, it is pretty apparent that he had no

---

[395] Bruce M. Metzger, *The Text of the New Testament: Its Transmission, Corruption and Restoration* (New York: Oxford University Press, 1964), p. 200, though he would not have countenanced my application of this principle to 1 John's clashing statements on perfectionism.

[396] Metzger, *Text of the New Testament*, p. 62.

[397] Bart D. Ehrman, *The Orthodox Corruption of Scripture: The Effect of Early Christological Controversies on the Text of the New Testament* (New York: Oxford University Press, 1993); A.J. Mattill, Jr., *Polluted Texts and Traditional Beliefs* (Gordo, AL: Flatwoods Free Press, 1998), p. 32.

[398] F.F. Bruce, *The New Testament Documents: Are They Reliable?* (Grand Rapids: Eerdmans, 1960), pp. 19-20.

great agape-compassion for these "heretics," whom he brands as the spawn of Satan (3:8-10), like Cain (3:12a), murderers (3:12-15) and liars (2:22). "Because... Christ's work has created a total division between the circle of light and 'the world' which lies under the Antichrist's power (5:19), there can be no obligation... beyond the bounds of the brotherhood (3:14ff)."[399]

First John displays a keen expectation of the soon-coming end of the world. "This is the last hour!" (2:18). What a great slogan for a sandwich sign! Not only has the Antichrist appeared as predicted (4:3), but it turns out there are many of them (2:18). As in 1 Corinthians 15:49-50 and Philippians 3:20-21, 1 John anticipates a miraculous transformation of believers when Christ appears (3:2), a transfiguration so radical that it cannot be imagined until it happens (3:2; cf., 1 Cor. 13:12). We obtain a very different picture from certain passages in the Gospel of John (5:25; 11:23-26; 14:22) which, in its original Gnostic form, rejected futuristic eschatology in favor of realized eschatology. Like 2 Thessalonians 2:1-2 and 1 Corinthians 15:12, the Ecclesiastical Redactor rejected the fully realized eschatology and restored futuristic expectation (5:28-29; 6:54). It looks like 1 John comes from the party to which the Ecclesiastical Redactor belonged. It used to be thought that the Johannine Epistles were the work of the author of the Gospel of John because of the large number of phrases and ideas they share, but nowadays most think these similarities stem not from a common author but from a common milieu, a "Johannine School,"[400] which I think we must identify as the circle of the Elder. Or, as Bultmann[401] suggested, maybe the author of the Johannine Epistles simply drew upon the Gospel of John in writing his epistles.

[399] J.L. Houlden, *Ethics and the New Testament* (Baltimore: Penguin Books, 1973), p. 39.

[400] E.g., Houlden, *Ethics*, p. 38; R. Alan Culpeper, *The Johannine School: An Evaluation of the Johannine-School Hypothesis Based on an Investigation of the Nature of Ancient Schools* (Society of Biblical Literature Dissertation Series 26 (Chico: Scholars Press, 1975).

[401] Bultmann, *Johannine Epistles*, p. 1.

27
The Book of Revelation
The Seven-Sealed Scroll

Let the Reader Understand

I believe that Paul D. Hanson[402] is correct: we may discover the inception of the apocalyptic movement in the religio-political struggles of the returned Exiles in Palestine. But first we must take a step back and take a brief look at the ideologies of the prophets and the monarchy in pre-Exilic Judah.

The monarchy was an importation from the surrounding countries, as 1 Samuel records. Hitherto rule had been by sporadic, charismatic Judges, if at all. When the institution of kingship was imported, the accompanying royal ideology came along with it. The New Year's Festival reenacted the primordial victory of the god Yahweh over the sea monster Yamm/Rahab/Leviathan, and the subsequent exaltation of Yahweh over the rest of the gods (thereafter "sons of God") as divine king. The human king of Judah, his earthly counterpart and vicar, was his Son and his Anointed, reigning at his right hand. He could even be called "Mighty God" or simply addressed as "God." He sprang from the womb of the Jerusalemite dawn goddess Shahar (Istahar, Ishtar), like the theocratic priest-kings of pre-Davidic, Jebusite Jerusalem. In this scenario, repeated every year for the sake of cosmic as well as regime renewal, history was static, ever-returning,[403] to be renewed by its intersection with the sacred springs of Being. The heavens were simply an exalted projection of the earthly status quo invoked to supply the unalterable mandate of heaven.

The prophets, popular spokesmen like Amos and Jeremiah (at least as represented in the books ascribed to them), challenged the monarchy and its ventriloquist dummy prophets ("court prophets") in the name of a very different conception of history. They saw ongoing history as linear, directional, the theater of the acts of God not quite hidden behind apparently mundane events. It was the task of the

---

[402] Paul D. Hanson, *The Dawn of Apocalyptic: The Historical and Sociological Roots of Jewish Apocalyptic Eschatology* (Philadelphia: Fortress Press, 1975).
[403] Mircea Eliade, *The Sacred and the Profane: The Nature of Religion.* Trans. Willard R. Trask. A Harvest Book (New York: Harcourt, Brace & World, 1959).

prophets to discern God's hand as he moved the chess pieces of the nations over the game board of the world. In this way the prophets sacralized history or, alternatively, secularized the acts of God into historical events not in some mythical world but in this one. In the name of this conception of history they challenged the kings and their machinations. History did *not* repeat an endless cycle, like a treadmill, but, instead, new things could and did happen, including Yahweh's abandonment of his people if they were unfaithful to him.

Things changed drastically once Nebuchadnezzar destroyed the monarchy and the Exile began. The common people were left behind in Palestine, while among the deported aristocracy, the priestly caste ("hierocrats," the "hierocracy") assumed what sovereignty they could in exile, hoping one day to take up the reins of power back home (perhaps for their successors). The former Temple scribes formulated the Deuteronomic view of history, and in their version it was not the sins of kings and aristocrats that had brought on the Exile as divine chastisement, but rather the peoples' (see Isaiah 53).

The old language of royal mythology, including the imagery of Yahweh the divine warrior and dragon slayer, once the property of the royal and priestly establishment, was now free for use by the prophets, since the kings were no more. So we find Deutero-Isaiah (author of Isaiah 40-55[404]) employing it on the eve of the end of the Exile to describe the imminent historical purposes of God: the restoration to the land will be like the primordial victory of Yahweh over Rahab. The nations will see the return from exile and glorify the God of Israel.

Ironically, once the return occurred, there was a split among the priestly classes, between the Aaronide and Zadokite hierarchy on the one hand and the lower echelons on the other. These latter included Levites, Korahites, temple singers, scribes, local village priests (like Zechariah in Luke 1:5-10) and their sympathizers among the "people of the land" (am-ha-aretz). During the Exile, these latter groups, remaining in Palestine, had anticipated a glorious democratization of the Holy, all Israel being now a holy and priestly people[405] with God dwelling freely in their midst, with the Temple restored and served by defeated pagan kings, and described in terms of mythic glory.

---

[404] As you'll recall, I side with C.C. Torrey in accepting the earlier opinion that Second Isaiah consists of chapters 40-66, but here, so far, I am outlining Hanson's view with which I do otherwise agree.

[405] An idea revived by Martin Luther: "the priesthood of all believers."

By contrast, the returning hieratic (priestly) elite, abetted and bankrolled by the Persian state, dug in and began to implement a more mundane, hard-nosed agenda: power politics. For them, the community must be carefully segregated from the Holy, and only the highest ranks of the priesthood might act as mediators between the two. The result was a colossal disappointment for the lower echelon and the common people, who now found themselves subject to a new group of oppressors, this time fellow Jews.

Ironically, the hierocratic party were now the heirs of the prophetic theology of history, viewing themselves as the virtuous Righteous Remnant of Yahweh. God had brought them to their present position (had not Jeremiah predicted he would?), so who dared challenge them? What they had done was to turn the old prophetic view of God's acts in ongoing history into its opposite: a new ideology to legitimate a new status quo. We find the program of the hierocratic faction in Ezekiel 40-48, the platform of their opponents in the so-called Trito-Isaiah (3 Isaiah), chapters 60-62, as well as in Deutero-Zechariah (Zechariah chapters 9-14, a later add-on).

What was left for the lower-class group, now on the outs? They emulated 2 Isaiah and appropriated the old language of the royal mythology. But the idea was not to legitimate a status quo, old or new. Rather, it was to predict a drastic change, an overthrow of the status quo. God would move again to destroy Leviathan, who this time stood for the arrogant faction controlling the emerging Temple State. But, though dynamic, the new view was not as dynamic as that of the old prophets had been, since the new postexilic prophets were disillusioned with the idea of God making history go their way. There surely had been a bad track record thus far! Thus the difference they expected would be the *discontinuance* of history, a drastic suspension of it from outside, a direct intervention by God on Judgment Day.

The old stock in trade of the prophets, oracles of salvation and doom, were reapplied. There was now a bifurcation in Israel, and now the oracles of doom were directed not at the heathen nations, but at the corrupt Jewish leadership. The oracles of salvation, of course, were reserved for the prophetic/popular, non-hierocratic faction.

Here we see the origin of two of the main features of developing apocalyptic thought and writing: first, the dehistoricizing of history. This was not, however, some sort of mystical otherworldly flight from historical concerns, but a greater emphasis on direct divine intervention, snapping the links of the chain of historical causation, a replacement of Providence with miracle. Second, we find a division opening up within Israel between saints and sinners, replacing the longstanding dichotomy "Israel versus the nations."

The increased attention to Satan and the angels, as well as the sudden appearance of the resurrection doctrine, which we begin to see a bit later and by no means in all apocalypses, are in all probability derived from Zoroastrianism,[406] which Jews encountered during the Babylonian Exile once the Persians took over.

The universal practice of pseudepigraphy (writing under a pseudonym, that of some ancient biblical figure) begins with the anonymity of the prophets whose work we now find in Deutero-Isaiah and Deutero-Zechariah. The hierocratic group had begun to form, then close, the canon of scripture. The word went out that there would be no new prophets from God, and that any who might claim the prophetic mantle must be stoned as imposters. The doctrine of the cessation of prophecy is of course *prescriptive*, not *descriptive*. It is an attempt to clamp the lid on new prophets, not an observation on a curious lack of them. Thus the post-exilic prophets who belonged to the hierocratic faction (Zechariah, Haggai, Malachi, parts of Ezekiel) were admitted to the canon with no problem, but the popular prophets were included only on the margins, if they could sneak in under some acceptable name of the past (hence *Deutero*-Zechariah; *Deutero*-Isaiah).

And for precisely the same reasons, the later apocalypses had to be written under the names of inspired figures of the past like Moses, Enoch, Baruch, Ezra, and Daniel, who had lived before the ban on new words from the Lord. They even sprang from the same circles: the lower post-exilic echelon of scribes, the same group associated with the Levitical choristers, the ones who codified the Psalms, adding a few important sapiential (Wisdom) psalms of their own (1; 19; 119; etc.) in the process. One would wear the cloak of pseudonymity only if one had something to fear from those who proclaimed that prophecy had ceased. Outside those circles, if you were somebody like John the Baptist or Jesus ben-Ananias, you would prophesy in your own name, and let the chips fall where they may. The scribal-sapiential character of apocalyptic was pointed out by Gerhard von Rad[407] and, later, by Jonathan Z. Smith.[408]

---

[406] Norman Cohn, *Cosmos, Chaos and the World to Come: The Ancient Roots of Apocalyptic Faith* (New Haven: Yale University Press, 1993), Chapter 13, "Jews, Zoroastrians and Christians," pp. 220-226.

[407] Gerhard von Rad, *Old Testament Theology, Volume II: The Theology of Israel's Prophetic Traditions*. Trans. D.M.G. Stalker (New York: Harper & Row, 1965), pp. 306-307.

[408] Jonathan Z. Smith, *Map Is not Territory: Studies in the History of Religions* (Chicago: University of Chicago Press, 1993), Chapter III, "Wisdom and Apocalyptic," pp. 67-

Enoch, Baruch, Daniel, Moses, and especially Ezra, were all scribes. Enoch[409] was the legendary inventor of writing (like Thoth and Cadmus in other myths). The disclosure of the secrets of the heavens and of nature is a preoccupation of later scribes under Egyptian influence (when Judea was under the Ptolemaic Empire of Egypt). The agonizing concern with theodicy (explaining the evil of a world created and run by an ostensibly good God) that we see especially in 4 Ezra (= 2 Esdras) is a traditional Wisdom concern, as is the appearance of the Wisdom myth in 1 Enoch.

Christopher Rowland[410] shows how there is a great deal of overlap between the apocalyptists and the later esotericism of the rabbis, e.g., Merkabah mysticism (visionary journeys to behold the Throne Chariot of God as in Ezekiel chapter 1) and the Lore of Creation,[411] both forbidden to anyone under 40 and not widely discussed. Bruce J. Malina[412] has shown how the Revelation of John is thoroughly permeated with ancient astronomy/astrology, another concern of the Wisdom movement. Joachim Jeremias[413] was probably right that apocalypticism was the hidden wisdom of the scribes, even though their successors put the damper on it after the failure of the Bar-Kochba messianic revolt of 134-136 C.E.[414]

Ironically, once the hierocratic party were themselves brutally driven from power during the crisis of Hellenization in the mid-second century B.C.E., fleeing from the Seleucid persecutors into the desert, they repeated the theological shift of their own opponents. In the Dead Sea Scrolls we find a marginalized Hasidean or Zadokite (i.e., priestly) conventicle awaiting the day God will vindicate them with armies of angelic storm-troopers from the skies. This faction, too,

---

87.

[409] Margaret Barker, *The Lost Prophet: The Book of Enoch and its Influence on Christianity* (Nashville: Abingdon Press, 1989).

[410] Christopher Rowland, *The Open Heaven: A Study of Apocalyptic in Judaism and Early Christianity* (London: SPCK, 1982), Part Four: "The Esoteric Tradition in Early Rabbinic Judaism," Chapter 11, "The Meditation of Rabban Johanan Ben Zakkai and His Circle on the Chariot-Chapter," pp. 282-305; Chapter 12, "The Problems Posed by the Esoteric Tradition in the Time of Rabbi Akiba," pp. 306-348.

[411] Gershom G. Scholem, *Major Trends in Jewish Mysticism.* Trans. George Lichtheim (New York: Schocken Books, 1973), Second Lecture: "Merkabah Mysticism and Jewish Gnosticism," pp. 40-79.

[412] Bruce J. Malina, *On the Genre and Message of Revelation: Star Visions and Sky Journeys* (Peabody: Hendrickson Publishers, 1995).

[413] Joachim Jeremias, *The Eucharistic Words of Jesus.* Trans. Arnold Ehrhardt (Oxford: Basil Blackwell, 1955), pp. 75-76.

[414] C.K. Barrett, *The Gospel of John and Judaism* (London: SPCK, 1980).

revives the old Divine Warrior myths, which we find in the Qumran Hymns as well as in the War Scroll.

As to this matter of the crisis of Hellenism, Richard A. Horsley[415] and John Dominic Crossan[416] have suggested that apocalypticism, with its apparent quietism, yet simultaneously rooting for the overthrow of the evil powers, must be seen as the impotent response of the retainer class. The ruling class (e.g., high priests Menelaus and Jason, the latter paying for Olympic sacrifices to Hercules!) sees nothing amiss, since they are collaborating with the Hellenizing foreigners. The lower classes and the dispossessed, more suited to pragmatic action, less literate and less likely to live in a world of abstractions, pay little heed to written apocalypses and instead field actual warrior messiahs. But the retainers (scribes, lower priests, etc.) merely dream of a better day. Their response to the crisis is to write down their dreams and pass the writings around. Robert Jay Lifton[417] and John G. Gager[418] explain that what we see in written apocalypses are scripts for a kind of play, a miracle play or mystery play, a "finite province of meaning"[419] in the "as if" mode.[420] It is like a stage play, a TV show, a film, a religious service in which we temporarily enter into a different state of mind and live for a few moments as if by different assumptions or in a different world—until the lights come up. It is a compensatory zone of imagining in which "time and death vanish"[421] and abreaction, a psychodramatic catharsis of pathological tensions, may occur.[422]

---

[415] Richard A. Horsley, *Jesus and the Spiral of Violence: Popular Jewish Resistance in Roman Palestine*. Facet Series (Minneapolis: Augsburg Fortress Press, 1993), p. 17. Actually, as I read him, Horsley sees apocalyptic literature as a kind of coded and/or artistic representation of concrete political (revolutionary) *samizdat*. The scribes wrote it this way, but the common people were inspired by it to act, or at least to dream of acting.

[416] John Dominic Crossan, *The Historical Jesus: The Life of a Mediterranean Jewish Peasant* (New York: HarperOne, 1993), p. 157.

[417] Robert Jay Lifton, *Boundaries: Psychological Man in Revolution* (New York: Random House/Vintage Books, 1969).

[418] John G. Gager, *Kingdom and Community: The Social World of Early Christianity*. Prentice-Hall Studies in Religion Series (Englewood Cliffs: Prentice-Hall, 1975), pp. 54-55; cf., John Wick Bowman, *The Drama of the Book of Revelation* (Philadelphia: Westminster Press, 1955), who argued that Revelation was actually the script for a play.

[419] Berger and Luckmann, *Social Construction*, p. 25.

[420] Michael Saler, *As If: Modern Enchantment and the Literary PreHistory of Virtual Reality* (New York: Oxford University Press, 2012).

[421] Lifton, *Boundaries*, p. 23; Eliade, *Sacred and Profane*, p. 205: "an 'escape from time.'"

[422] Gager, *Kingdom and Community*, p. 55; William Sargant, *The Mind Possessed: A Physiology of Possession, Mysticism and Faith Healing* (Baltimore: Penguin Books, 1975),

If you have ever seen one of those fundamentalist movies dramatizing the Second Coming of Christ on a low budget, you know what Gager means: the audience has been raised on the imminent coming of Jesus. It never seems to happen. Things grow worse and worse. The viewers would dearly love to see the End come for real, but in the meantime, playing pretend with these awful movies is about all they can do. But it's good enough for the moment. That's what the written apocalypses were for, too.

Understanding apocalyptic as crisis literature (some of it originating as underground pamphlets in time of persecution) even helps us make sense of the evolution of the genre, as well as specific, otherwise puzzling, details in the texts.

John J. Collins[423] outlines a workable paradigm for understanding apocalypses. They are narratives in which a supernatural revelation is made to a mortal by a heavenly messenger, concerning the secrets (vertically) of the heavens and (horizontally) of future history. Collins adds that these disclosures are made by way of exhortation or consolation of a persecuted group. And there are two main types. The first, constituting the earlier texts, are the "historical survey" apocalypses, where we tend to find an *ex eventu* (after the fact) review (posing as a *preview*) of history (fictively couched as prediction as from the standpoint of the ancient writer to whom the book is pseudonymously ascribed), including persecution, vindication, and the resurrection of the dead. These documents appear to be products of the crucible. Their point is to reassure readers that, despite appearances, God is still in charge: he has guided history to this point and has a plan that will soon eventuate in salvation for the living and the dead.

Second, we also find heavenly journey texts in which the main attraction is the description of the heavenly bodies, the compartments of heaven, ranks of angels, etc., but even here there is a corporate eschatology awaiting, i.e., a blessed conclusion for all Israel. In my opinion, there is little real difference between these two types, since even the element of historical prediction originally stemmed from the heavenly New Year vision of the ascended sacred king to behold the events of the following year inscribed on the heavenly Tablets of

---

pp. 4-17; Claude Levi-Strauss, *Structural Anthropology*. Trans. Claire Jacobson and Brooke Grundfest Schoepf (Garden City: Doubleday Anchor Books, 1967), Chapter X, "The Effectiveness of Symbols," pp. 181-201.
[423] John J. Collins, *The Apocalyptic Imagination: An Introduction to Jewish Apocalyptic Literature* (Grand Rapids: Eerdmans/Livonia, MI: Dove Booksellers, 1998), pp. 6-7.

Destiny. So future history, as in astrology, is itself one of the secrets of the heavens.[424] The combination still appears explicitly in some apocalypses, including some of the Enoch texts.

Later we find heavenly journeys in which the revelation skips any historical dimension and depicts only the fate of single individuals after death, and in them salvation is largely heavenly and spiritual, with no prospect of resurrection (e.g., Testament of Abraham, 3 Baruch, Apocalypse of Zephaniah). These late texts stem from after the once-imminent crisis of persecution when history had disappointed. We are on the way to Gnosticism here.

We might suggest that 4 Ezra shows evidence of the crisis psychology described by Lifton. Why does Ezra insist that he is as much a sinner as the Jerusalemites who died in the crisis (c. Luke 13:1-5)? Perhaps because he is like Lifton's Hiroshima survivors, wracked by survivor guilt.[425] Why them and not their loved ones? The boundary between the living and the dead had become unclear. And for the same reason, Ezra's comfort is not in his survival in the present life but in the prospect of resurrection, with the righteous dead, into the future world. Resurrection belief is another way of fantasizing the return of the unjustly killed, as well as pretending to share their present death. Throughout his dialogue with Uriel the angel, Ezra protests his unworthiness; it almost sounds like we are overhearing someone with survivor guilt cross-examining his own conscience.[426]

---

[424] Geo Widengren, *The Ascension of the Apostle and the Heavenly Book* (King and Saviour III). Uppsala Universitets Arsskrift 1950: 7. Acta Universitatis Upsaliensis (Uppsala: A.B. Lundequistska Bokhandeln, 1950).

[425] There is a huge cycle of twentieth-century "apocalypses" of survivor guilt: the 1954 Toho Studios movie *Godzilla the King of the Monsters* and its numerous sequels and imitators. Godzilla, a giant mutated dinosaur reminiscent of the biblical Leviathan, devastates Tokyo, both by stomping the buildings into matchwood and incinerating fleeing crowds by spewing radioactive fire. Very clearly, the early Toho films were based on a subtext of survivor guilt: Godzilla was giving those Japanese who had avoided destruction in Hiroshima and Nagasaki a mere nine years earlier the opportunity to cast off the guilt of having survived where so many others had not. Now the living could stop subsisting on borrowed time and join those whose death they felt they should have shared. These movies provided abreaction and catharsis, at least for the original generation of viewers.

[426] Thanks to my professor at Drew University, Lala Kalyan Dey, for this way of viewing 4 Ezra.

The Revelation of John

The Greek word for the title of this book is the *Apocalypse* of John. "*Apo-calypso*" means the lifting away, the peeling back, of a hitherto-drawn veil to disclose what lies behind it. There are many such ancient and medieval books, most of them located in the Jewish, Christian, and Islamic traditions, though they are not altogether absent from other religions. Their collective genre has rightly taken on the name of this one book; hence, all are "apocalypses," revelations. John's was by no means the first, despite having shared its name with the rest.

Now, how do these considerations weigh upon the Revelation of John? First, we must suppose it to be pseudonymous, though we cannot identify either the actual author or the fictive narrator. As Benjamin W. Bacon[427] pointed out, if the Revelation of John is not pseudonymous, it has the improbable distinction of being the only apocalypse that isn't! And we have no reason to assume it is an exception to the rule. The seer of Patmos is supposed to be someone named John, and a John of such prominence, at least within the circle of the seven churches of Asia Minor, that he will need no further identification. Traditionally he was identified as John, son of Zebedee, though when Eusebius, an Amillennialist who thought Constantine's empire embodied the Kingdom of Christ, decided he did not favor the millenarianism of the Revelation, he posited a distinct character, a "John the Elder" separate from the Apostle John,[428] to have written it. His denial of apostolic authorship was no historical judgment but only a function of his distaste for the content of the book. But John was a common name, and we may guess that anyone who attached particular importance to any John thought his John so important as to need no epithets or patronymics to distinguish himself: let others be known as "John the less," "John of Schenectady," or whatever.

It is only a further complication to raise the issue of a connection between the Revelation of John and the gospel and epistles ascribed to the same name, for there we have anonymous

---

[427] Benjamin W. Bacon, "The Authoress of Revelation - A Conjecture," *Harvard Theological Review* 23 (July 1930), pp. 235-250.

[428] Papias of Hierapolis listed various men whom he believed had heard Jesus' teaching, including John the apostle as well as one "the elder John," who might or might not have been a second reference to the apostle. The passage is ambiguous. Eusebius may have been the first to distinguish them as separate individuals, taking advantage of the ambiguity in order to cut loose the Book of Revelation.

works without even a pseudonym. Tradition alone dubs that author or those authors as "John." While our author cannot be the same as any of those writers (style precludes it), it is not unlikely there is some connection, that this apocalypse represents a late stage of sectarian debate, the opposite extreme from the original version of the Gospel of John which did away completely with futuristic eschatology.[429] Revelation, like the other "Johannine" writings, does call the heavenly Christ the Word and the Lamb (or perhaps just picks up on the same Aramaic pun, since the two words are very close in that language.).

Who *did* write it? Once we get past the red herring of John the Elder versus John the Apostle, and few commentators have, we find a small but wide range of suggested candidates, including the one of the prophesying daughters of Philip who married and settled in Hierapolis (B.W. Bacon); Jesus (the seven letters), John and James bar Zebedee, Tychicus, and a Deutero-John (Barbara Thiering);[430] and John the Baptist (Josephine Massyngberde Ford).[431] Who knows? But we can take a guess at the writer's stance, which may be more important anyway. It appears, as F.C. Baur[432] suggested, that the Revelation stems from non- or anti-Pauline Jewish Christianity. Paul's is conspicuously absent from the list of apostolic names carven upon the foundation stones of the New Jerusalem (21:14).

The book would also seem plainly encratite in its sympathies. That is, it envisions the salvation of a celibate elite (14:4). The celibacy gospel was rife in the very area of Asia Minor to which the work is addressed. The Revelator vilifies a former colleague, a prophetess, as "Jezebel," no doubt only a spite-name for her. He says she entices the servants of Christ to prostitution or fornication, but this may be nothing. Remember, we are hearing the fulminations of the Anti-Sex League here. As in the Dead Sea Scrolls, "fornication" probably meant some perceived sexual infraction like sex during the menstrual period (or perhaps having sex *period*).

When was Revelation written? Depending upon how one

---

[429] Robert T. Fortna, *The Fourth Gospel and Its Predecessor: From Narrative Source to Present Gospel* (Philadelphia: Fortress Press, 1988), Part 2, section E., "Eschatology and Community," pp. 284-293.

[430] Barbara Thiering, *Jesus of the Apocalypse: The Life of Jesus After the Crucifixion* (New York: Doubleday, 1995).

[431] Josephine Massyngberde Ford, *Revelation*. Anchor Bible 38 (Garden City: Doubleday Anchor, 1975).

[432] F.C. Baur, *Church History of the First Three Centuries*. Trans. Allan Menzies. Theological Translation Fund Library (London: Williams and Norgate, 1878), Vol. I, pp. 84-86.

identifies the eight emperors in chapter 17, the narrator would seem to be positioning himself during the reign of Vespasian, fictively predicting the reigns of Titus and Domitian. And since he veers off the historical track after Domitian, predicting the overthrow of Rome by the Parthians as the culmination of his reign (and as the immediate precursor to the second advent of Jesus), we should accept Irenaeus' placement of the book during Domitian's reign (81-96 C.E). It works out pretty well. We have traditionally spoken of a widespread persecution engineered by Domitian, but a second look reveals that the evidence for this is pretty slim.[433] Nonetheless, the writer of Revelation may have *expected* imminent persecution from the Emperor given his brazen claims to divinity, something made on behalf of all Caesars, but not taken seriously by most. What is John predicting? He has in mind neither the events of the twenty-first century nor a survey of the whole of church history,[434] though these interpretations are popular today.

No, John's symbols make most sense as referring to figures and events of his own time.[435] For instance, who is the Beast with the number 666 (13:17-18), with the fatal wound that has been healed (13:3), that is simultaneously the eighth in a series of kings and one of the previous seven (17:9-11)? He must be Domitian, understood as the return of the deposed Nero (as John the Baptist was the return of Elijah). "Neron Caesar" has the number value 666. Who is the Great Harlot who sits upon the seven hills (17:16)? She must be Rome, built on seven hills. Underlying all this is the contemporary legend that Nero had not really died, as he seemed to, but escaped. Or he did die but would rise. Either way, he would retreat to Parthia across the Euphrates and from there lead the innumerable legions of the Parthian Empire into Rome to destroy her, gaining revenge upon Rome for deposing him. Revelation casts Domitian in this role, *Nero Redivivus*. This is why he is the eighth emperor yet one of the seven. That is why he is alive (again) despite a mortal wound. This is why his name in common cipher code comes out to 666. This is why he leads

---

[433] Collins, *Apocalyptic Imagination*, p. 273.

[434] Henry H. Halley, *Halley's Bible Handbook: An Abbreviated Bible Commentary* (Grand Rapids: Zondervan, 1965), pp. 684, 711-733.

[435] J. Stuart Russell, *The Parousia: A Study of the New Testament Doctrine of Our Lord's Second Coming* (London: T. Fisher Unwin, 1887; rpt. Grand Rapids: Baker Book House, 1983), Part III, "The Parousia in the Apocalypse," pp. 365-537; R.H. Charles, *A Critical and Exegetical Commentary on the Revelation of St. John*. International Critical Commentary (Edinburgh: T&T Clark, 1920), Vol. I, p. 274, calls this approach "the Contemporary Historical Method."

a host of demons (whose accoutrements resemble those of the Parthian cavalry, right down to the horsehair crests of their helmets, "hair like the hair of women") across the Euphrates and destroys his old consort, the Whore of Babylon.

John joins this popular Roman legend with the Jewish myth of the Antichrist who seizes control of the world during a famine, trading grain rations for oaths of fealty, and finally blasphemously proclaims his own divinity in the Temple. John thought the Roman Empire would soon collapse. When he actually starts predicting, as in all apocalypses, he veers off the track, and thus do we date apocalypses.

Is the Revelation of John actually based upon visions experienced by the unknown author? There is no particular reason to think so. To an astonishing degree the book is knit together from phrases and paraphrases of Old Testament apocalyptic and prophetic books, especially Isaiah, Zechariah, Daniel, and Ezekiel. This is, of course, no criticism; what it borrows it uses to considerable effect.[436]

The scribal origin of the apocalyptic genre explains one of its most puzzling features: the riddling cipher-language. It used to be thought that the baffling symbolism was a code language made needful because of the persecution setting of the genre: what if a clear and gloating prediction of the doom of Rome were to fall into the wrong hands? The faithful are in enough trouble already! Best write in code. But no persecution seems to be in view in most apocalypses, a fact which must make us guess again, and the prevalent guess today is that the puzzle element is just the language of the scribes who wanted to make their readers work for it: He who has ears to hear, let him hear. Everyone else? Work on getting some ears!

We probably also have scribalism, with its love of antiquity and antique lore, to thank for the appearance in Revelation of archaic mythemes such as that of Leviathan the seven-headed dragon, as well as stray bits of unassimilated Greek myth including Hades, Argus, Baucus and Philemon, and Gaia. How striking that the Revelator vilifies Pergamum as the place "where Satan has his throne" (2:13), referring to a great shrine of Zeus there, and yet he applies the old

---

[436] Kim Mark Lewis, *How John Wrote the Book of Revelation: From Concept to Publication* (Lorton, VA: Kim Mark Lewis, 2015), deconstructs the present Book of Revelation, delineating successive stages of revision and supplementation by focusing on clusters of allusions to any single Old Testament text. When we find several such citations, then another later on, he suggests that the intervening material with its own scripture citations is an insertion by the author.

myth of Zeus and his father Kronos to the infant messiah in 12:4b-6, 13-14.[437]

Chapter and Verse

The opening phrase, "A revelation of Jesus Christ" (1:1), functions as the book's title but also refers to the scene in the heavenly court (5:1-7) in which God gives the seven-sealed scroll to the exalted Christ. That scroll is the "revelation which God gave him" to show John the Revelator, and through him, the readers (hearers) the secrets of the hastening future. This he did by "sending his angel to his servant John" (1:1), and it is this angel whom we see appearing (1:12-15) in the guise of Gabriel from Daniel 10:2-10. The epithet "one like a son of man" derives from the triumphant dragon-slayer Yahweh, about to assume the throne of creation (Dan. 7:13a). The snowy, wool-white hair is that of El Elyon, the god "ancient in days" (Dan. 7:9). The detail of feet so bright they look not only like polished bronze but like bronze in the furnace comes from the "fourth man" who protected Shadrach, Meschach, and Abed-Nego[438] in the furnace of Nebuchadnezzar, "one like a son of Elohim" (Dan. 3:25). The speaker is an angel; just as the Seven Spirits of 1:4 are angels,[439] so is this angel called "the Spirit" in each of the seven letters to follow.

But wait—isn't this supposed to be Jesus? He certainly speaks in the persona of Jesus in the letters. This is a "Christophany," an apparition of Christ who remains in heaven but projects his image in exactly the fashion of the Old Testament theophanies in which the angel of God or angel of Yahweh appears to Abraham, Hagar, Gideon, the parents of Samson, etc. It is his angel ("messenger"), yet anyone who sees him has seen God (Gen. 16:7-14; Judg. 6:11-23; 13:1-23).[440]

It is interesting that the revelation should be prefaced by a set of cover letters to the seven congregations in Asia Minor over which

---

[437] James M. Robinson, "On the *Gattung* of Mark (and John)," in David G. Buttrick, ed., *Jesus and Man's Hope*. A Perspective Book I (Pittsburgh: Pittsburgh Theological Seminary, 1970), pp. 99-129.

[438] This name means "Servant (i.e., worshipper) of Nergal," a Babylonian deity.

[439] These are the archangels, or angel princes: Gabriel, Michael, Raphael, Uriel, Sauriel, Jeremiel, and Raguel. (There are different lists with different names, just like the lists of Jesus' disciples in the gospels.)

[440] Hugh J. Schonfield, in *The Authentic New Testament*. A Mentor Religious Classic (New York: New American Library, 1958), p. 440, calls him "the Angel-Messiah."

the author had some sort of jurisdiction. Why only to them?[441] Did the Revelator suppose other bishops or apostles were receiving their own visions with instructions to other congregations? There is no sign of that, and we have to suspect that the restriction of the readership denotes the fictive character of the whole thing. In view of the gravity and urgency of the contents, it is rather like a gospel depicting Jesus charging the disciples to make sure they preach the gospel message only to a handful of Galilean villages. In fact, wasn't this one of the criteria employed in choosing books for the New Testament canon: "catholicity"? The book would have to be the property of the church as a whole.

Verse 7 ("Behold! He is coming with the clouds") uses the ancient imagery common to Yahweh and his Syrian counterpart Baal Hadad, both of whom were gods of storm and war. See Psalm 104:3b; Daniel 7:13; 2 Samuel 22:10-15; Psalm 18:10-14. That "every eye will see him, even those who pierced him," comes directly from Zechariah 12:10. And note that "all the tribes of earth shall wail at the sight of him" becomes a saying of the earthly Jesus in Matthew 24:30. Likewise, the admonition, "He who has an ear, let him hear" (2:7) will be attributed to a historical Jesus of Nazareth in Mark 4:9, 23; Matthew 13:43, etc. The gospel context is that of Jesus telling parables. The transition from the apocalyptic genre to the parabolic was natural, since the former is also basically a matter of unraveling puzzles and riddles. Cf. Mark 13:14; Revelation 13:18.

Who were the Nicolaitan sect (2:6, 15), or the followers of a prophetess whom our writer disdainfully calls "Jezebel," the Israelite queen who promoted Baal worship (1 Kings 16:30-33)? We know of a group of Gnostics called the Nicolaitans, and Baur[442] was no doubt correct in seeing in them the more religiously adventurous Pauline "stronger brethren" with whom the Apostle dealt in 1 Corinthians. The "fornication" and the eating of meat previously sacrificed to idols reflect (in loaded, pejorative terms) the more liberal behaviors of these Corinthian Gnostics. William Ramsey[443] thought that this "Jezebel" might actually have been Paul's convert Lydia from Acts 16:14-15.

The various promises the Son of God makes to those who last

---

[441] Raymond F. Jones, "The Lions of Rome" in Roger Ellwood, ed., *Flame Tree Planet: An Anthology of Religious Science Fiction* (St. Louis: Concordia Publishing House, 1973), pp. 103-124, suggests that these seven congregations were the only franchises still in business!

[442] Baur, *Church History*, Vol. I, pp. 84-86.

[443] William M. Ramsey, *The Letters to the Seven Churches of Asia and their Place in the Plan of the Apocalypse* (New York: A.C. Armstrong & Son, 1905), pp. 336-337.

out the expected persecution often refer to events discussed at greater length in subsequent chapters. Verse 7 promises that the overcomer "will... eat of the Tree of Life which is in the Paradise of God,'" which appears in Revelation 22:1-2. In The Life of Adam and Eve 41:1-2; 42:1 (or the related Apocalypse of Moses 13:1-5), Seth and Eve leave Adam on his deathbed and travel back to Eden to ask for healing oil from the Tree of Life to save Adam. Their request is turned down, but the archangel Michael promises them that the Tree of Life should again become available to mankind in the Last Days, at the resurrection of the dead. This is assumed in Revelation's promise in 2:7. The promise is for participation in the resurrection.

Verse 8 warns readers in Smyrna that Satan "is about to throw some of you into prison to test you." The role of Satan ("the Adversary," just the opposite of the Paraclete, the courtroom Advocate) here is exactly as in Job 1:9-12; 2:4-7; 1 Chronicles 21:1-7; Zechariah 3:1-5; Mark 1:13; Mark 8:33; and Luke 22:31, namely, to put the ostensibly righteous to the test lest a gracious God be too lenient. There is nothing evil in this. Satan becomes an evil being only where he has been conflated with originally independent mythical villains such as Ahriman, Leviathan, and Beelzebul.

The church in Pergamum lives in the shadow of Satan's throne (2:13), i.e., the great statue of the enthroned Zeus located in the city. Some church members are flirting with the Nicolaitan sect active in Pergamum, and if they do not think better of it, warns the Angel-Messiah, "I will attack them with the blade of my mouth" (cf., 2 Thess. 2:8)! But if they do straighten out and fly right, this reward awaits them: "I will give [them] some of the hidden manna," namely the manna stored away in the Ark of the Covenant (Exod. 16:32-34). In Revelation 11:19, the Ark of the Covenant is opened to reveal the manna and the other relics. But that's not all: "I will give him a white stone." Deuteronomy 10:5 has the original tables of the Law deposited in the Ark. The Deuteronomist, as we have seen, liked to indulge in historical revisionism, and he probably substituted these orthodox sancta for others, since fallen under theological suspicion, namely the divination stones, the Urim and Thummim[444] (Exod. 28:30; Lev. 8:8; Num. 27:21). These were probably black on one side and white on the other. "And on that stone is inscribed a new name, which no one knows except him who receives it!'" There may be a reference here to

---

[444] Cf., Margaret Barker, *The Older Testament: The Survival of Themes from the Ancient Royal Cult in Sectarian Judaism and Early Christianity* (Sheffield: Phoenix Press, 2005), pp. 97, 222.

Isaiah 62:2, but I believe the new name is a token of an initiation ritual, receiving a new name in baptism, which, however, one is not to disclose, like the mantra assigned new initiates into Transcendental Meditation today.

The note to Thyatira gives "Jezebel" and her fans quite the bruising. She was a Gnostic mystagogue, as is evident from the description of her teaching as "the deep things of Satan." Of course she must have, like Paul himself, promised her initiates "the deep things of God" (1 Cor. 2:10). Again, a la Baur, these Nicolaitans sound remarkably Pauline. The threat to strike down the Gnostic prophetess-harlot anticipates the fate awaiting the Great Harlot, Rome, in chapters 17-18. Faithful Johannine Christians, by contrast, will receive authority over the pagans, ruling them with an iron sceptre (2:26-27). This comes true when we get to Revelation 12:5; 20:4. The promise extends the prerogatives of the messianic reign (Psalm 2:8-9) to the Messiah's loyalists. These include the splendid seats that the sons of Zebedee coveted (Mark 10:35-37). The saying found in Revelation 2:26-27 is one of a number of versions of the same promise, others being Luke 22:28-30; Matthew 19:28; 2 Timothy 2:12a; and 1 Corinthians 6:2-3.

In Revelation 22:16, the Angel-Messiah reveals himself as "the bright morning star," whereas in 2:28 he promises to give the morning star to his overcomers. In Isaiah 14:12 the king of Babylon is called the Morning Star, the son of the dawn goddess Shahar, as is any newly crowned king of Judah in Psalm 110:3b. Thus, for Jesus to be called "the Morning Star" denotes kingly sovereignty, which he promises to extend to his followers (as in Luke 22:8-29). Also compare Revelation 2:26-27 with Psalm 2:9.

The righteous in Sardis are promised radiant resurrection bodies (for which "white robes" were a traditional Jewish and Christian metaphor). The names of these are already registered in the Book of Life (3:4, anticipating 20:12) and will not be crossed off the list (3:5), the fate in store for apostates on the Day of Judgment. That is the day predicted in Mark 8:38 and Matthew 10:32-33 when Jesus will gladly acknowledge those who have fearlessly confessed their faith in him but will repudiate all who buckled under persecution and denied their faith.

The reward promised to the faithful in Philadelphia is to become "a pillar in the temple of my God, and [they] will never have to leave it again" (3:12), the very boon granted to faithful Baucis and Philemon by Zeus (Ovid, *Metamorphoses*, Book 8; see also Luke 2:36-37; Ps. 84:1-4, 10; 1 Kings 7:15).

The letter to the church at Laodicea (not the letter mentioned in Colossians 4:16) presents several interesting features. For one, the Angel-Messiah speaks of himself as "the beginning of the creation of God" (3:14).You can't prove it doesn't mean that the pre-existent Logos was the one who initiated the creation. But that interpretation seems to me a strained harmonization to safeguard Nicene "Jesus is God" Christology. Wouldn't it sound less forced if you took it to mean "the first one created," precisely parallel to Colossians 1:15, "the first-born of all creation"?

Second, there is the surprising statement in Revelation 3:15-16 that Jesus has more regard for people who are spiritually uninterested or actively hostile than he does for complacent, unenthusiastic Christians.

Third, we find one of the most beloved (and perhaps most misused) passages in the book (3:20) that supposedly asks the individual to invite Jesus into his heart as Savior and Lord: "Behold! I stand at the door and knock! Whoever *hears my voice* and opens the door, I will come in to him and will dine with him, and he with me." I think that, as with the previous promises in these chapters, this one points forward, this time to the Marriage Supper of the Lamb (Rev. 19:7-9), the Messianic Banquet. Also in the writer's mind, I think, is the Eucharist as a proleptic foretaste of that eschatological feast. Christ is invisibly present at the Communion table, as in Luke 24:28-31, as he will be *visibly* present at the Marriage Supper. Just as Jews at Passover believe themselves to be mystically present at the original Passover in Egypt, so Christian communicants understood themselves to be somehow already present at the Messianic Banquet in the future.

So far, so good. But where is the challenge, the victory, in hearing his voice and opening the door? I suggest the point is the same as that in John 5:25; 10:3-5; and Mark 13:5-6: discerning the true voice of the returning Christ and not being deceived by impostors. The familiar "Come to Jesus" reading of the passage is, I believe, an invention of seventeenth-century German and English Pietism.

The Starry Wisdom

Here is my translation of chapters 4-6, set in the heavenly throne room. Bruce J. Malina,[445] who qualifies as something of a Revelator himself, given what his research has brought to light concerning this passage, shows how the author of the Apocalypse by no means made the modern distinction between the metaphysical heaven and the starry heavens of outer space.[446] In fact, for him, as for all the ancients, to say God's throne was in heaven meant that it was smack-dab in the center of the starry sky, and Revelation describes it in precisely those terms. For instance, things look quite different (and make more sense) once we realize that "horses, horses' manes, trumpets, and bowls are, among other labels, common names for comets and that comets invariably have negative effects on human beings."[447]

> After these words, I looked and, behold! A door standing open in the sky! And the voice I heard initially addressing me, the one like a trumpet, was saying to me: "Come up here, and I will show you events which must transpire after this!" At once I passed into a trance. Behold! A throne was set up in the sky, and on the throne one sat in state. And the one enthroned there appeared somewhat like a jasper stone and a sardius, and a nimbus radiated about the throne like a great emerald.[448] And around the throne was a circle of twenty-four thrones, and on these thrones sat twenty-four elders, clad in white robes, with golden crowns on their heads. And from out of the throne resound lightnings and reverberations and thunders, and seven lamps of fire blaze before the throne, which are the Seven Spirits of God. And in front of the throne was a glassy sea as if made of crystal.[449] And in the middle of the throne-room and circling the throne were four life-forms[450] covered with eyes in front and in back. And the first life-form was like a lion. The second life-form was like a

---

[445] Malina, *Genre and Message.*

[446] Nowadays, since cosmonaut Yuri Gagarin reported the lack of Pearly Gates up there, believers have shifted over to science fiction conceptuality, reinterpreting "heaven" as some sort of "other dimension," whatever that means.

[447] Malina, *Genre and Message*, p. 51. Also "horns," p. 103.

[448] A detail derived from Ezekiel 1:26-28.

[449] This is supposed to be the divine prototype according to which the "molten sea" in Solomon's Temple was designed (1 Kings 7:23-26).

[450] Perhaps suggested by the four beasts in Daniel 7:2-7, they are intended here as constellations reminiscent of the thousand-eyed Argus, and the eyes are stars. As astronaut Dave, gazing into the Monolith, says, "My God! It's full of stars!" (*2001: A Space Odyssey*).

calf. The third life-form had a human face. The fourth life-form was like a flying eagle.[451] And the four life-forms, considered one by one, had six wings, and each is circled with many eyes, inside and out. And they cry out unceasingly, day and night, "Holy! Holy! Holy is the God Adonai, the Almighty! The One Who Was, and the One Who Is, and the Coming One!"[452] And whenever those life-forms render worship and honor and thanks to the one seated upon the throne, to the one who lives for ages multiplied by ages, the twenty-four elders drop to the ground before the one seated upon the throne and prostrate themselves before him who lives for ages multiplied by ages and toss their crowns at the foot of the throne, singing:

"Worthy are you, our Lord and God,
to receive the worship and the honor and the power,
because you created the All!
By your fiat they existed and were created!"

As Malina[453] shows by comparison with astronomical/astrological texts from the ancient world, the door into heaven (4:1) reflects a common belief among the ancients that there was such a door opening between the visible vault overhead and the divine habitation on the other side. Ancient temples were themselves scale models of the firmament and thus contained openings at the top, a "sun roof," as it were, only its purpose was to symbolize the *Axis Mundi*[454] connecting heaven and earth. The same idea is presupposed in Genesis 28:12, where Jacob beholds the ladder (or staircase) to and from heaven, with angels going up and down it, like bees in a hive, on errands for God, like Clarence in *It's a Wonderful Life* or Cavender in the *Twilight Zone* episode "Cavender Is Coming" (May 29, 1962).[455]

---

[451] These are the four faces of each cherub in Ezekiel 1:10. In the *X-Files* episode "All Souls" (April 26, 1998), we see one of the Seraphim whose face shifts from one of the four visages to the next.

[452] The six wings are those of the seraphs of Isaiah 6:2-3, from whose celestial worship the Trishagion ("Holy, holy, holy!") is also derived.

[453] Malina, *Genre and Message*, pp. 80-81.

[454] Eliade, *Sacred and Profane*, pp. 26-27 ("doors of the gods"), 36-42 (*axis mundi*), 57-62 (temple architecture), 174-180 ("the eye of the temple"); Malina, *Genre and Message*, pp. 80-81.

[455] A stinker, by my reckoning, despite a good cast.

Much speculation, all of it more or less plausible, none of it very persuasive, has surrounded the twenty-four elders surrounding the throne[456] in 4:4, 10. Who are they? The twelve tribal patriarchs (Judah, Reuben, Gad, Zebulun, etc.) plus their New Testament counterparts, the twelve apostles (Peter, Lebbaeus, Bartholomew, Simon Zelotes, et. al.)? Good guess! But wrong. Malina discloses their identity as a group of stars called the *decans*, which were believed to control events, each for one hour of the day (cf., Gen. 1:14-18).[457] One of Malina's axioms is that John the Revelator understood the constellations of the night sky as living entities,[458] and that this is why we hear of gigantic angels looming above the horizon (10:2). He observes that the twenty-four elders (decans) on their thrones, directing events down on earth (as the ancient astrologers believed), must be identified as among the angelic ranks of Principalities, Powers, Thrones, Rulers, etc. (Rom. 8:38-39) with whom Ephesians tells us we are engaged in combat: "we are not contending against flesh and blood, but against the principalities, against the powers, against the world rulers [Gnostic archons] of this present darkness, against the spiritual hosts of wickedness in the heavenly places" (Eph. 6:12), i.e., the malevolent stars in the sky above.

The clashes between and among the heavenly Powers (e.g., 12:7-9) presage events down below. But there is a time-lag between momentous events in heaven and their manifest impact here in the sub-lunar world.

> There existed a twofold world, and thus also a twofold occurrence of events. The world of men and history is only the lower floor of the world's structure. The world of the angels and spirits is erected above that. Both parts make up the cosmos (1Cor. 4:9). Moreover, what happens on earth has its exact parallel in heaven. All history is only the consequence, effect, or parallel copy of heavenly events. Thus an event which on earth is only just beginning to take place may not merely be already determined, but even already enacted in heaven. [...] But while these realities have transpired in the realm between heaven and earth, they must now be fought out on earth. (Johannes Weiss)[459]

---

[456] Malina, *Genre and Message*, pp. 52, 69-70.
[457] Malina, *Genre and Message*, pp. 93-95.
[458] Malina, *Genre and Message*, p. 18.
[459] Johannes Weiss, *Jesus' Proclamation of the Kingdom of God*. Trans. Richard Hyde

This last observation helps explain an otherwise puzzling aspect of Malina's schema. Malina interprets many of the epic celestial events in Revelation as reviews of ancient scenes from Genesis chapters 1-11, as if to provide the back-story for the Final Judgment soon to befall the world of his time. For example, he takes the Fall of Satan and his angels in 12:7-9 as a replay, in the starry void, of the Fall of the sons of God in Genesis 6:1-4. He understands the Fall of Babylon in Revelation 18 as a retelling of the Fall of the Tower of Babel in Genesis chapter 11. It is almost like modern astronomers telling us that, given the unthinkably vast scope of the universe, the light we see from distant stars represents the state of those stars zillions of years ago. Even so, John the Revelator looks to the night sky and sees ancient biblical events played out before his eyes. Thus it becomes possible, I think, to broadly harmonize Malina's perspective with the "Contemporary Historical" interpretation of R.H. Charles, J. Stuart Russell, and others who see John predicting soon-to-come catastrophes for his own generation. We need only say that the Revelator beheld the ancient events in the heavens and predicted their imminent manifestation here on earth below.

Think, too, of Isaiah 14, a famous example of stellar mythology anticipating earthly events. The story of Helal, son of Shahar, relates, as if it were a one-time event, the hubris and fall of the ambitious godling, but the story symbolizes a celestial event that occurs *over and over again every day*. And Isaiah applies that astro-myth to the king of Babylon, a specific historical individual who suffers his fate once and for all. Likewise, we must assume, Revelation describes as definite events of epic proportions what are actually celestial events that occur with clocklike regularity, albeit at a glacial pace. These mythic phenomena of the realm eternal appear, translated into mundane circumstances, as fleeting (supposedly) historical events, whether in the primordial era or in the future. And there is no reason to assume these earthly copies of heavenly events cannot happen more

---

Hiers and David Larrimore Holland. Lives of Jesus Series (1892; English translation, Philadelphia: Fortress Press, 1971), pp. 74-76. See also C.G. Harrison, *The Transcendental Universe: Six Lectures on Occult Science, Theosophy, and the Catholic Faith.* (London: James Elliott and Company, 1894; rpt. Hudson, NY: Lindisfarne Press, 1993), pp. 128-129: "all great movements in the external world have their origin in the spiritual world, and... the conflict of ideas which marks the transition period between one historical epoch and another is, as it were, a copy of a battle already fought and won in the spiritual region [...] but some years must elapse before its effects begin to show themselves plainly in the world."

than once.[460] The events in outer space function as paradigms enabling the wise to "discern the signs of the times" (Matt. 16:3).[461] And this is why, as Hermann Gunkel observed, the *Endzeit* is the same as the *Urzeit* (the End Times recapitulate the Time of Origins).[462] The four living beings at "four equidistant and opposing points along the comic circle around the throne,"[463] "the celestial equator,"[464] are probably intended as the constellations Leo, Taurus, Scorpio (who bore a human face),[465] and Pegasus (with eagle wings).[466]

Here is chapter 5.

And I saw, held in the right hand of him who sat upon the throne, a scroll written on both sides[467] and sealed up with seven seals. And I saw a mighty angel proclaiming in a loud voice: "Is anyone here worthy to open the scroll and to break its seals?" And in all the heaven and on the earth and underneath the earth there was no one equal to the task of opening the scroll or even of peeking into it. As for me, I cried bitterly that no one was found who could open the scroll or look into it. But one of the elders says to me: "Do not cry! See? The Lion of the tribe of Judah, the root of David, has been deemed worthy to open the scroll and its seven seals!" And I saw, standing in the middle of the throne-room, amid the four life-forms, among the twenty-four elders, a Lamb looking as if it had been slain,[468] possessing seven horns and seven eyes, which are the Seven Spirits of God sent out

---

[460] "'Megiddo was Armageddon. The end of the world.' Jennings walked forward, shaken by what he'd seen. 'You mean... "Armageddon" has already been?' 'Oh, yes,' replied Bugenhagen. 'As it will be many times again.'" David Seltzer, *The Omen*. A Futura Book (London: Futura Publications, 1976), p. 175.

[461] Jacob Neusner, "History, Time, and Paradigm in Scripture and in Judaism" *Journal of Higher Criticism* 7/1 (Spring 2000), pp. 54-84.

[462] Hermann Gunkel, *Creation and Chaos in the Primeval Era and the Eschaton: A Religio-Historical Study of Genesis 1 and Revelation 12*. Trans. K. William Whitney, Jr. Biblical Resource Series (Grand Rapids: Eerdmans, 2006), p. 233.

[463] Malina, *Genre and Message*, p. 52.

[464] Malina, *Genre and Message*, p. 100.

[465] Come to think of it, just like Spider-Man's barb-tailed nemesis Mac Gargan, the Scorpion.

[466] Malina, *Genre and Message*, p. 100. This constellation was known to the Babylonian Magi as "the Thunderbird." I wouldn't be much surprised if some wild-haired "expert" on The History Channel cited that fact as proof that space aliens drove cars through the streets of ancient Babylon.

[467] Based on Ezekiel 2:10.

[468] Could this be a stray bit of docetism? I.e., "*as if* it were slain"?

into all the earth.[469] And he entered. Now he has taken the scroll from the right hand of the one seated upon the throne. And when he took the scroll, the four life-forms and the twenty-four elders fell prostrate before the Lamb, each one having a harp and golden bowls full of incense, namely the prayers of the saints. And they sing a new song which goes like this:

"Worthy are you to receive the scroll
and to open its seals,
because you were slain,
and with your blood you purchased for God
those belonging to every tribe and language group
and people and nation,[470]
and made them into a kingdom
and a priesthood to serve our God,
and they will rule the earth!"[471]

And I saw and heard a voice of many angels circling the throne with the life-forms and the elders, and in number they were myriads of myriads and thousands of thousands, exclaiming with a loud voice, "Worthy is the slain Lamb to receive the power and riches and wisdom and strength and honor and worship and blessing!" And every creature in the sky and on the earth and underneath the earth and on the sea, yes, all that people them, I heard exclaiming: "To the one seated on the throne and to the Lamb be all bliss and honor and worship and rule through ages multiplied by ages!" And the four life-forms said, "Amen!" And the elders fell and prostrated themselves.

Who is the Lamb? Here it does not seem to mean the same thing as in John 1:29 which makes Jesus the Passover lamb, a sacrifice. In Revelation, the Lamb is the constellation Aries,[472] understood by the

---

[469] Zechariah 4:10b. They are called seven lamps and seven eyes; hence they represent the seven planets known to ancient astronomy: Sun, Moon, Mercury, Venus, Mars, Jupiter, and Saturn. See Margaret Barker, *The Gate of Heaven: The History and Symbolism of the Temple in Jerusalem* (London: SPCK, 1991), pp. 29, 90-95; Malina, *Genre and Message*, p. 68. They are also, as we have seen, the seven angel princes.

[470] Dan. 7:13-14.

[471] Dan. 7:18; Rev. 1:5b-6.

[472] Unless, as Malina (*Genre and Message*, pp. 102-103) suggests, the original

ancient star-gazers to have occupied "mid-heaven," the very summit of the universe, and the first of the Zodiacal constellations. Hence the Angel-Messiah calls himself "the beginning of God's creation" (3:14). He possesses seven horns and seven eyes.[473] We know by now that "horns" means comets, while "eyes" are planets. Hence he is cognizant of all that happens in the universe and knows where to aim his hurtling comets portending doom.

Is there a hint that the Lamb was somehow the victor in a contest to see who might be worthy or able to open the scroll, like Arthur drawing Excalibur from the stone when all competitors had failed? Or was the Lamb the only one who stepped forth? When he receives acclaim from all beings in the three-leveled universe, we can't help thinking of the confession of fealty wrung from the lips even of the demons and ghosts under the earth (Phil. 2:9-11).

At this point I cannot resist providing a parallel text from a twelfth- to thirteenth-century Catharist scripture, the name of which seems not to have survived.[474]

> Thereupon the Father began to write a book, which He composed in the space of forty years. In this book were written in detail the sufferings, losses, sorrows, poverty, infirmity, shame, injuries, envy, hatred, malice and generally speaking all the penalties which can befall men in this life. And therein it was stated that he who was willing to endure all the aforesaid penalties and to teach them also should be a Son of the heavenly Father. And when the holy Father began the book, Isaiah the Prophet began to prophesy that a Branch or Bough was to come who should redeem human souls. And when the holy Father had composed that book, He placed it in the midst of the heavenly spirits who had remained with Him in heaven[475] and said: "He who shall fulfil the things which are written in this book shall be My Son."

---

significance of the Passover had to do with Aries, not improbable given the still-evident character of the rite as a shepherds' "feast of firstlings."

[473] For a striking depiction of the Lamb with sevenfold horns and eyes, see the 1981 film, *Altered States*.

[474] Duncan Greenlees, ed. and trans., *The Gospel of the Prophet Mani*. World Gospel Series 12 (Adyar: Theosophical Publishing House, 1956), pp. 349-351. The text was reconstructed from the interrogation of the heretic Bavilus. Maybe, lacking an original title, we ought to call it the Gospel of Bavilus.

[475] That is the two-thirds of the angels who had not defected to Satan, as in Revelation 12:4, 7-9.

And many of the heavenly spirits, wishing to be Sons of the holy Father and to be honoured above the rest, went up to that book and opened it; but when they read therein the penalties which he must needs suffer who should desire to come among men and uplift the human race, after reading a little in that book, they fell fainting in a swoon. None of them was willing to forfeit the glory he possessed and subject himself to the penalties of this life, in order to become the Son of God. Then, seeing this, the holy Father said: "So then there is not one of you who desires to be My Son?" Then one of the spirits standing by who was called Jesus, rose up and said: "I myself am willing to be the Son of the Father and to complete all things which are written in that book." Then he went up to that book and opened it, and read therein four or five pages; and he fell in a swoon beside the book, and so remained for three days and nights. Then having awakened from his swoon he grieved much and mourned; but because he had promised that he would fulfil these things which were contained in that book, and because it was right for him not to lie, he told the Father that he himself desired to be his Son and to fulfil all things which were written in that book, however grievous they might be. Then he descended from heaven and appeared as a newly-born Boy in Bethlehem.

This story looks to me like a variant of the heavenly throne room scene in Revelation chapter four; note the reshuffling of the same cards we saw on the table there. And some things implicit in Revelation are explicit in the Catharist version, perhaps implying they share some original in common. We find ourselves in the celestial court with a divine book. There is a contest of sorts among the attendant angels, and only Jesus proves himself worthy of the challenge. As in Revelation, Jesus *is* an angel. In both accounts the book turns out to be a book of prophecy. In Revelation the prophecies depict the impending future unto the end of the age; in the Catharist gospel, the prophecies are predictions of the Passion of the Redeemer—whoever that turns out to be! In Revelation the book would seem to be that of the biblical prophets. It is they who set out the vicissitudes awaiting the Christ, and we are shown Isaiah prophesying as a cameo of the book's contents. The angel Jesus, about to be inaugurated as the Son of God, proleptically undergoes his scheduled destiny, albeit in a different order: his fainting spell models his death, and his awakening *after three days and three nights* models his resurrection. Only then do we witness an anticipation of the agony in Gethsemane. And *then* the incarnation begins! All this, strange as it sounds, fits quite well with the ancient apocalyptic schema of "as above, so below," whereby what happens on earth reiterates accomplished events up in heaven.[476]

Malina notes that ancient drawings of the Zodiac depict Aries with his head looking backward toward Taurus. If John the Revelator had this image in mind, he might have intended that the Lamb's neck had been broken preparatory to slaughter.

> And I saw it when the Lamb opened the first of the seven seals, and I heard one of the four life-forms saying like a thunderclap: "Come!" And I saw, and, behold! A white horse! And the one mounted upon it held a bow, and a crown was set on his brow, and he rode out conquering and meaning to conquer ever more.
>
> And when he broke open the second seal, I heard the second life-form exclaiming: "Come!" At this another steed sprang forth, fiery red, and to its rider was assigned the task of depriving the earth of peace, that its inhabitants should slay one another, and he was given a huge battle sword.
>
> And when he broke the third seal, I heard the third life-form cry out, "Come!" And I saw, and, behold! A black horse, and one mounted upon it holding a balance scale in his hand. And I heard a sound like a voice from among the four life-forms, saying, "A measure of wheat shall cost a denarius! Let three measures of barley command a denarius! But do not blight the oil and the wine!"
>
> And when he opened up the fourth seal, I heard the voice of the fourth life-form cry out, "Come!" And I saw, and behold! A nag of leprous green, and the one who sat upon it was named Death, and Hades rode behind him, and authority was given them over a quarter of the earth, to kill with sword and with famine, and with death, and by the wild animals of the earth.
>
> And when he broke the fifth seal, I saw beneath the altar the souls of those who had been slain for the sake of the message of God and for the sake of the witness they bore.

---

[476] Weiss, *Jesus' Proclamation of the Kingdom of God*, pp. 74-76.

And they moaned with a loud voice, saying: "When, O Despot holy and true, will you finally judge and avenge our blood on those who live on the earth?" And each of them was given a white robe, and they were told they must needs wait but a little longer, until the allotted quota of their fellow-slaves and brothers should be killed as they had been.

And I saw when he opened the sixth seal: a mammoth earthquake shook the world, and the sun turned black as sackcloth, and the full moon became like blood, and the stars of the sky crashed to the ground like a fig tree scattering its unripe figs onto the earth when a strong wind shakes it, and the sky retracted like a scroll rolling up,[477] and every mountain sank and each island was thrust up from the sea floor. And the kings of the earth and the grandees and the commanders and the wealthy and the strong, and every slave and free citizen took refuge in the caves and in the rocky mountain crags, and they wail to the mountains and to the rocks, "Fall upon us! Conceal us from the scrutiny of the one who sits on the throne and from the fury of the Lamb, because the great day of their wrath has arrived, and who can stand against it?"

There is more unsuspected astro-theology[478] on display in chapter 6. The horses are comets, ushering in various dooms. The horsemen represent four of the Zodiacal constellations (Leo or Sagittarius, Virgo, Libra, and Scorpio) each of which rule one successive year of a twelve-year cycle, and the horrors each unleashes reflect the standard conditions expected (feared) for that (ill-omened) year.[479]

The third horseman brings universal famine. In 13:16-17 the Beast 666 will take advantage of this scarcity to secure loyalty by rationing grain. See 13:16-17. This stratagem is an infernal version of the strategy of Joseph in Egypt, who stockpiled grain in advance of the coming famine, in order to sell it to the people, but as mercy, not

---

[477] Isa. 34:4; Thom. 11.

[478] I prefer this term, which I borrow from my late friend and colleague D.M. Murdock (Acharya S.), to "astrology" or "astronomy," both of which are appropriate but do not quite capture Malina's fascinating interpretation of what is going on in Revelation.

[479] Malina, *Genre and Message*, pp. 121-128. One is reminded of the Plagues of Egypt in Exodus, where adverse conditions ensuing upon the yearly flooding of the Nile have been collected and magnified as a sequence of supernatural torments. The same thing has happened here.

blackmail.

The notion of an altar in heaven does not sound so strange when we recall that Moses was told to copy the pattern of the celestial Tabernacle, and, since the resultant earthly Tabernacle had an altar, the heavenly prototype must have had one as well. But wait a minute. For *what*? To appeal for help to higher gods? According to the Roman astronomer Manilius, author of the fabled *Astronomicon*, Jupiter feared the long-imprisoned Giants as they smashed through the earth's surface from caverns below. Would the Olympians be capable of putting them down? "Then even the gods sought aid of mighty gods, and Jupiter himself felt the need of another Jupiter, fearing lest his power prove powerless."[480]

Something similar comes up in L. Sprague de Camp's novel, *The Tritonian Ring*, when the pantheon of ancient Poseidonis gathers to discuss impending doom threatened by one Prince Vakar.

> Entigta's tentacles writhed. "If we cannot communicate with this mortal, how shall we deflect him from his intended path?"
>
> "We might pray to *our* gods for guidance," said the small bat-eared god of the Coranians, whereupon all the gods laughed, being hardened skeptics.[481]

The heavenly altar itself is a constellation, able to speak (16:7). Underneath it one finds the righteous dead clothed in white. These are the faithful martyrs of Daniel 12:3; 4 Ezra 7:97; 4 Maccabees 17:4-5, who shine like stars in the firmament. The pagans, too, believed the righteous heroes of the past survived as stars in the celestial river called the Milky Way.[482] Significantly, that is where the constellation of the heavenly altar was located. Revelation 22:1-2 speaks of the River of Life gushing forth from beneath the throne of God. Presumably this is the (future) earthly instantiation of the heavenly prototype: the starry tide of the Milky Way.

In chapter 7 we see a couple of items borrowed from Ezekiel. Verse three harks back to Ezekiel 9:4, where an angel tattoos the

---

[480] Quoted in Malina, *Genre and Message*, p. 129.

[481] L. Sprague de Camp, *The Tritonian Ring* (New York: Paperback Library, 1968), pp. 9-10.

[482] Malina, *Genre and Message*, pp. 129-131. Who knew there'd be candy bars in heaven? But then again, how could there *not* be?

righteous to exempt them from the soon-coming catastrophe.[483] Revelation 7:13 ("And one of the elders remarked upon it, asking me, 'These people dressed in white robes: who are they? Where do they come from?' And I replied, 'My lord, you know!'") comes right out of Ezekiel 37:3, where the angel asks a similar Socratic question of the seer. This is interesting because the Ezekiel passage gives us the vision of the Valley of Dry Bones: "Son of man, can these bones become people again?" John the Revelator must have seen in that text a prediction of the eschatological resurrection, and that is what he is implying in Revelation 7, the ultimate triumph of those who experienced the Great Tribulation.

You might notice something odd in the enumeration of the twelve tribes of Israel in verses 4-8. A tribe of Joseph has replaced Ephraim. Ephraim and Manasseh were "half-tribes" hailing from Joseph. Levi, not listed in Old Testament territorial allotments, appears here instead of Dan, possibly because of a contemporary belief that the Antichrist would be born from Dan.

Every reader of Revelation 8:1 has wondered what to make of the mysterious half hour of pregnant silence following the opening of the seventh seal. At the very least, it functions as a suspense-building device.[484] But the specific connection with the incense offering suggests a traditional ritual protocol seen in a couple of other ancient sources where the heavenly Powers pause for some period before the offering.[485] As in the Dead Sea Scrolls, it was probably imagined that unseen spirits and angels in heaven performed the same rituals as mortals do on earth, and at the same time.

The Cometeers[486]

The seven archangels are given "trumpets," meaning "comets" signaling "natural" disasters about to befall the earth. But before they

---

[483] Albert Schweitzer thought this was the real point of John the Baptist's immersion, to mark out the elect, like the lamb's blood on the lintels and doorposts of Goshen, to preserve them from the impending Tribulation. Schweitzer, *Paul and his Interpreters: A Critical History*. Trans. W. Montgomery (New York: Schocken Books. 1964), pp. 242-243.

[484] Take a look at the effective use of this passage in the denouement of Ingmar Bergman's *The Seventh Seal*, as Antonius Block and his companions await the arrival of the Grim Reaper.

[485] Malina, *Genre and Message*, p. 136.

[486] Jack Williamson, *The Cometeers* (Reading, PA: Fantasy Press, 1950).

"go on stage," they wait while another angel collects various kinds of incense and sends the stuff wafting "heavenward" as he stands upon the celestial altar. Uh, where exactly is this incense aimed? The angel swinging the censer is in heaven already! Remember, that puzzle is built into the very notion of a heavenly altar. At any rate, the incense is explicitly symbolic of the prayers of the righteous, but *which* righteous? Presumably those whose disembodied souls float in the Milky Way that issues from beneath the altar/throne.

And what were they praying for? We already know: vengeance on their torturers and executioners (Rev. 6:10). And it looks like they're going to get it. The trumpeters unleash a series of environmental catastrophes, all of a meteorological nature. Several of these are comet-like, reinforcing the imagery behind the "trumpets": a flaming meteor the size of a mountain crashes into the sea (verse 8). A massive star, blazing like a torch, plummets out of the sky (verse 10). In 9:1 a "star" (an angel) descends to the earth and opens the shaft of the Abyss. The ancients believed there was a Hades beneath the earth, but that there was another in outer space! It was a mega-constellation including/combining Scorpio, Ophiucus the Snake-handler, Sagittarius, the Altar, and the Centaur. One entered the celestial-infernal realm just between Sagittarius and Scorpio.

From this "heavenly hell" swarms a legion of chimera-like locusts. "And these locusts might be compared to horses caparisoned for battle, on their heads something like crowns made of gold, with their faces resembling human faces. And they had hair like the hair of women,[487] and their teeth were like the fangs of lions, and their thoraxes looked as if armored in iron breastplates, and the sound of their wings was like the sound of many horse-drawn chariots clattering to war" (verses 7-9). Ancient Babylonian and Egyptian iconography depicts such monsters, which seem to be the troops of Sagittarius, who is similarly described.[488] Their earthly counterparts must be the Parthian cavalry and chariots, feared enemies of Rome who, it was believed, would one day sweep across the Euphrates to conquer Rome.[489] The long hair matches the horsehair crests of the Parthian horsemen, while the breastplates and war chariots are self-explanatory: here the veil of metaphor has grown exceedingly thin.

---

[487] Long hair was yet another (and very obvious) metaphor for comets. Our word "comet" actually comes from the Greek for "long-haired."

[488] Malina, *Genre and Message*, pp. 144-145.

[489] Surprisingly, R.H. Charles understands the locust hordes as purely mythological monsters, not as Parthian cavalry.

In verse 15 four more angels let loose a cavalry of two hundred million strong. Verse 17 describes the horsemen and the nightmarish mounts they ride: "wearing breastplates of fiery bronze, of jacinth, and brimstone, with the heads of the horses like lions' heads, and out of their mouths stream fire and smoke and sulfur." "For the power of the horses lies in their mouths and in their tails. For their tails are like snakes, each having multiple heads, and with these they wreak havoc" (verse 19). These delightful pets are the minions of the Centaur constellation.[490] Their earthly instantiations are, again, the Parthians.

Chapter 10 owes a pretty obvious debt to the Revelator's predecessor Ezekiel. The description of the angelic colossus, with his rainbow halo, comes from Ezekiel 1:27-28. When he gives the "little scroll," sweet like honey, to the Revelator to swallow (sort of like eating the menu rather than ordering from it), it comes from Ezekiel 2:9-3:3, only this one packs a nasty aftertaste. It looks like our author is signaling his incorporation of an earlier "little apocalypse," probably the basis of 11:1-12.[491] In just the same way, Timotheé Colani argued that Mark 13:5-31 was a separate apocalyptic tract subsequently incorporated into Mark.[492]

Things get really weird in verses 3-4, another hint at textual funny business. The gigantic angel roars like the MGM lion, prompting a reply: "the seven thunders spoke with their own voices. And when the seven thunders spoke, I was ready to write, but I heard a voice speaking from out of the sky, saying: 'Seal up what the seven thunders have spoken, nor may you transcribe them!'" That textual cul-de-sac vanishes without issue when the business about the little scroll resumes, implying the abortive revelation of the seven thunders is another interpolation, followed by a scribal excision of the interpolation! Let's take it step by step. In view here is *brontology*,[493] the technique of telling the future by interpreting thunderclaps, an art practiced by the Dead Sea Scrolls community. "Seal up" implies there is already a written text, but that it is intended for some future readership, exactly as in Daniel 12:9 and in Isaiah 8:16, implying the pseudepigraphical nature of the writing in which this device appears.

---

[490] Malina, *Genre and Message*, pp. 146-147.

[491] R.H. Charles, *Revelation*, vol. I, pp. 270-271.

[492] Timotheé Colani, "The Little Apocalypse of Mark 13." Trans. Nancy Wilson. *Journal of Higher Criticism* (10/1) Spring 2003, pp. 41-47. Excerpted from Colani, *Jesus-Christ et les croyances messianiques de son temps*, 1864, pp. 201-214.

[493] Cf., *Brontosaurus*, "thunder lizard," whose mighty steps shook the ground.

THE BOOK OF REVELATION

The pseudonymous author is pretending the identity of some ancient prophet, as if he had anticipated issues of the actual writer's own day. (By contrast, the Revelator is charged *not* to seal up the Book of Revelation for the future, 22:10, since there isn't going to *be* one. The whole thing is coming down so soon, there is no longer time for the sinners to repent, 22:11).

But the angel nips this particular thunderous revelation in the bud. The Daniel and Isaiah passages actually do share with their readers the message in a bottle addressed to the ostensible future. But here we are left wondering what on earth the eloquent thundering revealed. Thus I suspect a fuller version had first been interpolated into Revelation, then subsequently censored (though why not verses 3 and 4 along with it?) by a scribe who did not like what he read there.

So what *did* the seven thunders reveal? I have a hunch it is still available in the Nag Hammadi text *Thunder: Perfect Mind*, a Nicolaitan scripture.[494] Remember, this sect comes in for unfavorable mention in Revelation 2:6 and 15. There are Nicolaitans within the very congregations (Ephesus and Pergamum) to whom the Revelator's cover letters are addressed, and my guess is that one of them, when he made a new copy of Revelation, added the Seven Thunders Apocalypse, interrupting the Little Scroll introduction. (This, I think, is exactly what happened in 1 Corinthians 2:6-16, which reads like a subsequent Gnostic rejoinder to the anti-Gnostic context into which it has been interpolated. This Corinthian Gnostic material even claims knowledge of the "deep things of God," verse 10, just like the heretics condemned in Revelation 2:24, probably Nicolaitans.) This sort of scribal mischief is just what the author of Revelation hoped to avoid (22:18-19). By threats of damnation (in the absence of copyright laws) he wanted to safeguard the integrity of his text. His was no idle fear, as we can see from the manner in which both Matthew chapters 24-25 and Luke 17:22-37; 21:5-36 treated Mark 13!

The text of the Little Scroll seems to begin with chapter 11. The Revelator goes easy on us in 11:1-2, which borrows from Ezekiel chapters 40-42. Given the tedium of the detail in Ezekiel's version, in which the seer is ordered to go over every inch of the heavenly Temple

---

[494] For a couple of fictional treatments of the Seven Thunders' revelations, see Robert M. Price and Peter H. Cannon, "The Curate of Temphill" in Price, ed., *The Shub-Niggurath Cycle: Tales of the Black Goat with a Thousand Young*. Call of Cthulhu Fiction (Oakland: Chaosium Publishers, 1994), pp. 187-200; Price, "The Seven Thunders" in Brian M. Sammons, ed., *Tales of Cthulhu Invictus* (Queens Village, NY: Golden Goblin Press, 2015), pp. 101-114.

with a tape measure, we can be grateful for the *Readers Digest* version. Two chapters reduced to two verses? Not bad! Having invoked the visions of Ezekiel concerning the Temple, albeit very tersely, the text follows this up with a reference to a feature of Temple décor as mentioned in Zechariah 4:3, 11-14, "the two olive trees and the two lamp stands which stand before the Lord of the earth." Zechariah intended them to stand for Zerubbabel, Davidic heir and Persian governor of Judea, and the high priest Joshua, but for the Revelator they symbolize the Two Witnesses. God sends them to prophesy imminent doom in Jerusalem, presumably at the hands of Rome. This has caused some interpreters to date the Book of Revelation to just before or after 70 C.E., but if chapter 11 is in fact an earlier, short apocalyptic tract subsequently repurposed as a chapter of Revelation,[495] then the extant Book of Revelation need not be dated so early. (This issue comes up again when we get to the infamous Mark of the Beast in chapter 13.)

Given their *modus operandi* of inflicting plagues (Exod. 17:17, 19) and droughts (1 Kings 17:1) and summoning fire from heaven (2 Kings 1:10; 1 Kings 18:36-38), the Two Witnesses are clearly supposed to be Moses and Elijah returned to earth, just as they made a cameo appearance on the Mount of Transfiguration (Mark 9:2-8; Matt. 17:1-8; Luke 9:28-36). Revelation does not presuppose that scene, but it shares with it the assumption that Moses and Elijah were available for an encore, seeing that neither man had died but had ascended bodily into heaven. The caginess of Deuteronomy 34:5-6 concerning the location of Moses' burial (plus the fact that Yahweh himself acted as grave-digger, implying no witnesses!) led Josephus, Philo, and others to infer that Moses had not really died.[496] And 2 Kings 2:11 could not be clearer in its assertion that Elijah was assumed bodily into heaven. But if in ancient times these two were lucky to have escaped death, their luck runs out in Revelation 11:7. Never fear, though: three days later, a heavenly voice summons them back to the sky and resurrects them in a scene recalling the language of Ezekiel 37:5, 10.

During the three days when the Two lay exposed in the gutter (Rev. 11:8), there is wild celebration, parties thrown, gifts exchanged

---

[495] Just as Mark 13 looks like a redactional insertion into the gospel, and as 2 Peter took over Jude as a chapter of his own work.

[496] To say, "God alone buried Moses," is to say "No one buried Moses" just as, when Origen said, "Only God knows who wrote the Epistle to the Hebrews" he meant, "No one knows who wrote the Epistle to the Hebrews." And if no one buried Moses, it can't mean they left his corpse to be eaten by jackals. It has to mean he didn't really die.

(11:10). I can't help wondering if this seemingly gratuitous detail is a clue that the whole sequence reflects, with some re-ordering, the rites of the various dying and rising gods, e.g., Attis, whose resurrection was celebrated three days after the ritual charade of his interment.

Who killed the Two? Verse 7 blames the Beast rising up out of the Abyss (cf., Dan. 7:3). It is taken for granted that we know this villain already, but he is introduced over in 13:1, to which this present verse seems to refer *back*, again implying that the "little scroll" was an originally independent patch sewed in here by our author who had already composed chapter 13. As if heeding the urging of the reporter in the movie *The Thing from Another World*, our Revelator "keep[s] watching the skies," and what he sees is the rising of the constellation Virgo. She is swathed in the sun, the moon beneath her feet, with a crown of twelve stars (the Zodiac) resting on her brow. This is how Virgo (and analogous figures like Isis) were depicted.

She writhes in the pre-Lamaz agonies of childbirth. And at this worst of all possible moments, she finds herself being chased by a hungry red dragon! And not just any old dragon, but our old friend Leviathan from whose powerful breast no less than seven heads sprout and wave on serpentine stalks.[497] Each scaled and horned head wears an ascending cone of concentric diadems (each one like Caesar's laurel wreath or the tiara resting upon the Statue of Liberty's brow).

> And the Dragon stood poised in front of the woman who was about to give birth, to be ready to devour the baby as soon as she might deliver it. And she bore a son, a male, who is destined to shepherd all the nations with an iron crook. And her child was snatched up to God and to his throne. As for the woman, she took flight into the desert, where she is to find a place of refuge prepared by God, where she will be taken care of for one thousand two-hundred and sixty days. (Rev. 12:4-6)

> And when the Dragon realized he had been exiled to the earth, he went after the woman who bore the male. And they

---

[497] See the very effective depictions of Leviathan/Hydra (give or take a head or two) in the movies *Hercules* (1957), *Jason and the Argonauts* (1963), *Gidorah the Three-Headed Monster* (1965), and, especially, *Yamato Takeru* (1994). Why, oh why, doesn't Toho Studios make a straight cinematic version of the whole Book of Revelation? Or maybe Guillermo del Toro? I'm telling you, this would have real value for the study of the book.

gave the woman the two wings of the great eagle, for her to fly to the desert, to her retreat, where she is cared for and hidden from the questing snout of the Serpent for a time, times, and half a time. And the Serpent, pursuing the woman, spewed out of his mouth a river of water to sweep her away. And Gaia came to the woman's rescue, opening her mouth to swallow the river that the Dragon has released from his own mouth. And the Dragon was infuriated over the woman and stalked off to renew the battle against the rest of her sons, those who keep the commandments of God and bear witness to Jesus. (12:13-17)

It is the constellation Draco, the Dragon, rising over the horizon as the wheel of the heavens turns. He comes up just after Virgo and so appears to pursue her—every night! As we have seen, these eternally repeated celestial events may occur more than once on earth as well. The Revelator looks backward to two primordial events, which he combines: Yahweh's slaying of Leviathan (Psalm 74:12-14) and the Fall of the lustful Sons of God (Gen. 6:1-4). In his version of the latter he incorporates the myth of baby Zeus' deliverance from the cannibalistic appetite of Kronos, the Titan king, who stood ready to scoop up and eat each of Rhea's newborns in order to prevent an eventual usurpation. Finally, Rhea gave Kronos a stone to swallow instead, while her mother Gaia took the baby away to be raised on the island of Crete (Hesiod, *Theogony* 459-491).

The myth is also reflected in The Apocalypse of Adam 78:9-13, 19-23, and in the *Liqqute Midrashim* 156: "In those days [before the Flood] only one virgin, Istahar by name, remained chaste. When the Sons of God made lecherous demands upon her, she cried: 'First lend me your wings!' They assented and she, flying up to heaven, took sanctuary at the Throne of God, who transformed her into the constellation Virgo."[498] The myth can be discerned beneath the baptism and desert sequence in Mark 1:9-13, where the divine winged dove descends upon Jesus and impels him into the desert, where angels provide for him.[499] It reappears in Matthew 2:13-16's Slaughter of the Innocents episode. In this last case, the pursuing Dragon has been split between the persecuting Herod and the place of refuge, since in the Old Testament "Rahab" refers both to Egypt and to the

---

[498] Summary by Robert Graves and Raphael Patai in *Hebrew Myths: The Book of Genesis* (New York: Greenhouse / Crown Publishers, 1983), p. 101.
[499] Robinson, "On the *Gattung* of Mark (and John)," pp. 124-126.

Chaos-Dragon.

The myth of the Fall of the Sons of God is anticipated in verse 4 ("and his tail sweeps up a third of the stars of the night sky and flung them to the earth") and continues with the War in Heaven (verses 7-12).

> And a war erupted in the sky, Michael and his angel legions battling the Dragon. The Dragon fought hard, and his own angels [i.e., the stars he swept up in verse 4] alongside him, yet they did not win out, and it was clear there was no longer any place for them in heaven. And the great Dragon was expelled, the archaic serpent,[500] the one called the Accuser and the Adversary, the deceiver of the whole inhabited earth, he was hurled down onto the ground [Ezek. 32:4], and his angels were thrown down with him. And I heard a loud voice resounding in the sky, saying, "Now it has come! The salvation and the power and the kingship of our God and the authority of his Christ, because the Accuser of our brothers has been toppled, he who used to accuse us before God day and night. [Job 1:8-11; Zech. 3:1; Luke 22:31; Jude 9] And they vanquished him by the blood of the Lamb and their confession of faith at their martyrdom and the fact that they did not insist on holding onto their lives till the last. Therefore, rejoice, you heavens and those sojourning there! But woe to you, O earth and sea, because the Accuser came down to you livid with rage, knowing that little time is left to him.

How did the overthrow of the Accuser (devil) or Adversary (Satan) save the brethren? The blood of the Lamb as well as their own voluntary suffering seemed quite the adequate atonement for all the sins which the Adversary might press before God as proper grounds to damn one to hell, but there is also the implication that they are safe

---

[500] The reference is to the seven-headed dragon Lotan ("Baal will run him through with his spear, even as he did Lotan, the crooked serpent with seven heads."), i.e., Leviathan (Job 41; Psalms 74:12-14; 104:26; Isa. 27:1), also called Rahab (Psalm 89:10; Isa. 51:9), and Tiamat. The serpent in the Garden of Eden is not meant here, but that character does go back to the same mythic source: in Genesis 3 he is merely "Mr. Snake," father of all snakes, who get punished for their scaly progenitor's sin, just like Adam and Eve's cursed descendants. But this tale is a half-demythologized version of the primordial combat between Yahweh/Marduk/Baal and Leviathan/Tiamat/Lotan.

because their accuser is no longer around to draw attention to their faults.

Malina[501] believes it is the *unfallen* angels who opted out of the ancient angelic panty-raid who are depicted in 14:1-5.

> And I saw, and behold! The Lamb standing upon the peak of Mount Zion! And with him were one hundred forty-four thousand who had his name and the name of his Father imprinted on their foreheads. And I heard a sound from the sky like the sound of a crashing cataract, and like deafening thunder. And the sound I heard was like harpists strumming their harps. And they sing a new song before the throne and before the four life-forms and the elders. No one could learn the song except for the hundred forty-four thousand who had been ransomed from the earth. These are the ones who did not degrade themselves with women, for they are virgins. It is these who follow the Lamb wherever he may lead. These were purchased from among mankind to be dedicated as first fruits to God and to the Lamb. No lie was ever found on their lips. They are impeccable.

Malina's interpretation is very attractive, but there is a problem. The 144, 000 are explicitly described as "of mankind," those "ransomed from the earth," i.e., mortals. And when we first met the 144, 000 back in 7:4-8, we were told they were Israelites belonging to the twelve tribes, hence mortals. We might venture the harmonization that there were 144, 000 righteous angels and that they were the guardian angels of the same number of righteous Israelites. Again, "as above, so below." The trouble is that nowhere in the text is this connection made. But who knows? Think of 1 Corinthians 6:3, "Do you not know that we shall judge angels?" I have argued elsewhere[502] that the reasoning here is that those who embrace continence will be the natural ones to judge the ancient angels who did *not*, so maybe the same connection is implied here.

Next (13:1) we behold the rising of a great Beast from the sea, as in Daniel 7:2-3, with ten horns (as in Daniel 7:7) and seven heads crowned with ten diadems. Obviously, the Beast is the venom-spitting image of the Dragon, though with a few added details penciled in

---

[501] Malina, *Genre and Message*, p.56.

[502] Robert M. Price, *The Amazing Colossal Apostle: The Search for the Historical Paul* (Salt Lake City: Signature Books, 2012), pp. 115-116.

from the same chapter of Daniel already referred to (Dan. 7:3-6). "And the Dragon gave it his power and throne and great authority." I would suggest that the Dragon is the heavenly constellation, itself a gigantic living being, and that the Beast is, so to speak, his incarnation/counterpart on earth. This Beast becomes a world-ruling tyrant. He apparently acknowledges the Dragon as his parent or patron, and all his *Sieg-heiling* sycophants are happy to worship Satan. This, needless to say, is the only mention in the Bible of a Satanist cult.

One of the Beast's seven heads displayed a healed-over mortal wound, which implies that one had been killed, then revived. It is worth asking if this might perhaps refer to the power of the Hydra to replace any head that got lopped off with two more. But why mention that here? We find out later on:

> The Beast that you saw was, and is not, and is about to rise up out of the Abyss. It is destined for destruction. And all the people of the earth will marvel when they see the Beast that was, and is not, and is to come, at least those whose names are not to be found in the scroll of the living since the creation of the world. This calls for a mind adept in wisdom! The seven heads are really seven mountains, where the woman sits and where seven kings are. Of these, five fell, one rules now, and the other has not yet arisen, but whenever he does, he must remain a little while. As for the Beast which was and is not, he is an eighth and is yet one of the previous seven, and then he goes to perdition. (Rev. 17:8-11)

For decades following World War Two, one saw occasional tabloid stories about Hitler having escaped Germany and fled to South America, where he, e.g., masterminded the Argentine invasion of the Falklands. He was just too good a bad guy to let go! People could not believe the world had seen the last of *der Führer*. It was the same with the notorious Nero. Rumor had it that Nero had escaped the plot against him or had actually been killed but rose from the dead. In fact there were at least three Nero pretenders who tried to exploit this popular belief. "The Beast that you saw was, and is not," "the Beast that was, and is not, and is to come," is a Roman Emperor. He once appeared as Nero, then disappeared, presumed or actually dead after his Praetorian Guards attacked him, and then returned (disguised? reincarnated?) as Domitian. Five of the seven kings are dead and gone; they are Augustus, Tiberius, Caligula, Claudius, and Nero. Vespasian rules at the time of writing (or the time in which the Revelator has fictively placed himself). Another will follow him and enjoy only a brief reign. He is Titus. "As for the Beast which was and is not, he is an eighth," namely Domitian, "and is yet one of the previous seven," the returned Nero.

Apocalipstick

People expected that the returned/revived Nero would seek revenge on Rome which had rejected him (cf., Luke 19:27). Revelation depicts pagan Rome as the Great Harlot who sits atop the seven hills. And the Beast has a beef against her.

> And he says to me, "The waters you saw, where the Prostitute sits enthroned, represent populations and crowds and nations and language groups. And the ten horns you saw, together with the Beast, will turn on the Prostitute and will leave her naked and bereft of her riches. They will eat bits of her flesh and will incinerate what remains!" (17:8-16).

The vengeful Nero leads the mounted Parthian armies across the Euphrates to attack Rome (16:12). Her utter destruction is depicted at great length in chapter 18.

But there is yet another Beast (that makes two fewer than Daniel's four!), this one rising from caverns beneath the earth (13:11-18). He would seem to be "the Land Leviathan,"[503] Behemoth (from Job 40:15-24).[504] "It had two horns like a ram and spoke like a dragon." In other words, he is an Antichrist.[505] He has horns like the Lamb on the heavenly throne, but he speaks the words of Satan, the Dragon. He is a wolf in sheep's clothing. "You have heard that

---

[503] Michael Moorcock, *The Land Leviathan* (New York: DAW Books, 1976).

[504] Job seems to intend the mighty Hippopotamus, but Jewish tradition pictured him as a monster. Howard Schwartz, *Tree of Souls: The Mythology of Judaism* (New York: Oxford University Press, 2004), p. 146; Graves and Patai, *Hebrew Myths*, pp. 49-50.

[505] On the *Sopranos* episode "The Legend of Tennessee Moltisanti," (February 28, 1999) Anthony Junior hears someone mention the anarchist martyrs Sacco and Vanzetti, and he asks, "Weren't they the two antichrists?" His sister Meadow snaps, "How can there be two antichrists? There's only one Christ!" Ah, but her stupid little brother was right! There *are* two antichrists in Revelation: Leviathan and Behemoth, the Beast and the False Prophet.

antichrist is coming, so now many antichrists have come; therefore we know that it is the last hour" (1 John 2:18). He whips up the crowds to worship the Beast. "And it performs great signs, calling down fire out of the sky onto the earth before mortal eyes" (verse 13). The reference is to Elijah's miracle contest with the Baal prophets in 1 Kings 18:24, in the light of which the point of this sign must be to prove that the Beast is the true god.

Another "miracle" he performs to dupe the people is to animate a statue of the Beast, even seeming to make it speak. Actually, this was a familiar ventriloquist stunt in the ancient world, but it may be intended as genuine, albeit wicked, magic along the lines of the Golem legends. The Chronicles of Jerahmeel 23:7 tells how

> Enosh then took six clods of earth, mixed them, and moulded them and formed an image of dust and clay. "But," said they, "this image does not walk, nor does it possess any breath of life." He then showed them how God breathed into his nostrils the breath of life. But when he began to breathe into it, Satan entered the image so that it walked, and they went away after it, saying, "What is the difference between bowing down before this image and before man?"[506]

The propaganda minister uses the stick as well as the carrot, issuing the decree that anyone who does not bow to the Beast's image shall pay with his life (a detail derived from Daniel 3:4-6). But it doesn't stop there: "he requires everyone, both peasants and nobles, both rich and poor, both free citizens and slaves, to receive a mark imprinted on their right hand or on their forehead, to make it impossible for anyone to buy or sell, except for those who bore the mark, the name of the Beast or the number of its name" (13:16-17). This tactic presupposes the famine anticipated in 6:5-6. The Beast is rationing precious grain, much as Joseph did in Egypt.

On another level, given the Jewish-Christian character of this book, we might wonder whether the Beast is intended as *Paul*, who was certainly regarded by Jewish Christians as the deceiver of the nations. The famine in question might then be identified with that

---

[506] Eleazar ben Asher ha-Levi, *The Chronicles of Jerahmeel or The Hebrew Bible Historiale being a collection of apocryphal and pseudo-epigraphical books dealing with the history of the world from the creation to the death of Judas Maccabeus.* Trans. Moses Gaster (New York: Ktav Publishing, 1971; rpt. CreateSpace, 2016), p. 64.

under Claudius in Acts 11:27-30. Since F.C. Baur, we are used to reading Acts 8:18-24 as preserving a Jewish-Christian, anti-Pauline, invidious interpretation of Paul's collection among the Gentiles on behalf of Jerusalem. Galatians 2:10 implies the collection was a condition for the Pillar Apostles' recognition of Paul's mission. Acts 8 makes it an attempt by Paul to buy apostleship, which is not all that different. It may be that Revelation 13 sees Paul extorting apostolic recognition as the price of relief aid for Jerusalem. In view of this, note the perhaps satirical analogy between Revelation 13:16 and Galatians 3:27-28.

What was the notorious *mark?* Malina identifies it as a religious allegiance tattoo (cf., Gal. 6:17),[507] while Schonfield decided it was a commerce stamp, of which ancient examples survive, bearing the name of the current Caesar and the year of his reign as the date of minting.[508]

"This requires wisdom: whoever has reasoning powers, let him reckon up the number of the Beast, for it works out to the number of a particular man. And the number of it is six hundred sixty six" (13:18). Greek, Hebrew, and Latin all used the same set of characters for both letters and numbers, context determining how to read it. People were amused to convert their names into number totals, rather as we use initials. Thus our author has chosen some name that converts to 666, and he knows it is a name already familiar to the reader. He means "Neron Caesar." This might imply that the book, or this portion of it, was written when Nero was still on the throne (he died in 68 C.E.). Or, as seems more probable, it stems from the reign of Domitian (81-96 C.E.) and identifies him as *Nero Redivivus.*[509] One might think it the better part of valor to avoid torture and death by bowing the knee to the Beast's statue or submitting to the branding, but then one would be very, very wrong: "Whoever worships the Beast and his statue and allows a mark to be

---

[507] Malina, *Genre and Message,* pp. 184, 245.

[508] Hugh J. Schonfield, *The Bible Was Right: An Astonishing Examination of the New Testament.* A Signet Key Book (New York: New American Library, 1959), Chapter 48, "The Mark of the Beast," pp. 177-181. Though these stamps were placed on documents and goods (exactly like the Stamp Act in colonial America), Schonfield thinks that branding them on the right hand and forehead was a blasphemous copy of the Jewish phylacteries (small leather boxes containing scripture verses and laced to the hand and forehead with leather thongs. They are mentioned in Matthew 23:5).

[509] Some manuscripts read "616," but this only represents an adjustment of the sum provided one drops the "n" from "Neron." In the same way, one might write either "Plato" or "Platon."

imprinted on his forehead or his hand, he shall choke on the wine of the fury of God, mixed full strength in the cup of his rage![510] He will be tortured by fire and sulfur to amuse the holy angels and the Lamb.[511] And the smoke from their torture rises up age after age,[512] nor have they any respite day or night, those who worship the Beast and his statue, and if anyone accepts the mark of his name." Or, as Luke 12:4-5 puts it so succinctly, "I tell you, my friends, do not fear those who kill the body, and after that have no more that they can do. But I will warn you whom to fear: fear him who, after he has killed, has power to cast into hell."

Two Suppers or One?

> And a voice echoed from the throne, saying, "Praise our God, all you his slaves, those who fear him, the small and the great!" And I heard a sound like that of a vast crowd, and like a crashing cataract, and like mighty thunderclaps, and it said, "Praise Yahweh! For the Lord, our God, the Almighty, has begun to rule! Let us rejoice, and let us exult! And we will give all credit to him, because the wedding of the Lamb has arrived, and his wife has prepared her finery." And she was given fine linen, bright and clean, for the fine linen signifies the righteous deeds of the saints. And he tells me: "Write this: 'Blessed are those invited to the wedding feast of the Lamb!'" And he says to me, "This is a promise of God you may rely upon!" And I fell at his feet before him to worship him. And he says to me, "Don't you see? I am only a fellow slave with you and your brothers who are martyrs for Jesus! Worship God! For martyrdom to Jesus is the theme of prophecy!" (19:5-10).

Who is the Bride of the Lamb? Is she the collective number of all the righteous (19:8)? Or are they specifically the martyrs who have washed their robes "as no launderer on earth could bleach them" (Mark 9:3)

---

[510] Isa. 51:17. Jer. 25:15-16; 49:12; 51:7.

[511] Luke 19:27 implies a similar scene of eschatological barbarism. As Alfred North Whitehead said, "It is, of course, the figure of an Oriental despot, with his inane and barbaric vanity." Lucien Price, *Dialogues of Alfred North Whitehead* (Boston: Little, Brown and Company, 1954), p. 277.

[512] Isa. 34:10.

in the sanguine detergent of the blood of the Lamb (6:11; 7:14; 12:11). I suspect the latter. It is the Tribulation martyrs who are accorded elite treatment, sitting to the right and the left of Christ in his glory (Mark 10:37-40[513]) while the remainder of the righteous idly watch the grass grow over their graves for a full thousand years (Rev. 20:4-6). Even so, here it is only the Tribulation martyrs who marry the Lamb and celebrate.

In 21:2, 9-10, we learn that the Bride of the Lamb is the New Jerusalem, floating down from the heavens. God will dwell there along with humanity, as he once dwelt with Israel in the desert, in the Ark of the Covenant. The city itself is his Tabernacle (21:3, not merely his "dwelling" as it is usually rendered). We read in 21:22 that the New Jerusalem contains no Temple because God himself is its Temple, but that is because the city is itself his Tabernacle. The Mosaic Tabernacle preceded the Jerusalem Temple, which replaced it. Now God has returned to a Tabernacle. Put another way, the city as a whole is a Temple, as implied in the fact that the Revelator borrows from Ezekiel chapters 40-42 the sequence of being given a tape measure by an angel who orders him to count every inch of the Temple, only this time it is the New Jerusalem that gets measured (Rev. 21:15-17). The New Jerusalem *needs* no Temple because it *is* a Temple, or Tabernacle.

Several times, in the hour of justice and vengeance, we hear the angelic choir (analogous to the Chorus in Greek plays) proclaiming that God has now *begun* to rule (11:15, 17; 12:10; 19:6b). What giveth? The royal marriage scene would seem to hark back to the ancient enthronement and kingship renewal ceremonies of Israel. It looks like the king would take a new wife every year, replicating on earth the *hieros gamos* (sacred marriage) of the King of Gods and his wives.[514] The whole thing was predicated on the myth of Yahweh's defeat of Leviathan (which morphs into the War in Heaven in Revelation 12:7-10). This primordial triumph eventuated in both the creation of the world and the ascension of Yahweh, the virile warrior God, to the throne. His kingship dates from that time. The Revelator saw this scenario played out again and again in the night skies. Down on earth, the Lord's Christ fulfills the role of his theocratic forbears of

---

[513] There, too, it is only those who have followed Jesus in martyrdom who are entitled to reign with him.

[514] Michael D. Goulder, *The Psalms of the Sons of Korah*. Studies in the Psalter, I. Journal for the Study of the Old Testament Supplement Series 20 (Sheffield: JSOT Press, 1982), pp. 122-130. Thus "the Bride of the Lamb" might well denote "the Harem of the Lamb."

David's line (Rev. 20:4, 11), playing, as every one of them did (Psalm 2), the part of the victorious King Yahweh coming to his throne. The proclamation of God's enthronement had always been a cyclical event, so its repetition in Revelation is nothing new.

But hark! There is word of another feast! Or perhaps another word of the same feast. When an angel calls mankind to the great slugfest of Armageddon (Rev. 16:16), he tells them not to forget the knives and forks, for it will be a veritable buffet of human organs and animal flesh, garnished with fragments of blood-spattered battle armor. "And I saw one angel eclipsing the sun and shouting with a loud voice to all the birds flying in the middle of the sky, 'Come! Gather for the great supper of God, where you may feast upon the flesh of kings and of commanders and of heroes, horseflesh and rider flesh, the carcasses of free and slave alike, both peasant and noble!'" (19:17-18). Can this be the same as the Marriage Supper of the Lamb, and its, er, menu?

As for Armageddon itself, there is a terrific build-up, but the battle is over before it starts. The armies of the Beast are gathered, awaiting the opposing forces on the way from heaven. In that expectation they are not disappointed. But it is over so fast, it is almost anticlimactic, making the supernatural Blitzkriegs of Joshua look like military quagmires. From the skies descends the heroic Word of God, fiery-eyed, vesture soaked in blood and mounted upon a white stallion, the white-clad hosts of heaven in tow. One might easily plug in Wisdom of Solomon 18:14-16 right at this point.

> For while gentle silence enveloped all things,
> and night in its swift course was now half gone,
> thy all-powerful word leaped from heaven, from the royal throne,
> into the midst of the land that was doomed,
> a stern warrior carrying the sharp sword of thy authentic command,
> and stood and filled all things with death,
> and touched heaven while standing on the earth.

His word of command is itself a sharp sword, dividing joints and marrow (cf., Heb. 4:12; John 18:6). By himself, the Word speaks death to every single soldier of the Beast, who, with his ram-horned Goebbels, is unceremoniously pitched into the great magma pit, the Lake of Fire. Their patron, the Dragon, receives similar treatment, only he is said to be chained up in a subterranean Abyss, awaiting eventual release. His confinement is just like that of the Uranian Giants of Hesiod and the fallen angels in 2 Peter 2:4 and Jude 6, chains and all.

In light of this, it is interesting that, when the Satan-Dragon is finally paroled, he goes right back to his infernal work, summoning to his banner vast armies of the wicked (Psalm 2:1-6), restive and chafing under the messianic yoke after a thousand years of galling righteousness.[515] Those diabolical nations are called Gog and Magog, well known from Ezekiel 38:1-6 but ultimately echoing Hesiod's *Theogony* 147-153, where Gog (Gyges) is one of the fifty-headed, hundred-handed giants, children of Uranos and Gaia, chained beneath the earth's crust—until, like Satan, he escapes. Though their gathered armies cover the earth, surrounding Jerusalem (again, playing out Psalm 2), they are incinerated in an eye-blink by an obliterating firestorm, Elijah-style (2 Kings 1:10-12), from the sky. After this abortive attempt to cast off the yolk of Yahweh and his anointed, Satan is hurled into the lake of molten sulfur, where the Beast and his prophet had long been awaiting him. And the Unholy Trinity scream in harmony day and night, world without end, amen.

Finally, it's time to face the music. All the dead of past and present ages mill about, each waiting for his case to come up. The Messianic King will make his own decision, render his own verdict, objective and incorruptible (Isa. 11:3-4). Nothing is said here of a set of beliefs being the shibboleth. No, it is an audit of righteous versus unrighteous deeds, precisely as in 2 Corinthians 5:10. Those who do not measure up will join the Beast, the Devil, and the False Prophet. There being no more use for them, the custodians of the dead, Hades and the Grim Reaper, end up there, too, with their former charges.

After the Judgment, the earth we know is destroyed (something one might have expected to be dealt with a bit more extensively!), then replaced. Why was this necessary, given that the Christ had finally secured the kingdom of God on earth, destroying all evil? Are we to infer that Armageddon and the Siege of Gog and Magog had devastated the earth's surface beyond repair? But it is hard to imagine the world defaced and degraded worse than it had been during the Tribulation, yet it remained serviceable for a thousand years thereafter. Perhaps the new creation mytheme is simply a matter

---

[515] Has the writer really taken seriously the implied scenario, that wickedness only grows, and that exponentially, under the glorious reign of Jesus Christ? He sounds more like a prison warden than a king.

of tradition. As R.H. Charles[516] notes, there were two alternate eschatological patterns: if the End Time intervention was the direct work of God himself, the world would be recreated at once. But if a human Messiah was to be his instrument, a messianic interregnum would precede the new creation. This pattern appears not only in Revelation, but also in 1 Corinthians 15:24-28 and 4 Ezra 7:28-31.

The Book of Revelation ends with pointed reiterations of the warning that the things predicted in the book will take place very shortly (22:6, 10, 12, 20). Obviously, they did not. Doesn't that make it technically a "false prophecy"? For fear of this verdict, fundamentalists remain stubbornly in denial, pretending that the text warns that the End *may* erupt *at any time*, hence one must be ready. This is not the same as saying, as the text actually does, that it *will* come *soon*. And this refusal to face reality has occasioned a phantasmagoria of contrived and fanciful (mis)interpretations, ranging from Hal Lindsey's to Charles Manson's. We could have avoided all this had the churches followed Martin Luther's advice to dump the book into the River Elba. But personally, I am glad they did not. I regard the Book of Revelation as a mesmerizing epic of dazzling imagery and echoing poetry.

---

[516] R.H. Charles, *Eschatology: The Doctrine of a Future Life in Israel, Judaism, and Christianity: A Critical History* (New York: Schocken Books, 1963), pp. 327, 330-333.

Printed in Great Britain
by Amazon

44274292R00149